J

M

F

Nolo's Pocket Guide to

Consumer Rights

2ND CALIFORNIA EDITION

formerly
Barbara Kaufman's Consumer Action Guide

by Barbara Kaufman

NOLO PRESS BERKELEY

YOUR RESPONSIBILITY WHEN USING A SELF-HELP LAW BOOK

We've done our best to give you useful and accurate information in this book. But laws and procedures change frequently and are subject to differing interpretations. If you want legal advice backed by a guarantee, see a lawyer. If you use this book, it's your responsibility to make sure that the facts and general advice contained in it are applicable to your situation.

KEEPING UP-TO-DATE

To keep its books up-to-date, Nolo Press issues new printings and new editions periodically. New printings reflect minor legal changes and technical corrections. New editions contain major legal changes, major text additions or major reorganizations. To find out if a later printing or edition of any Nolo book is available, call Nolo Press at (510) 549-1976 or check the catalog in the *Nolo News*, our quarterly newspaper.

To stay current, follow the "Update" service in the *Nolo News*. You can get a two-year subscription to the paper free by sending us the registration card in the back of the book. In another effort to help you use Nolo's latest materials, we offer a 25% discount off the purchase of any new Nolo book if you turn in any earlier printing or edition. (See the "Recycle Offer" in the back of the book.)

PRINTING HISTORY

Second Edition	FEBRUARY 1994
Editor	ROBIN LEONARD
Book Design	JACKIE MANCUSO
Cover Design	TONI IHARA
Proofreading	ELY NEWMAN
Production	DAVE McFARLAND
Index	JANE MEYERHOFFER
Printing	DELTA LITHOGRAPH

Kaufman, Barbara, 1993-
    Nolo's pocket guide to consumer rights :
/ by Barbara Kaufman. -- 2nd California ed.
        p.   cm.
    Rev. ed. of: Barbara Kaufman's consumer action guide. 1st ed.
1991.
    Includes index.
    ISBN 0-87337-218-2
    1. Consumer protection--Law and legislation--California--Popular
works. I. Kaufman, Barbara, 1933- Consumer action guide.
II. Nolo Press. III. Title.
KFC375.Z9K38 1994
343.794'071--dc
[347.940371]   94-2698
                                                    CIP

DEDICATIONS

To Ron Kaufman, for his love and incredible patience.
To Steve, Karen and Lauren, for their support and encouragement.

ACKNOWLEDGMENTS

Many thanks to Karen Kaufman, Juliana McCrary and Pat Nelson for reading and editing the first draft before it was ever submitted to the publisher.

I also want to express my gratitude to Robin Leonard, the toughest editor in California (but so lovable), for her outstanding editing, hard work, stamina and patience, as well as her hard questions, which helped make the book far better than I ever anticipated. (She was even tougher than my editor on the first edition, Jake Warner.) Without Robin and Jake's help, this book wouldn't have happened.

The "family" at Nolo Press is incredible. My thanks to all the folks who contributed to this book, namely Nolo editors Lisa Goldoftas, Mary Randolph, Steve Elias and Patti Gima; Nolo authors Dave Brown, Denis Clifford, Steve Fishman, Cora Jordan, Tony Mancuso and Ira Serkes; Nolo comptroller Barbara Hodovan; Nolo insurance guru, Mike Mansel, of the Insurance Associates of Northern California; and Nolo mortgage guru, Michael Cohen, of Schnell Investments. An extra special thanks to Marcia Stewart and Barbara Kate Repa for their tremendous contributions to the second editions; and Jane Meyerhoffer for compiling the index. I want to thank Ely Newman for his excellent proofreading, fact-checking and copyediting; Jackie Mancuso for her fine book design; and Dave McFarland for his rapid and conscientious production.

Special thanks, too, to Robert Bruss, the syndicated newspaper columnist and real estate expert, for his good information and editing; and Judy Gaither of the Human Investment Project of San Mateo for her help on reverse annuity mortgages.

ABOUT THE AUTHOR

In November of 1992, Barbara Kaufman was elected to the San Francisco Board of Supervisors. Previously, she was the founder of the all-volunteer public service KCBS Call For Action, in San Francisco. This community service, staffed by 45 volunteers, provides consumer information, referrals with follow-up calls and problem-solving ombudsmen services for Northern Californians. In addition to having run this nonbroadcast service for the past ten years, Barbara hosted a live, daily call-in, consumer-oriented, problem-solving radio program for many years on KCBS. Many people call her a consumer advocate; she calls herself a problem-solver and an "information junkie." For three years, she served on the Federal Reserve Board's Consumer Advisory Council, which met with the Board of Governors of the Federal Reserve in Washington, DC. Barbara and her husband, Ron Kaufman, live in San Francisco and have three grown children.

CONTENTS

Introduction

This book is designed to provide Californians with practical and legal information to effectively solve hundreds of consumer problems. It provides a single place to turn for answers to a wide variety of consumer questions—the kinds we all encounter everyday. And, if your rights have been violated, this consumer guide tells you where to complain to get action.

Here are examples of the kinds of problems I cover:

- Your new car won't start for the fourth time in a month.
- A store won't give you a cash refund.
- Your former landlord won't return your security deposit.
- Your car sustained $1,600 of damage in an accident, but your insurance company will pay only $1,200.
- A contractor you hired and paid to remodel your kitchen hasn't paid his subcontractor, who puts a lien on your house.
- An airline loses your luggage and offers much less than what you think is fair to cover your loss.

One of the objectives of this book is to help consumers figure out which of the literally hundreds of federal, state, local and private agencies and businesses can help with their problems. Often help is available in unexpected ways from surprising places, and many busy consumers needlessly give up important rights because they don't have the time or energy to find the right help.

To help consumers find out what to do and/or where to go, I've divided this book into approximately 200 topics, organized alphabetically by larger categories, such as Motor Vehicles and Travel. Each entry covers basic information, including your legal rights, as well as what help may be available from government and private organizations with relevant addresses and phone numbers. If you're having difficulty getting your problem addressed and there's a possible remedy, I tell you how to proceed. If you need additional information on the topic and it can be obtained for little or no cost, I tell you how to get it.

For example, suppose your new car develops engine failure that the dealer fails to fix after repeated attempts. What can you do? In the chapter Motor Vehicles, look under the entry Automobile Repairs. There you'll find the subhead "If Your Car's a Lemon." In this section, I describe what government agencies may investigate your problems with an auto dealer or manufacturer; how you can try to get a new car or refund by invoking your rights to an arbitration hearing under California's "lemon law;" where you can get a free booklet on the state's lemon law; what books are available to help you prepare and perhaps win your arbitration hearing; and how to find a list of lawyers who specialize in lemon law if you decide to sue in court.

It's fair to ask how I collected all the information in this book. As the founder of KCBS Radio's Call For Action, an entirely volunteer-run community service, I spent 11 years working with 45 dedicated Call For Action volunteers to provide off-air consumer information to individuals, make appropriate referrals with follow-up phone calls and provide hands-on problem-solving (ombudsman) services. Together, we handled over 100,000 telephone calls and helped consumers recover over $7,000,000. In addition, for many years I hosted a daily, hour-long call-in radio program on KCBS and currently provide daily consumer reports. In short, I've learned, on the job, what consumers want to know and how to get the answers.

Finally, a personal request. If I haven't covered a topic you think should be included, or I didn't cover it thoroughly enough, please complete the feedbak card in the back of this book, and return it to Nolo Press . I will try and answer your question and, if it's of widespread interest, include it in the next edition of this book.

Barbara Kaufman

San Francisco, California

Banking

CROSS-REFERENCES

DEPOSIT INSTITUTIONS (BANKS, CREDIT UNIONS, SAVINGS AND LOAN ASSOCIATIONS)

Shopping for a conveniently located bank that is fiscally safe and offers a good deal can be time-consuming and confusing. Deposits of a $100,000 or less are safe (meaning that if the deposit institution goes under, you can still get your money) if the bank, credit union or savings and loan association has federal deposit insurance. All deposit institutions are overseen by a regulatory agency.

Credit Unions

Credit unions are increasingly popular because they offer slightly higher rates of interest on savings accounts, and slightly lower rates of interest on loans, than many traditional financial institutions. Credit unions are often more competitive than banks and savings and loans because their nonprofit status makes their operating costs lower. Also, because they are member-owned, credit unions use volunteers, which helps cut down expenses. Credit unions, just like banks and savings and loans, are either state or federally chartered. Make sure your credit union is federally insured by the National Credit Union Administration, which means accounts are insured up to $100,000.

Some people think it is easier to get a loan from a credit union than from a bank of savings and loan. That is not necessarily true. Credit unions are just as concerned about your credit-worthiness as are other financial institutions. Like banks and savings and loans, credit unions offer automatic payroll savings plans—a set amount is deducted from your paycheck and put in a savings account. If your financial history shows you are a consistent saver, you may have a better chance of qualifying for a loan.

Automated Teller Machines (ATMs) or 24-Hour Tellers

ATMs are electronic terminals that allow you to withdraw cash, make deposits, transfer money between different bank accounts, make loan and/or credit card payments and verify your current balance. Most ATMs have 24-hour access.

If you think money is missing from your account (or has been withdrawn by an unauthorized person), you will have a hard time convincing the bank that it made a mistake. Money can be withdrawn from an ATM only by using your ATM card and your Personal Identification Number (PIN). When cardholders insist they did not take money out of their account, the culprit usually turns out to be a family member or friend. When this happens, you are responsible, not the bank. Some banks have cameras recording ATM transactions for proof.

Debit Cards/Electronic Fund Transfers (EFTs)

A debit card looks like an ATM card or a credit card, but using one is the equivalent of writing a check—the money is automatically deducted from your bank account. You can use your debit card at some grocery stores, gas stations and a few retail stores, and to get cash from automatic teller machines. Unfortunately, the debit card gives you fewer legal rights than does a credit card. For example, you cannot dispute the quality of goods or services purchased with a debit card. If you generally pay your credit card bills in full each month without paying finance charges, you are better off using a credit card because the money accrues interest longer in your bank account (assuming you have an interest-bearing account) than if it is automatically deducted.

Debit cards are particularly attractive to merchants because the money is immediately, or within a day or two, transferred to the merchant's account, eliminating the possibility of bounced checks. Debit cards are attractive to consumers who prefer to pay at the point of sale rather than charge their purchases, but do not want to carry their checkbook or large amounts of cash.

EFT Consumer Protections

The federal Electronic Fund Transfer Act protects you against a deduction for a purchase not made, an incorrect deduction or an error. You should call or write your financial institution as soon as you notice the error, but you must contact the bank no later than 60 days from when the monthly statement showing the error is mailed to you. If you call, you may be asked to send the information in writing within ten business days. You are always better off putting a dispute in writing because you will have proof of notification. The financial institution must resolve the problem within 45 days. If it takes longer than ten days, it must put the disputed amount of money back into the account until the investigation is completed. If the institution finds no error, it can take the money back, but only after sending a written explanation of why it believes the statement was correct. 15 U.S.C. § 1693f.

Lost or Stolen ATM and EFT Cards

Once you report your ATM or EFT card missing, you are not responsible for any unauthorized withdrawals. If you notify your financial institution within two business days after learning of the loss or theft of your ATM or EFT card, your maximum liability is $50. If you fail to notify the bank within two business days after you realize the card is gone but do notify the bank within 60 days from the date the statement is sent to you, your maximum liability is $500. Your liability is unlimited if you do not report a theft or loss within 60 days from the date the monthly statement is mailed to you. Check your statements carefully in a timely fashion and you won't have this problem. 15 U.S.C. § 1693f.

Direct Deposits/Withdrawals and Pre-Authorized Payments

Direct deposits allow your paychecks or Social Security checks to be deposited directly into your bank account. You can also authorize certain recurring bills, such as monthly utility bills, mortgage payments or insurance premiums, to be paid automatically from your bank account. You can stop most automatic payments by calling or writing your financial institution at least three business days before the transfer takes place. It's always a good idea to follow up in writing. In fact, your institution may require you to submit a written request within 14 days of your call.

Pay-by-Phone (Telephone Transfer) Plans

Pay-by-phone or telephone transfer plans allow you to pay bills or transfer money between accounts by calling your financial institution and giving your "Identification Number." Generally, you must sign a written plan or agreement with your financial institution before telephone transfer authorization goes into effect.

MONEY TRANSFER RECORDS

If you are in the habit of transferring money between accounts, make sure you receive written confirmations so you can verify that the transactions went through correctly. Good, up-to-date recordkeeping will not only help you keep track of your money, but also will be useful if you ever have a problem with your account.

Certificate of Deposit (CD) Accounts

A CD is a contract between a depositor and a financial institution. You agree to leave your money on deposit for a specified time period while the bank agrees to pay a set amount of interest for that same length of time.

Cashing a CD Before Maturity

A financial institution can refuse to cash a CD before it matures. Most, however, will cash the CD but charge you an early withdrawal penalty.

Penalty for Early Withdrawal

The federal government does not require that a financial institution fine you for taking money out of a CD before it matures. A financial institution can charge a penalty, however, for early withdrawal—and most do. For CDs of one year or less, the typical penalty is one-to-three months' interest. The penalty on longer term deposits is three-to-six months' interest.

Early Withdrawal When the CD Holder Dies

Federally insured banks and savings and loan associations are prohibited from charging a penalty when a CD is cashed early because of the death of a primary or joint CD owner.

More Information/Where to Complain—Banks

If you have a problem with a bank and cannot satisfactorily resolve it, you can file a complaint with the appropriate regulatory agency. Regulators handle only certain kinds of complaints. For example, many consumers complain about high fees that banks charge for various services, such as for closing an IRA account. Regulatory agencies have no enforcement powers over that type of complaint—banks can charge what they want for services. Regulators will handle complaints about a bank not complying with the law. For example, if you can't get satisfaction from a bank that cashes a check with a forged signature, you can complain to a regulatory agency. Also, it's appropriate to go to a regulatory agency if you have disputed something on your credit card bill and your bank is not responding.

If you are not sure where to complain, your financial institution or any of the regulators can tell you which agency to contact.

- Nationally chartered banks (any bank whose name contains the word "national" or the initials "NA" or "NT and SA"). Comptroller of the Currency, Consumer Department, 50 Fremont Street, Suite 3900, San Francisco, CA 94105. Send a written recap of the facts. Or call (415) 545-5900, between 3:00 p.m. and 4:00 p.m., Monday through Thursday, or between 2:00 p.m. and 3:00 p.m., Fridays, to file a complaint or request a complaint form.
- State chartered banks that are members of the Federal Reserve. Federal Reserve Bank, Consumer Affairs Department, P.O. Box 7702, San Francisco, CA 94120, (415) 974-2967.
- State chartered banks that are not members of the Federal Reserve are regulated by the California Department of Banking. The main office is located in San Francisco, with regional offices in Sacramento, Los Angeles and San Diego. The Department of Banking will accept complaints on its toll-free number, (800) 622-0620.

    You can also file a complaint against a state chartered bank that is not a member of the Federal Reserve through the Federal Deposit Insurance Corporation (FDIC), Office of Consumer and Compliance Programs, 25 Ecker Street, Suite 2300, San Francisco, CA 94105, (415) 546-0160. You can also reach the FDIC through its toll-free number, (800) 934-3342, Monday through Friday, 6 a.m. to 2 p.m. pacific time.

More Information/Where to Complain— Savings and Loan Associations

- State chartered savings and loans. You can file a complaint regarding the computation of interest on loans or savings accounts, homebuyers' impound accounts for taxes and insurance, late charges on loan payments, unfulfilled loan commitments, improper foreclosure on real estate or discrimination in lending through the California Department of Savings and Loans, 300 South Spring Street, Suite 16502, Los Angeles, CA 90013, (213) 897-8242.
- Federally chartered savings and loans. Contact the Office of Thrift Supervision, Regulatory Compliance, P.O. Box 7165, San Francisco, CA 94120, (415) 616-1500.
- You may be able to file a complaint (regarding deposit insurance) about some savings and loans through the Federal Deposit Insurance Corporation (FDIC), office of Consumer and Compliance Programs, which has taken control over the former Federal Savings and Loan Insurance Corporation (FSLIC). FDIC's California office is listed above, under "More Information/Where to Complain—Banks."

More Information/Where to Complain—Credit Unions

- Federally chartered credit unions. National Credit Union Administration, 2300 Clayton Road, Suite 1350, Concord, CA 94520, (510) 825-6125.
- State chartered credit unions are regulated by the California Department of Corporations, which has four offices: 3700 Wilshire Blvd., Suite 600, Los Angeles, CA 90010, (213) 736-2741; 1115 11th Street, Sacramento, CA 95814, (916) 445-7205; 1350 Front Street, San Diego, CA 92101, (619) 525-4233; 1390 Market Street, Room 810, San Francisco, CA 94102, (415) 557-3787. The toll-free number for general information and complaints is (800) 347-6995.

Additional Resources

Consumer Action, a nonprofit consumer education and advocacy group, does annual surveys of bank, savings and loan, and credit union checking and savings accounts, comparing services, interest rates and costs. Consumer Action's publications are free; send a self-addressed, stamped, business-size envelope with 52¢ postage to Consumer Action,116 New Montgomery Street, Suite 233, San Francisco, CA 94105. Consumer Action also has a "Credit and Finance Project," to provide banking information to people with disabilities, communities of color and low-income, immigrant, senior and limited-English-speaking consumers. Write to Consumer Action or call (415) 777-9648 to find out more about the "Credit and Finance Project."

CHECKS

The variety of checks and checking accounts is so vast that you have many choices. Be aware of the following rules that affect your writing and cashing of checks.

Check Holds

You can withdraw money deposited from government checks, cashier's checks and money orders the day after you deposit them.

Under the federal Expedited Funds Act, local checks payable through the Federal Reserve's check-clearing system (or commercial banking check-clearing systems), cannot be held more than two business days, and nonlocal checks more than five business days. A local check is one written on Northern California (and parts of Nevada) financial institutions for people living in Northern California. A local check is one written on Southern California (and Las Vegas area and Arizona) financial institutions for people living in Southern California. All others are nonlocal checks.

For example, a local check deposited on Monday will be available for withdrawal on Wednesday. A nonlocal check will be available for withdrawal the following Monday. Even though many banks are open on Saturdays, Federal Reserve business days are Monday through Friday.

In the following situations, holds c.re seven business days for local checks and 11 business days for nonlocal checks:

- new accounts fewer than 30-days old
- accounts often overdrawn
- checks over $5,000
- re-deposited bounced checks, and
- checks the bank has reasonable cause to believe will be uncollectible.

Money Market Checking Accounts

Money market accounts are not the same as bank, savings and loan or credit union accounts. The instruments used to spend the funds are not checks, but share drafts. Money market accounts are not insured or regulated by the federal government, and are therefore not subject to the Expedited Funds Act described above.

Bounced Checks

Checks bounce usually for one of three reasons:

- insufficient funds in the account
- no bank account exists (usually the account has been closed), or
- the person who wrote the check ordered a stop payment.

If a check you *receive* bounces, California law gives you the right to collect the amount of the check plus additional "punitive" damages—damages meant to punish. Send a demand letter, by certified mail, giving the check-maker 30 days to make good on the check. Make it clear that if he fails to do so, you intend to take him to Small Claims Court and ask the judge to award you triple damages. Civil Code § 1719.

Once you're in court, the judge can award you the amount of the check plus triple damages as follows:

- In general, you are entitled to three times the amount of the check.
- In no case will the court award you less than $100.
- In no case will the court award you more than $500.

If the check is for $25, the judge will award you the minimum $100 plus the $25. If the check is for $150, the judge will award you three times the $150, or $450, plus the original $150, for a total of $600. If the check is for $500, the judge will award you the maximum penalty of $500 plus the original $500, for a total of $1,000.

If a check you *write* bounces, no law limits the amount that a financial institution can charge you. California banks assess a fee on average of $12, with the general range between $8 and $15. You may take comfort in knowing that California's average is much lower than most states, where the typical fee charged for a bounced checked is close to $25.

Stopping Payment on a Check

You can usually stop payment on a check that hasn't been cashed simply by calling your financial institution. Some banks, however, require a written request, which you can deliver in person. Banks charge $5 to $10 to stop payment on a check. Some stop-payment orders last only six months. If you are concerned that the person to whom you wrote the check will try to cash it more than six months from when you first stop payment, you may have to pay another $5 or $10 for a second stop payment order. Once a stop-payment order goes into effect, your bank won't honor the check when it's presented for payment.

In general, you can legally stop payment on a check if:

- You have the merchant's consent, such as when a check gets lost in the mail and you write a replacement.
- You have an honest dispute over a purchase. A merchant who believes it is right, however, may pursue legal remedies, including suing you.
- A purchase includes a "three-day cooling-off period" and three days have not yet elapsed.
- You clearly didn't get what you paid for. Again, a merchant may dispute this and sue you.
- A merchant deceived you.
- You were seriously confused or under real duress when you wrote the check.

In general, you don't have the right to stop payment on a check if:

- You simply change your mind about a purchase. Once you hand over a check, the merchant is entitled to be paid.
- It will look like you never intended to honor the check; it's a crime to write a check you don't intend to honor.

If you stop payment without explanation—especially if you don't return the merchandise—the seller will likely assume you intended a rip-off. You may face criminal charges as well as a civil lawsuit. Whether you are returning a product or have already received a service that can't be returned (you ate a meal or had repair work done), always write a short, polite letter to the merchant explaining why you stopped payment on the check. Be sure to date the letter and keep a photocopy. If the merchant sues you, you'll want evidence that you communicated your reasons for stopping payment in writing.

Endorsed Checks

When you cash or deposit a check made payable to you, you are normally required to endorse it (sign your name) on the back of the check. This endorsement identifies you as the correct recipient of the check. This endorsement also means you accept legal responsibility for the check. Even if you deposit a check without first endorsing it, you still accept responsibility for it. (If you lose an endorsed check and someone else cashes it, you're out of luck.) In addition, if the check bounces, you must reimburse the bank for any money you withdrew.

Old or "Stale" Checks

Generally, a check is considered stale when it is older than six months or 180 days. Banks are not obligated to honor a check more than six-months old; however, banks can, at their discretion, cash older checks if the funds are there. In California, most banks will cash stale checks unless the check says "void after six months." Commercial Code § 4404.

Postdated Checks

A postdated check is one dated later than the date it was actually written. If you receive a postdated check and present it to a bank for cashing prior to its date, a bank may legally cash the check, although it may refuse to do so.

 Don't write a postdated check. It is better to wait until you have the funds in your account so that the recipient can cash it.

Undated Checks

An undated check is valid and payable immediately.

Check Cashing for Non-Customers

Banks are not required to cash checks, make change or provide any other services to people who are not bank customers. Some banks charge non-customers a fee for cashing checks, even if the check is drawn on that bank.

Must a Merchant Accept Checks?

California law does not require merchants to accept checks, but many do.

Can the Merchant Ask for Identification?

In years past, many merchants required two pieces of identification to cash a check—a California driver's license or ID card, and another form of identification, such as a major credit card.

Today, however, merchants cannot require you to show a credit card or write down your credit card number on the back of a check. Nor can a merchant refuse your check just because you won't show a credit card. A merchant can require a reasonable form of identification, however, such as a driver's license—and can record the number on your check. Merchants may also ask you to voluntarily show them a credit card and then record the type of card, the issuer of the card and expiration date, but not the card number, on the back of your check. If you refuse to show the card, however, you cannot be denied the right to complete your purchase.

If a merchant violates the law, the fine for the first offense is $250. Each subsequent violation can cost the merchant a $1,000 fine. In addition, the merchant may be sued in a civil action by the person paying with a check, the attorney general, or the district attorney or city attorney where the violation occurred. If the merchant shows that the violation was not intentional and was the result of an honest error, the merchant will not be penalized.

Checks Marked "Payment in Full"

If you write a check for less than the full payment yet mark it "payment in full," a creditor can strike out the notation, cash the check and pursue you for the remaining balance. Even if the creditor cashes the check without striking out the "payment in full" language, he can still come after you for the rest.

If you want to ensure that the creditor can't come after you for the balance, before sending the check you must give the creditor at least 15 days' (but not more than 90 days') notice of your intention to send a check for less than the disputed amount with a "payment in full" notation. Once you send the check, if the creditor cashes it, he really does accept it as full payment and can't sue you for the rest. Civil Code § 1526.

Lost Government Checks

If you do not receive an expected government check, contact the issuing agency (such as the Social Security Administration or Internal Revenue Service) as soon as possible. The agency first checks to see if in fact a check was issued to you. If a check was issued, the agency investigates, with the help of the Post Office and Treasury Department if necessary, to determine if the check has been cashed.

The agency will send you an investigation form with a claim number. If the agency determines the check has not been cashed, the agency will order a stop payment on the missing check and send you a replacement check within a few weeks. If the check has been cashed, the agency will do a signature check to determine whether you or an unauthorized person cashed the check. This investigation may take as long as six months.

More Information

Money Troubles: Legal Strategies to Cope With Your Debts, by attorney Robin Leonard (Nolo Press), contains extensive information on using checks to pay your bills. It's available in bookstores and libraries. ∎

BUSINESSES AND CORPORATIONS

BETTER BUSINESS BUREAU (BBB)

BBBs are nonprofit organizations, sponsored by local businesses, that provide general information on companies, such as the nature of the business or how long it has been in business. BBBs maintain and disclose records of consumer satisfaction or dissatisfaction on individual companies. Just because a local BBB doesn't have any complaints on record about a particular company doesn't necessarily mean the company is okay. But if the local BBB's records include numerous complaints about a company, be on guard.

Local BBBs provide free arbitration or mediation services for any type of dispute if both sides are willing to participate.

Autoline is one of the BBB's mediation/arbitration services for many auto manufacturers. It is the authorized third-party dispute-resolution provider for Acura, Alfa Romeo, American Izuzu, Audi, General Motors (Buick, Cadillac, Chevrolet, Oldsmobile, Pontiac), Honda, Infiniti, Jaguar, Maserati, Nissan, Peugeot, Range Rover, Rolls-Royce, Saab-Scania, Saturn and Volkswagen.

BUSINESS LISTINGS

Most large libraries have a Business section with directories and reference materials containing the names and addresses of the president, chairman of the board and chief executive officer of private and public corporations. Reference librarians may help you by phone if they are not too busy when you call.

If you want to register a complaint or compliment with a company, write to the vice-president for public relations, or a similarly titled person, at the main headquarters.

Finding the Owner of a Business

Here are several reasons why you might want to find the owner of a business:

- The business establishment closes its doors with no advance notice to the public. The company may have your money or your goods, such as shoes or jewelry left for repair.
- The employees of a business may not be cooperative, and you would like to discuss the situation with the owner.
- You would like to sue the owner in Small Claims Court.

The following offices or businesses may have records which may help you track down the owner of a business:

- The Business License office in the city where the business is located. Licenses and permits to operate a business are controlled at the city or county level.
- The Tax Collector's office, which can tell you if the business owner is also the property owner. If the business is renting or leasing space, the tax collector can tell you who owns the property. The property owner may give you the name of the tenant—the business owner.
- For corporations, the California Secretary of State requires incorporated businesses to file Articles of Incorporation. These list corporate directors and the "agent for service"—who you need to serve any court papers to. You can write to the California Secretary of State, Corporation Status Unit, 1230 J Street, Sacramento, CA 95814. Enclose a $5 check. The California Secretary of State also maintains a list of out-of-state corporations doing business in California.
- For partnerships or unincorporated businesses, the County Recorder's office requires "fictitious name" (for example, the XYZ Candy Store) or "doing business as" (DBA) firms to be formally filed, published and recorded.
- The landlord (owner of the real property where the business is located) may tell you who owns the business if you explain why you want this information.
- Public libraries.

BUSINESS COUNSELING

The U.S. Small Business Administration (SBA) provides a wide variety of business counseling on finance, accounting, recordkeeping, business start-up and management, taxes, marketing, sales promotion and advertising, as well as special areas of retailing, manufacturing, sales and service businesses. Under SBA sponsorship, retired business executives—Service Corps of Retired Executives (SCORE)—and non-retired executives—Active Corps of Executives (ACE)—volunteer their services to small business owners and managers and to people planning to go into business. SCORE and ACE programs are located all over the state in SBA offices and Chambers of Commerce. For information, check the phone book white pages listings under United States Government Offices—Small Business Administration—SCORE Counseling.

CORPORATIONS

The California Department of Corporations licenses and regulates loan and finance companies, escrow companies, state-chartered credit unions and health maintenance organizations (HMOs). It also regulates and watches many investment activities—sales of corporate securities, limited partnerships and commodity option contracts—in addition to regulating investment counselors, commodity option issuers and security brokers. The Department of Corporations handles complaints about check-sellers and -cashers, and trading stamp companies.

Forming a Corporation

Small business owners often incorporate to protect themselves from personal liability for the debts and claims of the company. Incorporating also provides the owners with tax-free fringe benefits and allows them to split business income between themselves and their corporation. Because corporate tax rates are less than individual rates for lower levels of corporate taxable income, incorporating can reduce the small business owner's overall income tax liability.

Forming a business corporation is accomplished by filing Articles of Incorporation with the California Secretary of State. Forms and instructions for Articles of Incorporation as well as other corporate forms are contained in the *Corporation's Check List,* available from the Sacramento office of the Secretary of State for a small fee. Call (916) 445-0620 for current ordering information. You can pick up this information in the following Secretary of State offices:

- 107 S. Broadway, Suite 4001, Los Angeles
- 455 Golden Gate Avenue, Suite 2236, San Francisco
- 1350 Front Street, Suite 2060, San Diego.

Nonprofit Corporations

Arts, environmental, health, social service and countless other charitable, educational, religious, scientific and literary groups form nonprofit corporations to qualify for state and federal tax exemptions, public and private grant funds and tax-deductible contributions from donors. Most seek tax-exempt status under § 501(c)(3) of the Internal Revenue Code. Forming a California nonprofit involves filing nonprofit Articles of Incorporation with the Secretary of State and filing state and federal tax exemption applications. Sample Articles and the state FTB 3500 tax form are free from the California Secretary of State by calling (916) 445-0620. The IRS 1023 application package can be obtained from a local IRS office, or by calling (800) 829-3676.

More Information/Where to Complain

The California Department of Corporations has four locations:
- 3700 Wilshire Blvd., Suite 600, Los Angeles, CA 90010, (213) 736-2741

BUSINESS AND CORPORATIONS

- 1115 11th Street, Sacramento, CA 95814, (916) 445-7205
- 1350 Front Street, San Diego, CA 92101, (619) 525-4233
- 1390 Market Street, Room 810, San Francisco, CA 94102, (415) 557-3787.
  The toll-free number for general information and complaints is (800) 347-6995.

Additional Resources

How to Form Your Own California Corporation, by attorney Anthony Mancuso (Nolo Press), contains the forms, instructions and tax information you need to incorporate a small business yourself. *California Incorporator,* also by Anthony Mancuso (Nolo Press), contains the same information as *How to Form Your Own California Corporation,* but is for people who'd rather do the paperwork on their DOS computer.

The California Nonprofit Corporation Handbook, by Anthony Mancuso (Nolo Press), shows you, step-by-step, how to form and operate a nonprofit corporation in California. You can buy the book alone or the book with the forms on a DOS or Macintosh disk. It covers the latest corporation and tax law changes, including expanded protection from personal liability for corporate directors, as well as complete instructions for obtaining federal tax exemptions.

The California Professional Corporation Handbook, by Anthony Mancuso (Nolo Press), shows healthcare professionals, lawyers, accountants and other professionals how to form and operate a corporation in California. It's available in bookstores and libraries.

Taking Care of Your Corporation, by Anthony Mancuso (Nolo Press), shows you how to take care of day-to-day corporate business, including holding meetings, preparing corporate minutes, passing board resolutions, amending Articles and Bylaws, borrowing and lending money and making important tax resolutions. It's available in bookstores and libraries.

STOCKS, STOCKBROKERS AND SECURITIES FIRMS

Corporations issue stock to raise capital to operate and expand their businesses. When you buy stock, you become part owner (stockholder or shareholder) of the company or corporation. If the corporation does well, your ownership share (stock) will likely go up in value. If it does poorly, the opposite is usually true. In short, when you buy stock, even in well-run, conservative companies, you are taking a chance. Stockholders can benefit if they receive dividends or if they sell the stock for more than they paid for it.

You can easily buy stock in any publicly traded corporation through a stockbroker who is a member of the stock exchange that trades the particular stock. "Full service" stockbrokers research various investments and give investment advice to help their clients. Discount brokers, who charge lower brokerage commissions, only execute orders and do not offer investment advice.

If a Securities Firm Fails

The Securities Investor Protection Corporation (SIPC), a nonprofit membership corporation, protects securities customers of member broker-dealers. SIPC does not protect against losses from the rise or fall in market value of your investments. Nor does it protect investments in commodities or precious metals.

If your firm fails, you will have no problem if the broker sent you the securities certificates. If your cash or securities are on deposit at the failed brokerage house, SIPC will try to arrange for your accounts to be transferred to another broker. If that can't be done, SIPC will deliver to you any securities registered in your name. All remaining cash and securities held by the firm will be distributed to customers on a pro-rata basis. After that, SIPC funds are available to satisfy remaining claims of each customer up to a maximum of $500,000.

SPIC is located at 805 15th Street NW, Suite 800, Washington, DC 20005-6728, (202) 371-8300.

Price Disputes

The Wall Street Journal listing of stock market prices is usually considered the official record. You can also verify a price by calling the National Daily Quotation Bureau, (201) 239-6100. If you place an order at a certain price, you are entitled to get it at that price. If you place a market order (to buy or sell at the market), the broker is not required to buy or sell at the price quoted at that minute. Brokers work quickly, however, so your price will be verified promptly. If you are having a dispute about a price which was higher or lower in your trade than reported in *The Wall Street Journal*, ask your broker to get an official tape from the New York or American Stock Exchange to resolve the question. This does not apply to NASDAQ ("over-the-counter") stocks.

Complaints Against Stockbrokers

Churning an investor's account is one of the most frequent complaints against brokers. "Churning" means excessive trading in the account to generate commissions for the broker with little or no benefit to the investor.

Unsuitability for the investor and the account is another common complaint. "Unsuitability" means investing the client's money in stocks with too much risk that were inappropriate for the investor's means and objectives. For example, unsuitability is apparent when a broker invests the money of an 83-year-old retired school teacher, who depends on dividends from her stock portfolio to provide the extra money she needs to live on, in highly speculative stocks or stocks that pay little or no dividend (growth stocks). A broker must know the customer and use due diligence to determine the needs and facts of that customer/investor.

Unauthorized trading, failing to follow trading instructions and failing to perform timely transactions are other common complaints.

If you have a complaint against a broker, first discuss it directly with him. If that does not work, go to the branch or regional manager who has responsibility for that broker.

If your problem is still not resolved, consider arbitration. The securities industry operates a system of self-regulation through arbitration programs to help settle disputes and controversies. Each major stock exchange, New York or American, for example, handles disputes with its members. The largest arbitration program is run by the National Association of Securities Dealers (NASD), whose members are required to arbitrate. Although NASD deals with over-the-counter (OTC) stocks (sales of any securities not listed on an exchange—the great majority of stocks are traded on the OTC market), NASD will arbitrate any dispute a consumer has with a member.

Check your brokerage agreement. It probably stipulates that you must take your dispute to arbitration rather than go to court, and it may specify which arbitration program will be used. This is, generally speaking, fine. Arbitration is faster and cheaper than going to court. Unfortunately, most securities arbitration agreements call for arbitration to be carried out by an organization chosen by the broker. A 1990 New York State Court of Appeals case, however, upheld a customer's right to take certain stockbroker disputes to independent arbitration (such as the American Arbitration Association). This is a major consumer victory that could benefit consumers in every state.

To learn more about securities arbitration, ask for the "Uniform Information Packet" from the NASD, 525 Market Street, Suite 300, San Francisco, CA 94105, (415) 882-1200.

Securities and Exchange Commission

The Securities and Exchange Commission (SEC) administers federal laws involving securities. Some of their responsibilities include:

- protecting the public and investors by trying to prevent fraud and/or deception in the sale of securities
- making sure that companies making public securities offerings fulfill all the necessary financial and other disclosure requirements, and
- protecting investors' interests in corporate reorganizations.

More Information/Where to Complain

The SEC has two branch offices in California:

- 5670 Wilshire Boulevard, 11th Floor, Los Angeles, CA 90036-3648, (213) 965-3998
- 901 Market Street, Suite 470, San Francisco, CA 94103, (415) 744-3140.

The main office location is 450 Fifth Street NW, Washington, DC 20549, (202) 272-3100.

Old Stock Certificates

You may have some old stock certificates and may be wondering if they have any value. They probably do if the corporation or a successor corporation (in the case of a merger or acquisition) is still in existence. Here's how to find out.

California Companies—1850s through 1959

Stocks of companies incorporated in California from the 1850s to the 1950s may be researched by writing or calling the Secretary of State Archives, 201 North Sunrise Avenue, Roseville, CA 95661, (916) 773-3000. The Secretary of State Archives keeps Articles of Incorporation for both active and inactive corporations. The records will show the names and addresses of the members of the Board of Directors for as long as the corporation remained active. Beyond that, the records may indicate what happened to the corporation and the stock. The Secretary of State Archives charge 10¢ per page to photocopy, payable in advance.

California Companies—1960 to the Present

If the stock certificate of the California Corporation was issued after 1959, contact the Corporations Division of the Secretary of State's office, (916) 445-0620, for more information.

Non-California Corporations

If the stock was not from a California corporation, the Secretary of State (or Corporations Commissioner) in the state where the corporation was incorporated may have records to help you.

Commercial Services

There are a number of commercial services which will trace an old stock for an up-front fee (from $20 to $50). If the company finds a valuable stock, it will charge you a fee based on a percentage of the stock's value. A stockbroker or one of the stock exchanges can give you the names of reputable stock-tracing services.

Additional Resources

The Directory of Obsolete Securities, published by Financial Information Inc., and *The Capital Changes Reporter*, published by Commerce Clearing House, contain lists and information about many old securities. Also, some of the standard financial resources (such as *Standard and Poor's* or *Moody's*) may show if your stock has a new name or has been bought out by another company. A large public library, especially one with a Business section, will likely have these books.

The Securities and Exchange Commission has a two-page publication called "How to Find Current Information About Old Stock Certificates" which lists a number of books that may have information to help you. Write to: Office of Consumer Affairs and Information Services, Securities and Exchange Commission, 450 Fifth Street NW, Washington, DC 20549.

COMMODITIES

Commodities (such as wheat, sugar, pork-bellies, oil and rubber) are raw materials which make the products we use on a daily basis. Businesses which use or produce commodities buy and sell them; so do investors and speculators. The commodities futures market (a deal made to buy or sell commodities in the future) helps businesses minimize risks that prices will rise or fall.

More Information/Where to Complain

The Commodity Futures Trading Commission regulates the futures exchanges, commodity brokerage companies, brokers, salespeople and advisors.

If you suspect fraud, misrepresentation, unauthorized trading or misappropriation of your money by an agent or broker, contact the Commodity Futures Trading Commission, Murdock Plaza, 10900 Wilshire Boulevard, Suite 400, Los Angeles, CA 90024, (310) 575-6783.

The National Futures Association can tell you if a company is registered with it and if any disciplinary action has been taken against the company. It can be reached at (800) 621-3570, 6:00 a.m. to 3:00 p.m. pacific standard time. ■

CONSUMER RIGHTS

TOPICS

RESTROOMS
Restrooms in Public Places
Restrooms in Restaurants
Restrooms in Gas Stations
Where to Complain
STORAGE
TELEPHONE LONG DISTANCE COSTS

SALES
AUCTIONS
Automobile Auctions
Private Auctions
Public Auctions
California Real Property Auctions
U.S. Government Auctions
IRS Auctions
Other Government Auctions
Where to Complain
DOOR-TO-DOOR SALES
MERCHANT STAMPS
REFUNDS FROM MERCHANTS
RIGHT OF CANCELLATION (COOLING-OFF PERIOD)
Federal Right to Cancel
Home Loans
State Right to Cancel
How to Count the Days
How to Cancel
CHARITIES
More Information
Make-a-Wish Foundation
FOOD
Contamination
Short Weight
Meat and Poultry Information
Salt and Sodium Information
Truth in Menus

HOW TO WRITE A COMPLAINT LETTER

CROSS-REFERENCES
Business and Corporations—Better Business Bureau (BBB)
Courts and Legal Rights—Small Claims Court
Credit, Loans and Debts—Credit Cards
Credit, Loans and Debts—Credit Reporting
Government—Government Agencies—Federal Trade Commission
Government—Government Agencies—Postal Service
Government—Government Agencies—California Public
Utilities Commission
Motor Vehicles—Trucks/Truckers
Real Estate, Homes & Neighbors—Home Sales
Safety and Hazards—Consumer Product Safety Commission
Safety and Hazards—Structural Pest Control
Service Providers—Accountants

FRAUD AND POTENTIAL PROBLEMS

CONSUMER FRAUD

Consumer fraud occurs when a merchant or other seller of goods uses deceit, trickery or intentional misrepresentation to con a consumer into making a purchase. An example is when a jewelry store offers to sell 14-carat gold chains at a certain price; when you bring home your purchase, you discover it is gold-plated.

More Information/Where to Complain

If you suspect you are a victim of fraud, call the National Fraud Information Center at (800) 876-7060.

Also contact your county District Attorney's office immediately. District Attorneys are law enforcement agencies responsible for investigating and pursuing criminal activity. In addition to prosecuting cases of fraud (criminal cases), they also file unfair business practices lawsuits (civil cases).

Many county District Attorney's offices offer mediation services, with a lot of clout, to consumers having a dispute with a merchant or business. For example, if you gave a merchant a deposit for a chair that was promised to be delivered to your house in two weeks, and three months later you still don't have it and the store won't give you your money back, the mediation service probably can get you a refund. Unfortunately, some smaller counties do not have large enough budgets to offer mediation services.

If your problem or complaint has statewide implications, such as a health spa chain violating California law, the California Attorney General's Public Inquiry Office, (800) 952-5225, may be interested. In addition, contacting a newspaper, radio or TV station that does investigative reporting may help bring attention to a fraudulent business practice.

The California Department of Consumer Affairs provides information and educational materials regarding consumer rights and responsibilities. In addition to advising consumers on how to resolve complaints, the Department will try to mediate a complaint that is not within the jurisdiction of other local, state or federal government or consumer protection agencies. Submit your written complaint to the California Department of Consumer Affairs, Consumer Assistance Office, 400 R Street, Room 1040, Sacramento, CA 95814; or call (916) 445-1254.

In addition, the Department has a consumer information line, (800) 344-9940, with recorded messages on four consumer areas—landlord-tenant, sales and promotion, automobiles and credit.

SCAMS

I am amazed by the vast numbers of sophisticated, intelligent and educated people who continually fall for scams. I guess we all want to believe we have truly won something once in our life. Of course, scam operators figured this out a long time ago—that's why new rip-offs proliferate every week. And scam operators have learned, paradoxically, that a person who has already been ripped off by one scam is most likely to bite again.

Even though I describe mainly mail scams, many of these rip-offs happen by phone, and all scams can happen either way.

Any postcard or letter you receive that asks you to call a long distance or even an 800 number to claim a "guaranteed prize" or verify a sweepstakes entry is almost surely a scam—even if you're asked to call a nationally recognized sweepstakes company such as Publisher's Clearing House. (Recent scams involve people posing as representatives of sweepstakes companies. But they still require that you send in money.) Legitimate contests and sweepstakes usually deliver a prize to you without requiring you to do anything or call anyone.

Here is the typical anatomy of a mail scam. A mailer states you have been selected to participate in a national promotion and that by participating you are a "guaranteed winner of one of four prizes." The prizes named may include:

- an expensive vehicle
- a $5,000 bond
- a vacation for two or four people to Hawaii, the Bahamas or Mexico
- some type of diamond jewelry (his and hers matching watches)
- a home entertainment set
- a fur coat, or
- a $5,000 shopping spree.

Often, the mailer will state that the promotion is not a lottery or a real estate timeshare sales presentation, but is a "valid premium incentive offer," which means you must buy something to get the so-called prize. Or the mailer will claim "this offer is not available to the general public; only those notified by mail are eligible." If you make the long distance call, you will be asked a question, such as "what color vehicle do you prefer," to lure you into thinking you have won the car or van.

But then you will be given a long, slick, sales pitch to buy overpriced products, such as vitamins, cosmetics, water purifiers, credit card protection services and the like, in order to claim one of these prizes. The prices charged are typically anywhere from $300 to $600 or more, while the products are probably worth only $30 to $150, assuming you receive anything at all. In short, you pay far more than any alleged prize is worth.

What You "Win"

If you actually receive a prize, it will likely be one of the following:

- diamond jewelry where the diamond would fit in a flea's navel
- a $5,000 shopping spree, which really consists of discount coupons to be used only in a catalog of overpriced junk, or
- a vacation certificate.

Here are some examples of the numerous versions of the vacation rip-off:

- Vacation certificate scam. Here you must get to the destination on your own, but the seller will give you two or three nights lodging. Only rarely is this a good deal.
- Free or discounted ticket scam. You receive one free airline ticket if you purchase a second airline ticket. The scam is that you have to buy a Y class fare, which is two to four times the price of the cheapest economy ticket. For example, a cheap economy ticket to New York costs approximately $350, while a Y class economy ticket is approximately $1,100.

Sometimes, you're just sold a cheap ticket (such as $29 to Hawaii). But then you have to stay at a hotel of the promoter's choice for seven nights. If you get a hotel confirmation at all, it will be for a $50 room, for which you will be charged $125 a night for seven nights. And you must deal by mail with an out-of-state travel agency, giving it at least 45 days' notice of when you want to travel and three potential travel dates. Whatever dates you pick will likely not be available.

- Cruise scam. You pay your own transportation to the cruise location and supposedly get a cruise to the Bahamas with luxury accommodations at a modest price of about $300. The cruise turns out to be a 12-hour boat ride you can buy in Florida for $50. The hotels are second or third rate.

- Travel club scam. You join a travel club for many hundreds of dollars and then get one of the above deals (or something similar) as your joining premium, which means the only thing you get is aggravation and frustration.

- Hotel reservation scam. You are asked to send a "refundable" $100 or more, in order to make hotel reservations. Supposedly, the fee is credited to the price of your selected hotel room. The problem is that reservations are almost never confirmed at any hotel.

- Discount coupon scam. Some telemarketers try to sell you a book of discount coupons, accepted by numerous merchants, which includes a "free" trip to Hawaii. They offer to send a runner right over to your house to pick up $59.95 to $79.95. The "free" trip is the same nonsense mentioned above.

- Free boat scam. This is a popular scam, in which you are solicited to buy hundreds of dollars of overpriced novelty items such as $2.95 key chains that normally sell for less than $1.50. In order to get a "free boat," you have to pay the shipping and handling charges ranging in price from $99 to $119. What you get is an inflatable vinyl raft meant for use in a swimming pool. The vinyl is about as thick as a shower-curtain. The motor is a handheld battery-operated gadget. The retail value is approximately $50.

- Postcards/magazine scam. These mailers (which often claim "we've been trying to reach you about your sweepstakes entry") offer an 800 number for you to call because they are selling magazine subscriptions. The pitch goes like this: We will enter you in our sweepstakes contest (that does not exist), but at the same time we will send you free magazines just for the price of postage and handling of $1.50 a week. You get signed up for three to five years, at a cost of several hundred dollars. Often you are charged more than the newsstand price for the same magazines.

Where to Complain

If you paid by credit card but never received any merchandise, or if you have proof you returned the merchandise, you can refuse to pay your credit card bill. See *Credit, Loans and Debts* (Credit Cards—Disputes Over Merchandise or Service).

If you paid by check and it's too late to stop payment, you can try asking the company for a refund, but it's unlikely you'll get one. Contact the California Attorney General's office, (800) 952-5225, as well as the Attorney General in the state where the company is located. The California Attorney General can give you the out-of-state address.

HOW TO SPOT A SCAM

- If it sounds too good to be true, it probably is.

- No legitimate business gives away highly valuable items, such as a car, vacation, boat or TV.

- Anyone who claims you must make a decision now is a rip-off artist.

- Avoid anyone who will not send you written material. Scam operators rarely send information before they have your money or credit card number.

- Anyone who asks for your credit card number for verification purposes is a scam operator.

- Anyone who asks you to send money by overnight mail or by messenger to qualify for a prize is a scam operator.

Legitimate Lotteries and Sweepstakes

A lottery is defined as having three parts: a prize, a chance to win and a payment of money. The only legal lottery in California is the one run by the State of California.

If you receive mail offers to buy lottery tickets from Canada, Germany, Holland and other foreign countries, understand that these lotteries are probably legal in their countries. Federal law, however, makes it illegal for anyone to use the U.S. mail to participate in a foreign or another state's lottery. 18 U.S.C. § 1302; 39 U.S.C. § 3001. Postal inspectors aren't reading your mail to see if you're buying foreign lottery tickets, but it explains why people fly to other states to buy lottery tickets when a lottery is set to pay-off a huge sum—such as $50 million. To be legal, lottery participants have to buy those tickets in person, not by mail.

Legitimate sweepstakes (or contests) offer you an opportunity to win a prize just for the cost of a postage stamp. Many companies, such as publishers of magazines, sponsor sweepstakes because they find it a profitable way to attract attention to their products. You don't need to pay a fee or purchase anything to participate in a legal sweepstakes, and purchasing a product will not increase your chances of winning. If you are required to pay or buy something to be "considered" for the prize, do not participate—that offer is a scam.

Most legitimate sweepstakes will clearly disclose:
- that no purchase or payment is required
- sweepstakes rules in non-technical terms
- restrictions on the awarding of prizes (if any)
- identity and address of sponsor where you can make inquiries
- deadline for eligibility, including date of drawing

- approximate odds of winning (if they can be calculated)
- method of selecting the winner, including where the sweepstakes drawing will be held
- approximate retail value and the number of prizes
- availability of lists of prize winners, and
- sponsor's right to use winners' names for publicity purposes.

900 TELEPHONE NUMBERS

These are seven-digit telephone numbers that start with "900." Many provide information on subjects, such as legal advice, horoscopes, sports and sex-lines. Sometimes, they are part of a scam, where you call an 800 number and then you're told to call a second number—a 900 number. 900 numbers always cost money to call—sometimes as much as $100 per call.

California 900 Numbers

Most 900 numbers in use are outside of California. The California Public Utilities Commission (CPUC) requires 900 in-state numbers to:

- charge no more than $5 for the first minute and $2 for each additional minute, with a $50 maximum for one call, and
- disclose within the first 15 seconds the name of the company and the cost of the call, allowing the caller to hang up without being charged.

Consumers can get a one-time refund for California 900 number calls from their home if:

- the call was made by a child without the parent's knowledge or permission
- the call was made without your permission
- you did not know the price of the call, or
- you apply for the refund within 60 days of the charge appearing on your bill.

Consumers may be able to get refunds (not subject to one-time only) for calls with poor sound quality, if the cost was not announced or advertised, or if other regulations were violated.

Non-California 900 Numbers

Out-of-state 900 calls are not regulated by the CPUC. The Federal Trade Commission requires all 900 number businesses to disclose their prices in print advertising and on radio and TV. Additionally, calls that cost more than $2 must begin with an identification of the company and the cost of the call, and inform you that charges will begin three seconds after the tone following the preamble unless you hang up sooner. You can dispute 900 charges within 60 days either in writing or by calling the billing company. The billing company must acknowledge your complaint in writing within 40 days of receiving it, and either correct the billing error or explain the reason for not doing so within 90 days or two billing cycles. The company cannot try to collect the debt or report the charge to a credit bureau until an investigation has been completed. Any billing company which doesn't comply with these rules forfeits the right to collect up to $50 of the amount of each disputed charge.

Where to Complain

For 900 services provided within California, contact the California Public Utilities Commission. (See *Government*.)

For 900 numbers outside California, complain to the Federal Communications Commission, Complaints and Investigations, 1919 M Street, NW, Washington, DC 20554, (202) 632-7048 and/or the Federal Trade Commission. It's also a good idea to use additional pressure by lodging a complaint with one of California's two U.S. senators, and your representative to Congress.

ADVERTISING

Most products are sold through advertising; we are bombarded with ads by mail, in newspapers and magazines, and on TV or radio. In order to be a smart shopper, comparison shop before you buy something. Your best protection against false advertising claims is common sense. A deal that sounds too good to be true probably is.

Advertisers' Claims

Under California law, advertisers must be able to prove any claims they make based on facts. If a dress shop advertises "the lowest prices in town" as opposed to "low, low prices" the advertiser must be able to support that claim. Business and Professions Code § 17508.

Misleading Advertising

Beware of "bait and switch" advertising. It typically works like this: A merchant lures you into his store by advertising a really low-priced TV (the "bait"). When you see its poor quality, the salesperson tells you that the TV is on sale because it's not really very good. He immediately suggests a much higher priced model (the "switch"). California law prohibits retailers from advertising goods or services which they don't intend to sell. Civil Code § 1770(i).

DON'T ALWAYS TRUST ADS

Just because an ad appears in a reputable magazine or newspaper, or on TV and radio stations, doesn't guarantee that the product or service is legitimate. Only a few publishers and broadcasters are cautious about what ads they run.

Government "Look Alikes"

California prohibits a business from soliciting information for funds by sending any mailing containing a seal, insignia, trade or brand name, or any other term or symbol, that reasonably could be interpreted as implying government connection, approval or endorsement unless:

- The business has an expressed connection with, or approval or endorsement from, the government agency.
- The mailing contains the following notice: "THIS PRODUCT OR SERVICE HAS NOT BEEN APPROVED OR ENDORSED BY ANY GOVERNMENT AGENCY, AND THIS OFFER IS NOT BEING MADE BY AN AGENCY OF THE GOVERNMENT."

- The envelope contains the notice: "THIS IS NOT A GOVERNMENT DOCU-MENT."
  Business and Professions Code § 17533.6.

Must a Merchant Sell an Item at a Wrong Price?

If there has been an honest mistake in an advertised price, or if a price tag on an item is wrong ($3.98 instead of $39.98), a merchant does not have to sell the goods at the wrong price. One reason is because consumers have been known to switch price tags.

Rain Checks

The law requires merchants to stock an advertised product in quantities large enough to meet reasonably expected demand, unless the ad states that stock is limited. The law does not require merchants to give a rain check allowing you to purchase the same merchandise at the same price at a later date. Many quality merchants do this as a matter of good business, however, so ask for a rain check if the merchandise is sold out. Civil Code § 1770.

Quantity Limitations

When a store advertises an item for sale, you are entitled to buy as many as you want unless its ad states a limit on the number to be sold to any one customer. (This law excludes sales to people who intend to resell the products.) For example, if a store advertises paper towels on sale for 89¢ but when you get there you find the shelf price states only two rolls per customer, you are entitled to buy more. If the store won't sell them to you, you can take the merchant to Small Claims Court for any money you lost (the amount of money you could have saved), plus $50. Business and Professions Code § 17500.5.

Used or Defective Advertised Products

Unless an ad states otherwise, you have the right to expect first-quality undamaged goods. If a store advertises an item at a reduced sale price because the item is used or defective, the ad must say this. Business and Professions Code § 7531.

More Information/Where to Complain

Consumer Reports magazine is an excellent source for product ratings which are often helpful for comparison shopping.

If you have a problem with an item you purchased, first ask for help from the merchant who sold it to you. If the salesperson cannot help, ask for the next person up the ladder—all the way to the president or chairman of the board, if necessary. If you can't get satisfaction from the merchant, there are several government and private agencies that may be able to help:

- Your county District Attorney, especially if it has a consumer fraud division
- The California Department of Consumer Affairs
- The California Attorney General's office
- Better Business Bureau
- Radio, TV or newspaper "Action Lines"
- For nationally advertised products, the Federal Trade Commission (FTC). While the FTC doesn't directly help individuals deal with particular problems, enough complaints can warrant an investigation, which in time can result in restitution for misled consumers.

UNORDERED MERCHANDISE

If you receive unordered merchandise, you can consider the item a gift to use or dispose of as you see fit. Although you have no legal obligation to do so, it is a good idea to write to the sender stating that you intend to keep the free gift. Whether you do this or not, you are under no obligation to pay for the unsolicited goods nor to return the item. Civil Code § 1584.5.

Few merchants send out unsolicited merchandise (other than in the case of honest error). In my experience, the only merchandise sent unordered consists of cheap key chains, greeting cards or name and address labels that some charitable organizations use to solicit funds. This is legal, although it's an expensive way to raise money and typically raises questions as to whether the charity really contributes much to its announced cause. Of course, you are under no obligation to contribute funds to these organizations just because they sent you a free gift.

Legitimate Shipping Errors

If you receive merchandise as a result of a legitimate mistake (a shipping error), you may want to offer to return it provided the seller pays for the postage and handling. Write or call the seller, giving a reasonable amount of time (30 days) for the company to pick up or arrange to have it returned at no expense to you.

Erroneously Ordered Merchandise

Many claims about unsolicited merchandise turn out to be the consumer's error. Frequently, "unordered" merchandise was actually ordered inadvertently. Sweepstakes (which are meant to sell merchandise, such as magazine subscriptions) fine print usually says that by entering the sweepstakes you have actually ordered something. In the case of magazines, you can usually cancel the subscription after one issue.

If you find yourself in this situation, don't pay anything. Simply return the merchandise (keep proof of the return) and write a separate letter explaining the mistake and indicating the merchandise was returned. Unfortunately, you may get future bills and have to repeat the process.

P R O D U C T S

APPLIANCES

Repair

The California Bureau of Electronic and Appliance Repair (BEAR) licenses appliance repair dealers, which must follow all BEAR rules and regulations. Repair dealers must provide written estimates of charges before making repairs. Dealers can charge for making a diagnosis and estimating repair cost, as long as you are told in writing that there will be a charge. Before making a home service call, appliance repair firms must inform you of the cost.

If you call BEAR to check on the reliability of an appliance repair shop, you will only be told if the business is registered properly. If you write to BEAR, you will be given the complaint history. (See below for address and phone number.)

More Information/Where to Complain

If you have a problem with an appliance, you'll want to start with the seller or manufacturer. (See Warranties at the end of this subsection.)

If the seller or manufacturer doesn't help, BEAR accepts and mediates complaints regarding the repair, service and maintenance of major appliances used in homes or private vehicles, including TV sets, radios, audio or video recorders or playback equipment, antennas and rotators, washers, dryers, dishwashers, refrigerators, ranges, ovens, microwave ovens, freezers, room air conditioners and home computers. BEAR investigates complaints using its two laboratories and undercover investigators. Contact BEAR at 909 S Street, Sacramento, CA 95814, (916) 445-4751.

BEAR does not handle repair complaints about countertop appliances (such as toasters, irons and mixers), sewing machines, vacuum cleaners, central air and heating systems or furnaces.

If the seller, manufacturer or BEAR cannot resolve the problem, contact the Major Appliance Consumer Action Panel (MACAP), 20 North Wacker Drive, Chicago, IL 60606, (800) 621-0477. This independent group will mediate with a manufacturer on your behalf if it believes you have a valid complaint concerning a clothes washer/dryer, dehumidifier, dishwasher, food waste disposer, freezer, microwave oven, range/oven, refrigerator, room air conditioner, trash compactor or water heater. MACAP has been around for years and has a good success rate, although it takes 40 to 60 days to settle a dispute.

When writing MACAP, give a concise description of the problem and what you want in terms of a refund or replacement; be reasonable—do not ask for a replacement of your ten-year-old stove. In your letter, include:
- your name
- your address
- your daytime phone number
- appliance information—brand name, model and serial number
- purchase date and price
- name, address and phone number of the repair service, and
- copies of all correspondence, service records and purchase receipts.

If BEAR or MACAP cannot or does not resolve the problem, you can take the seller or manufacturer to Small Claims Court. Also, a newspaper, TV or radio station "Action Line" may help you.

CARPETS

New Carpets: Defects and Installation Problems

Typically, carpet complaints concern poor installation or carpeting matting or wearing out too quickly. If the carpet store, manufacturer or installer has not responded satisfactorily to your complaint, contact an organization that does an independent inspection for a fee:
- Advanced Carpet Specialists at (510) 792-5758, charges $100 and 30¢ per mile (plus any other legitimate expenses, such as parking in downtown San Francisco) in the greater Bay Area. If the job is large enough, the inspectors will travel further.
- The Academy of Textiles and Flooring at (310) 698-1279, charges $75 for a report, $25 per hour in travel and 28¢ per mile in Los Angeles, Orange, San Bernardino, Riverside and San Diego counties. If the job is large enough, the inspectors will travel further.

Both organizations are funded by various manufacturers of carpet, linoleum/vinyl and hardwood flooring; however, they claim they give objective reports. For a referral to a third group, call the International Institute of Carpet and Restoration Certification, at (206) 693-5675.

With photographs and other good documentation of a carpet or installation problem, you may want to consider taking the installer, the seller and/or the manufacturer to Small Claims Court. And if the report is in your favor, you probably have a better chance of winning your case.

REQUEST A CERTIFIED CARPET CLEANER

When arranging for carpet cleaning, specify that you want a cleaner who has been certified by the International Institute of Carpet and Upholstery Certification. Just because a company advertises that it has certified cleaners doesn't mean the one who comes to your house is certified. With a particularly difficult cleaning job, you may be more likely to achieve a successful result using a certified cleaner.

Cleaning Problems

The Carpet and FabriCare Institute has a toll-free consumer hotline, (800) 227-7389, to handle problems with carpet cleaners. If the cleaner is a member, the Institute will contact her on your behalf. Even if the cleaner is not a member, file a complaint with the Institute and it will advise you on how to proceed.

CONTACT LENSES AND EYEGLASSES

To obtain contact lenses, you must have an eye examination and a fitting. The fitting can only be performed by an ophthalmologist (an MD) or an optometrist (an OD—doctor of optometry) who will measure the curvature of your eye and determine which lens is best for you. Opticians fill prescriptions written by ophthalmologists and optometrists. To obtain eyeglasses, you can have your eyes examined by an optician, ophthalmologist or optometrist.

The Federal Trade Commission requires eye examiners to give patients their eyeglass prescriptions, at no charge, at the time of the exam. This gives you the opportunity to comparison shop for eyeglasses. This rule does not apply to contact lens examinations; however, some ophthalmologists and optometrists will give you the prescription. And some write eyeglass prescriptions with a provision stating "approved for contact lenses."

Eyeglass Recycling

Eyeglasses no longer used by you can be used by others. New Eyes for the Needy, Inc., Box 332, Short Hills, NJ 07078, (201) 376-4903, distributes used eyeglasses to the needy. In addition, many local Lions Club and Kiwanis Club groups have eyeglass recycling programs.

Where to Complain

Ophthalmologists and Opticians: Medical Board of California, 1426 Howe Avenue, Suite 54, Sacramento, CA 95825-3236, (800) 633-2322 or (916) 920-6697.

Optometrists: California Board of Optometry: 400 R Street, Suite 3130, Sacramento, CA 95814-6200, (916) 323-8720.

Neither Board handles fee disputes. They handle complaints about negligence, incompetence, misrepresentation, unlicensed activity or fraud.

FURNITURE

The California Bureau of Home Furnishings enforces the laws governing safety issues (such as fire-retardant materials) of upholstered furniture, bedding, waterbeds and products with thermal insulation. Its jurisdiction covers items that contain filling materials, such as sofas, pillows and comforters, as well as any warranties and advertising for these products.

Special Order Furniture and Delivery

The biggest consumer problem with furniture is getting it delivered when promised. Often, an item must be special ordered from the factory or distributor. As a condition of doing this, most merchants require a substantial deposit, which is generally not refundable. The problem arises when the salesperson promises you it will take four to six weeks to get the furniture. But this simply may not be true. Furniture dealers are often at the mercy of the manufacturers. If you want furniture that must be special ordered, press for a realistic estimate of delivery time before you order. Be prepared to wait, because you don't have much recourse. Although it's not very likely, you can try to get the store manager to sign your order requiring your deposit be refunded if the store can't deliver as promised.

More Information/Where to Complain

If you have a problem with damaged or defective furniture or a delivery delay, first discuss it with the retailer who sold you the merchandise. If that does not resolve the problem, contact a radio, TV or newspaper "Action Line" or the Better Business Bureau for help. If all else fails, write to the Furniture Consumer Action Panel (FCAP), P.O. Box 951, High Point, NC 27261. Much U.S. furniture is made in North Carolina; this organization will intervene with the manufacturer, on your behalf, to seek a satisfactory solution to the problem.

For questions or problems with upholstered furniture or bedding, contact the Bureau of Home Furnishings in Sacramento at (916) 445-1254.

The Carpet and FabriCare Institute has a toll-free consumer hotline, (800) 227-7389, to handle problems with cleaning problems with furniture fabric. If the cleaner is a member, the Institute will contact the cleaner on your behalf. Even if the cleaner is not a member, file a complaint with the Institute and it will advise you on how to proceed.

HEARING AIDS

All retail hearing aid purchases in California must come with a written warranty stating that the hearing aid is fit for your particular needs. If you return the hearing aid during the warranty period, the seller must—without charge and within a reasonable period—adjust the hearing aid or replace it. If the seller cannot do either, he must refund the total amount you paid, including returning any trade-ins or security agreements.

If you do not receive a written warranty when you purchase a hearing aid, you are entitled return the device to the seller within 30 days of the completion of the fitting or of your receiving the aid, whichever occurs later. If you return the hearing aid during the 30-day period, the seller must either adjust or replace it, or promptly refund the total amount paid.

If you purchase a hearing aid away from the seller's normal place of business (for example, at a hospital, nursing home, group residence or private home), you have three days to cancel your purchase under California's door-to-door sales rule.

More Information/Where to Complain

The Hearing Aid Dispensers Examining Committee (HADEC) is part of the Medical Board of California. It licenses hearing aid dispensers and enforces regulations against them. HADEC encourages consumers to file a formal complaint if you have any concerns regarding care rendered by a hearing aid dispenser. HADEC will also answer your questions about hearing aids or hearing aid sellers. Contact HADEC at 1420 Howe Avenue, Suite 12, Sacramento, CA 95825-3230, (916) 263-2288. To obtain a complaint form, call (800) 633-2322.

MAGAZINES

If you have a problem with a magazine subscription, such as continuing to receive a bill after you have paid, or never receiving a magazine after you have paid for it, contact the Magazine Publishers of America, a trade association that can provide assistance in resolving magazine subscription complaints. MPA accepts written complaints only. Contact: Magazine Publishers Association, Director, Subscription Inquiry Unit, 575 Lexington Avenue, 5th Floor, New York, NY 10022.

People often complain that a particular magazine arrives completely unsolicited. Often, however, this isn't the case. If you enter a sweepstakes, you may automatically register to receive a magazine subscription. (This probably was disclosed in fine print.) If you do not want to continue to receive that magazine, write "cancel" across the bill and send it back to the publisher. You may have to do this several times if the magazines and/or bills continue.

When the Magazine Ceases Before Your Subscription Is Up

Generally, magazine publishers will offer a choice of substitute magazines to finish out your paid-up subscription. If it's a single magazine publisher, you should be given a refund. If the company folded and has no assets, however, you may be out of luck.

MAIL ORDER

Shopping by mail order can be a convenient way to save time and sometimes money. To make sure that mail-order companies do not cheat you, the Federal Trade Commission (FTC) instituted a "Mail Order Rule." Beginning March 1, 1994, this applies to all telephone, as well as mail order, purchases.

- The seller must ship your order within 30 days of receipt of your properly completed order and payment, unless the ad clearly states it will take longer.
- In case of a delay, the seller must notify you in writing, giving you the option of a definite new shipment date (if known), or the opportunity to cancel the order and receive a full refund. The seller must give you a postage-free way to reply. If you do not respond, it means you agree to the delay.
- If you cancel the order because of the seller's delayed shipping, you are entitled to a refund within seven business days of receipt of your canceled order. If you used a credit card, the credit must be issued within one billing cycle.
- Even if you consented to an indefinite delay, you still have the right to cancel the order anytime before it is shipped.
- If you cancel or never receive the merchandise, you do not have to accept a store credit in place of a refund.

This rule does not apply to mail-order photo finishing, spaced deliveries such as magazine subscriptions (except for the initial shipment), seeds and plants, COD orders or credit card purchases where your account is not charged before the merchandise is shipped.

Returning Mail-Order Merchandise

When returning mail-order merchandise, be sure to keep "proof" (postal or UPS receipt) that you returned the shipment. A few high-quality mail-order companies will reimburse your shipping costs, but most companies don't refund the cost. If, however, the seller shipped a wrong or defective item, postage should logically be refundable.

Unfortunately, whether or not you'll be refunded the shipping is determined by the seller's policy, not law.

Mail Order Insurance Coverage
Some companies charge a nominal amount of money for insurance on mail-order purchases. If the prices seem too high, shop elsewhere.

United Parcel Service (UPS) automatically insures the first $100 for free.

HOW TO PICK A REPUTABLE MAIL-ORDER COMPANY

One way to judge if a mail-order company is reliable is to ask about its credit card order policy. Reputable mail-order companies won't charge your credit card until they ship the merchandise. They usually do cash checks, however, so paying by credit card gives you more protection if you ultimately want to cancel your order because of delay.

More Information/Where to Complain
Always try to work out a dispute directly with the seller. If you are not satisfied, contact one of the following:

- Mail Order Action Line, Direct Marketing Association, 1101 17th Street, NW, Suite 705, Washington, DC 20036, (202) 347-1222. Briefly state the problem, name and address of the company, and include photocopies of canceled checks (front and back), order forms and other relevant correspondence.
- The magazine or newspaper publisher that carried the ad. Sometimes publishers will try to resolve a dispute between a reader and an advertiser.
- A radio, TV or newspaper "Action Line" in your own community, or the Better Business Bureau nearest the seller.
- Ask your local post office for the name and address of the appropriate "postal inspector-in-charge" to file a complaint.
- Federal Trade Commission. Although it does not solve individual problems, if the seller has developed a pattern of abuse, the FTC may take action.

MAILING LISTS
Direct mail advertising is a major communications vehicle—for businesses and nonprofit groups—as a means of advertising, fundraising and increasing consumer awareness for mail-order companies, telemarketers and almost anyone selling a product or service. Many businesses and organizations depend on the rental and exchange of mailing lists to find new customers and members. This renting and exchanging of names and addresses for mailing lists has become a major business.

Where Did They Get Your Name?

- Various companies compile lists from public records which indicate if you own a house, land, an automobile or a boat. Marriages, divorces, births and voter registrations are also matters of public record and also are used to compile these lists.

- One direct mail list is composed of all telephone-owning households listed in the more than 5,000 telephone books.

- The Department of Motor Vehicles (DMV), the credit reporting agencies, major merchants and financial institutions sell names for mailing lists. Many college alumni directories and professional organizations/associations also sell names.

- If you have ever purchased anything by mail order, including magazine and newsletter subscriptions, your name is likely to be sold by the company you bought from. Other mail-order sellers who sell the same or similar products will buy your name.

- Many major merchants ask for your name and address when you make a purchase—even if you pay by cash. They put you on their customer list. You can refuse to give this information.

- Four major direct marketing brokers—R.L. Polk, Donnelley Marketing, Metromail Corporation and Database America—keep and sell consumers' names, addresses and phone numbers to thousands of businesses that compile mailing lists.

- National Demographics and Lifestyles collects electronic and household good warranty cards. NDL keeps your name, address, phone number, age, income, marital status and "lifestyles" data. If you want to return the warranty card, but don't want to be inundated with mailings, just include your name and address and the information specifically pertaining to the product you bought, such as the item's serial number.

- Some mailing lists target you by your zip code, especially if you live in an affluent area. Similarly, some 800 and 900 telephone number switchboards have technology that can match your telephone number to your name and address to create customer lists.

Junk Mail—Removing Your Name

The Direct Marketing Association (DMA), a membership organization comprised of national companies and organizations that use the mail and/or telephone to sell their products or services, attempts to police their own members, to forestall governmental regulation. The DMA's Mail Preference Service (MPS) allows consumers to have their names removed, free of charge, from national mailing and telephone lists and databases.

To have your name removed from DMA's mailing lists, you (not a creditor or other third party) must send a written request to: Mail Preference Service, Direct Marketing Association, P.O. Box 9008, Farmingdale, NY 11735. Include your name (with variations if your name appears in different ways, such as with initials, your full name or with misspellings), address and zip code.

To have your name removed from DMA's telephone solicitation lists, send a written request to Telephone Preference Service, Direct Marketing Association, P.O. Box 9014, Farmingdale, NY 11735.

Making a request to DMA may take three to six months to get your name removed from about 70% of national direct marketers. This will not, however, get rid of all of your junk mail. To do that, you should contact the three major credit bureaus—TRW, Equifax and TransUnion—as well as National Demographics and Lifestyles, marketing brokers and numerous other companies.

You can contact the three credit bureaus as follows:

- TRW-Target Marketing Services, Consumer Opt Out, 600 City Parkway West, 7th Floor, Orange, CA 92668
- Equifax Options, P.O. Box 740123, Atlanta, GA 30374-0123
- TransUnion, Transmark, Inc., 555 West Adams Street, Chicago, IL 60601.

I don't have the space to list the addresses of NDL, the market brokers and other companies here. If you are serious about cleaning up your mail box, I highly recommend you order a copy of *Stop Junk Mail Forever*, by Marc Eisenson, Nancy Castleman and Marcy Ross, and "The Stop Junk Mail-Man." Send $3 to Good Advice Press, Box 78, Elizaville, NY 12523, (914) 758-1400.

HOW TO KEEP THE CATALOGS YOU WANT

Writing to DMA and the other companies will stop you from receiving some catalog mailings you want. Simply write those merchants directly and ask them to keep you on their in-house mailing list, but to not rent or share your name with anyone else. Whenever you buy anything by mail order, print this same request prominently on the order form and it should keep you from being buried in catalogs.

Some organizations have popped up trying to profit by charging consumers for name-removal from national mailing lists. Don't be fooled—the DMA's Mail Preference Service is the only national name-removal service recognized by federal, state and local regulatory agencies and used by direct mailers. And you can write to the others directly yourself. It's silly to pay for this.

TIMESHARES

A timeshare means you buy the right to use a vacation home/condo/apartment for a limited, pre-planned time, once a year, such as in the second two weeks in March. In addition to a down payment, you make monthly charges—which often are hefty and can be increased—to pay off the purchase price and annual fee assessments.

Types of Timesharing Plans

"Deeded plans" give the buyer an ownership interest (title) in a fraction of the unit (a small piece of real estate) in perpetuity.

"Non-deeded plans" give the buyer a lease, license or club membership which entitles the buyer to use the unit for a specified number of years, but does not give any ownership rights.

Three-Day Right to Cancel

California timeshare contracts must include a three-day "cooling-off period" in which you have until midnight of the third business day following when you signed your contract to cancel it. Timeshares located in another state or foreign country may not offer this protection.

Timeshares as Investments

Timeshares often have poor resale value and therefore tend to be bad investments. In an economic downturn, they may be impossible to sell. As a general rule, buy a timeshare from a reputable developer only in a situation where you and your family really want to use the time.

Resales—Beware of Scams!

If you are one of approximately a half-million owners trying to sell your timeshare, watch out for fraudulent resale schemes. For up-front fees of $400, phony companies typically offer a guaranteed sale or your money back. They won't sell your timeshare and you won't get your money back because you won't be able to find them. Some companies offer a $1,000 bond if they do not sell your timeshare. Not only will you never see your $400 again, the "bonds" have a 45-year maturity (which means in 45 years the bond will be worth $1,000) with a current value of less than $60.

More Information/Where to Complain

The following organizations have useful information on buying and selling timeshares:

- American Resort Development Association, 1220 L St. NW, 5th Floor, Washington, DC 20005, (202) 371-6700.
- Resort Property Owners Association, Box 2395, Northbrook, IL 60062, (800) 989-0710.

BEWARE OF "DREAM VACATION" PRIZES

A favorite giveaway (that sounds like a valuable prize) to lure you to timeshare and resort condo sales presentations is the promise of a "dream vacation" to Hawaii, the Bahamas or Mexico. In fact, what you get is a worthless vacation certificate. To take advantage of it, you must typically deal with an out-of-state travel agency by mail. It is difficult to get reservations, and even harder to get the name of a hotel where you are to stay. Ultimately, the vacation, if you ever get one, is apt to cost you more money than if you had booked your own travel plans. A variation on this theme is the vacation certificate which states you must get to the destination on your own, but the company will give you two or three nights lodging in a place you'd never want to stay.

DON'T FALL FOR THE PROMOTIONAL PRIZE TRICK ON TIMESHARE ADS

Timeshares mailers often tout the possibility of winning cash, a car, vacation, or some other prize just for coming to a 90-minute timeshare sales presentation. Don't be fooled. You will get the sales presentation—not a valuable prize. The true story is buried in the fine print because the mailer must spell out your chance of winning each prize. Typically, your chance is one out of 100,000. The other 99,999 receive a prize worth less than the gasoline you used to get there. Some mailers contain another deception. The odds of winning are shown as 1:100,000. When asked who won the car, the response is "that winning number never showed up."

According to the Resort Property Owners' Association, timeshare/resort owners pay the following for prizes, compared with the claimed retail value:

	Claimed Retail Value	Wholesale
• Three-piece luggage	$70	$10
• 35 mm camera	$79	$5
• Barbecue grill/hibachi	$45	$7
• Seiko sports watch	$80	$6

California real estate timeshares are under the jurisdiction of the California Department of Real Estate, Timeshare Division, P.O. Box 187005, Sacramento, CA 95818, (916) 227-0864.

California campground timeshares are under the jurisdiction of the Attorney General's office. The Attorney General's office will also pursue—for real estate and campground timeshares—the failure to state the odds of winning a prize, the failure to award prizes promised and any contract violation (such as not honoring a three-day cancellation). Contact the public inquiry unit at (800) 952-5225.

TIRES

Registration

New tires should be registered with the tire manufacturer, so you can be reached if a defect is found in the type of tire you bought. Ask if your tire dealer routinely does this. If not, ask for a tire registration form to send back to the manufacturer. If you receive a defect notification letter from the manufacturer, go to your dealer for an inspection or free replacement. When you buy a new car the tires do not need to be registered. If there is a problem, the dealership will provide your name and address to the tire manufacturer.

Tire Warranties

Almost all tires come with a warranty. Check warranties carefully before making a selection. Most tire warranties include coverage for defects in workmanship and materials, and offer replacement of the tire on a prorated basis. (A deduction will be made for the amount of use you had from the tire.) Many manufacturers, rather than giving cash, will give a credit which can be used to purchase the same tire by the same manufacturer. Tire manufacturers' warranties generally do not include coverage for damage due to road hazards or treadwear; however, you may be able to purchase that additional coverage from a retail outlet.

More Information/Where to Complain

For free information on treadwear, traction and temperature-resistant characteristics of tires, or for the uniform tire quality grading report or where to file a complaint, contact the National Highway Traffic Safety Administration, Auto Safety Hotline, 400 Seventh Street SW, Washington, DC 20590, (800) 424-9393.

WARRANTIES

Warranties (sometimes called guarantees) are promises by manufacturers or sellers to stand behind their products. A written warranty is a contract spelling out your consumer rights—a promise to fix, replace or refund your money if the product does not work properly within a given time period. Warranties are governed by the federal Magnuson-Moss Warranty Act and the California Song-Beverly law.

Kinds of Warranties

Warranties may be "full" or "limited" and may be "written" or "implied." (Most warranties are limited, not full.) Let's look at the rules for each:

Full Written Warranties (New Products)
Coverage includes the following:
- A defective product will be repaired or replaced for free—including removal and reinstallation if necessary—during the warranty period.
- The product will be repaired within a reasonable time period.
- You will not have to do anything unreasonable to get warranty service—such as returning a heavy product to a store.
- The warranty is good for anyone who owns the product during the warranty period.
- If the product has not been repaired after a reasonable number of tries, you are entitled to a replacement or refund.
- You do not have to return a warranty card for the warranty to be valid.
- Implied warranties (described below) cannot be disclaimed or denied or limited to any specific length of time.

Full warranty coverage *does not* necessarily mean that:
- The entire product is covered by the warranty.
- The warranty lasts for any particular time period except as specified in writing.
- The company must pay for "consequential or incidental damages" (such as towing, food spoilage or damage to the kitchen floor caused by water flooding out of the dishwasher).
- The product is warranted in all geographic areas.

Limited Written Warranties (New Products)
Coverage includes the following:
- You may have to pay for labor, reinstallation or other charges.

- You may have to bring a heavy product—such as a TV set—in for service.
- Your warranty may be good only for the first purchaser—a second owner may not be entitled to any warranty service.
- You may be given a pro-rata refund or credit—that is, you have to pay for the time you had use of the product, such as with an automobile tire.
- You do not have to return an owner registration card, even if the warranty says you must; however, you should keep the purchase receipt to prove when the warranty period began.
- Your implied warranty (described below) may expire when your written warranty expires—for example, a one-year limited warranty can state that the implied warranty lasts for only one year.

Limited warranty coverage *does not* necessarily mean that:

- Only part of the product is covered; a limited warranty may cover the entire product.
- The warranty only covers the cost of repair parts; it can include labor too.
- The warranty will last for any particular length of time except as specified.
- You can have warranty service done in only a few locations.

Combination Warranties

A product can come with a full warranty for some things and a limited for others. For example, a washing machine can have a full warranty on the entire product for one year and a limited four-year warranty on the gear assembly.

Federal Magnuson-Moss Warranty Act

This Act does not require manufacturers to give written warranties. If the seller or manufacturer provides a warranty, however, it must be as follows:

- written in ordinary language that is easy to read and understand, and
- labeled either full warranty or limited warranty—stating what the company will do for you under the warranty.

Sellers must have a copy of the written warranty available for you to see before you make a purchase (for products that sell for more than $15) and provide you with a copy of the warranty when you buy the product.

ORAL WARRANTIES AREN'T ENOUGH

Do not accept a salesperson's oral promise that the company will take care of anything that goes wrong. Proving such a statement is almost impossible. Get any such promises in writing and have it signed by a manager or someone else in authority. Of course, you may find that no one is willing to do this. If that's the case, you then know that the promise is worth exactly as much as the paper it's not written on.

Song-Beverly Consumer Warranty Act

This Act provides an "implied warranty of merchantability" on almost every new product purchase you make. This means that the manufacturer and retail seller have made an implied promise that the product is fit for its ordinary purpose. For example, when you buy a toaster, the "implied warranty of merchantability" promises that the toaster will be able to toast bread under all normal conditions. Similarly, if you buy a washing machine, it should do a credible job of washing a normal load of clothes.

The Act also provides an "implied warranty of fitness for a specific purpose" when a product is sold or marketed in a context where the specific needs or intent of the consumer is known. For instance, if you are sold a sleeping bag after telling the sporting goods salesperson that you plan to camp in sub-zero weather, the sleeping bag must be suitable for that specific purpose. If it isn't, this implied warranty has been breached.

Exceptions (items not covered by an implied warranty):

* food, personal care and cleaning products, and
* wearing apparel, including under and outer garments, shoes and accessories made of woven material, yarn, fiber, leather and similar fabrics (unless you receive a written warranty).

If a warranty has been breached, you may either have the item replaced—if the replacement will fulfill the terms of the warranty—or you can get your money back, less an adjustment for the use you got out of the product before the warranty breach was discovered.

How Long an Implied Warranty Lasts

When the product comes with a written warranty, the implied warranty lasts as long as the written one (generally not less than 60 days or more than one year). If there is no written warranty, the implied warranty on a new product lasts one year.

When the Item Is in Repair

For the period of time a product that cost more than $50 is being repaired, the duration of the implied warranty is extended, because you lost use of the product.

If a defect was present at the time of sale but you did not discover it until much later, the California Commercial Code implied warranty of fitness may apply, but you probably will need a lawyer to enforce it.

No Warranty—"As Is" Sales

"As is" sales may have no implied warranty. A seller can usually avoid any warranty, including implied warranties, by stating that it gives no warranty—that is, the product is being sold "as is." The Song-Beverly Act requires an "as is" sale on a new product without a warranty to have a disclaimer conspicuously attached to the product. There is one exception to this—if a seller gives a written warranty (even a short, limited one), he can't legally get out of an implied warranty. If you get any written warranty, you get implied warranties too, no matter what any disclaimers say.

Implied Warranties on Used Products

Implied warranties apply to used products only in transactions in which a written warranty is given, and then only last for as long as the written warranty, but no shorter than 30 days or longer than 90 days. Implied warranties on used goods imply that the item will work, given its age and condition.

When the Warranty Period Ends but the Problem Hasn't

Your warranty rights do not run out at the end of the warranty for problems you complained about during the warranty period. The company must still take care of these problems.

The Warranted Product Causes Other Damage—Who Pays?

Generally, your rights under a warranty include the right to "consequential damages" unless the written warranty specifically states "Full or limited warranty does not cover consequential damages." This means the company must pay to repair not only the defective product but must also pay for any other damage caused by the product. For example, if your refrigerator conks out and all the food in it spoils, the company must pay for the cost of the food you lost. Many warranties specifically exclude consequential damages.

Service and Repair of Products Under Warranty

Under the Song-Beverly Act, a manufacturer who gives a written warranty (full or limited) must maintain service and repair facilities in California reasonably close to all areas where its products are sold. The manufacturer can delegate repair and service facilities to retailers or independent repair shops. Repairs must be completed within 30 days, unless a delay is beyond the control of the manufacturer or its representative. Then the time can be extended, but only to the extent justified. Failing to stock parts without a satisfactory reason does not extend the 30-day period.

Most new products, such as refrigerators and stoves, come with warranties from the manufacturer, not the seller. Generally, warranties list the names of the authorized service repair firms, which may or may not include the retail store where you bought the appliance. The phone book yellow pages (under Appliances) should also list the names of factory-authorized dealers. If the authorized firm cannot repair your appliance, contact the manufacturer for further instructions; an 800 number is usually listed on the warranty. If the appliance is still under warranty (and, in some cases, even if it is not), the manufacturer must repair or replace the product.

There is one exception: The manufacturer or warrantor's obligation to repair does not cover any abuse you may have given a product. Unauthorized or unreasonable use of the product, too, including failing to do necessary maintenance, may invalidate your warranty.

Are You Entitled to Repair Service in Your Home?

If the product's size and weight or installation make it impossible or very difficult for you to return the product, the manufacturer or its authorized representative must provide warranty service at your home or arrange to have the malfunctioning product picked up without additional charges for transportation. If the manufacturer has not set up sufficient repair facilities in California, the seller must accept these obligations for repairs or service.

Where to Complain

Start with the warrantor of the product, most likely the manufacturer. Enlist the help of the retail seller, if necessary. If you do not get satisfaction, contact a newspaper, TV or radio station "Action Line" for assistance; or try a consumer protection office (such as a District Attorney's Consumer Fraud Unit). You may want to consider suing in Small Claims Court.

EXTENDED WARRANTIES OR SERVICE CONTRACTS

Many consumers are encouraged by merchants to buy extended warranties (also called service contracts) when they buy autos, appliances or electronic items. Service contracts are a source of big profits for stores, which pocket up to 50% of the amount you pay as a reward for just securing your business. In addition, the salesperson collects 15% to 20% of the value of the contract—almost double the commission on the sale itself—when you sign on the dotted line.

But do you need an extended warranty? Most of the time, no. Name-brand appliances usually don't break down during the first few years (and if they do they're covered by the original warranty), and often have a life span of eight to 15 years, depending on the product. The extended warranty usually lasts no more than five years, the period you're least likely to need it. Similarly, electronic equipment usually breaks immediately or within the first few months after purchase, and is thus covered by the original warranty. In fact, according to the president of the Professional Servicers Association, less than 3% of electronic goods actually break down during an extended warranty period.

And be aware that a company that sells extended warranties may go out of business, leaving you out in the cold if you try to make a claim under the contract. Your protections in California for service contracts for home appliances and electronic products include the following (Civil Code §§ 1794.4 and 1794.41):

- The extended warranty must fully disclose all contract terms.
- The extended warranty must identify (including name and address) the person who is financially and legally obligated to perform the services specified in the service contract.
- The extended warranty must be delivered to you within 60 days of purchase.
- The contract must provide you with a 60-day right of cancellation and full refund, starting with the day the written contract document was received.

More Information

If you're toying with the idea of buying a service contract, call or write the Federal Trade Commission (*see Government* chapter) and ask for a free copy of the pamphlet "Facts for Consumers—Service Contracts." Or, send a self-addressed stamped envelope to the Electronic Industries Association, 2001 Pennsylvania Ave. NW, Washington, DC 20006-1813, and request "What Consumers Should Know About Service Contracts and Repairs."

SERVICES

CAR WASH—DAMAGED AUTOMOBILE PARTS

If after driving your car through an automatic car wash, you come out with a cracked, broken or damaged windshield, it may not be the car wash that caused the dirty deed. The Automatic Car Wash Association (ACWA)—which claims to have done considerable research on the matter, working with automobile manufacturers and companies which manufacture automobile windshields—believes it is virtually impossible for damage to occur to windshields while going through a modern car wash operation. Glass companies claim the glass can withstand a temperature change from 140 to 150 degrees and that the water pressure exerted upon the windshield is not sufficient to cause a crack. ACWA claims that fine stone "bruises" occur during normal driving and from ordinary driving vibrations, that water hitting the windshield area in the car wash can turn this "bruise" into a "crack" and that the "bruise" caused the damage—not the car wash. I can't guarantee this information is unbiased, but I suspect this is what you would face if you take a car wash to Small Claims Court.

Sometimes car paint, mirrors and antennas get damaged in car washes. More than likely the car wash establishment will deny responsibility. Looking at it from the car wash's point of view, how does it know the damage wasn't done before you went through the car wash? You can try negotiating with the owner or manager of the business, but you will probably have to take the car wash to Small Claims Court. You will need to convince the judge that the car wash was responsible for the claimed damage.

CLEANERS

If you believe your dry cleaner is responsible for a missed or new stain, ask that the work be redone, at no charge. If damage is permanent or merchandise is lost, ask the cleaner for a reasonable amount of money for compensation, based on the age and condition of your garment. You are usually not entitled to full replacement cost unless your garment was new or nearly new. You may be asked to document the value of your claim based on the original cost of your garment.

CLEAN STAINED GARMENTS PROMPTLY

To avoid problems, get any stained garment cleaned promptly and always discuss the source of the stains with your dry cleaner. It's particularly important to point out light colored or invisible stains caused by soft drinks, white wine or champagne. These stains contain sugar which can caramelize and turn brown with the heat of drying unless flushed out with water before dry cleaning. If you wait too long before getting a stained garment dry cleaned, it may be too late and will not be the cleaner's fault.

If the Cleaner Claims It Is the Manufacturer's Fault

A dry cleaner who is a member of the International Fabricare Institute can send an item to the IFI for analysis (a report takes approximately three weeks) and possibly corrective measures, such as removing stains or stretching the fabric. (IFI does not deal directly with consumers. It charges your dry cleaner for these services; your dry cleaner will probably pass the cost on to you.) IFI will determine whether the dry cleaner, manufacturer or you are at fault. IFI appears to be fairly objective, although it is funded by dry cleaners. Normally, if the dry cleaner is found to be at fault, he will pay reasonable compensation. IFI is located at 12251 Tech Road, Silver Spring, MD 20904, (301) 622-1900.

Where to Complain

The California Fabricare Association is a membership organization that will mediate a valid complaint against members only. (Fewer than half the dry cleaners in the state are members.) You can request a complaint form, or check to see if your dry cleaner is a member, by calling (408) 252-1746.

Ask a radio, TV or newspaper "Action Line" to intervene on your behalf. Also, the Better Business Bureau or the District Attorney's mediation service may be able to mediate a dispute if the dry cleaner is willing to participate. Or, let a judge decide in Small Claims Court. If a garment has been damaged, be sure to bring it to court and be ready to document the garment's original cost.

HOME DELIVERY SERVICE

Merchandise Delivery

If you must be present at the time of delivery, California law requires retailers employing 25 or more people to specify a four-hour time period within which any delivery will be made, at the time of the sale or at a later date prior to the delivery date. For example, you bought a sofa at a department store and were given a Tuesday delivery date; the store, or the store's agent (if someone else is hired to make the delivery) must give you a set four-hour time period—such as 9:00 a.m. to 1:00 p.m.—for delivering your sofa on Tuesday. Civil Code § 1722 (a) (1).

Installation and Repairs

If you must be present at the time of installation, service or repair, California law requires retailers employing 25 or more people, whether or not the merchandise was sold by the retailer, to specify a four-hour time period within which the installation, service or repair will be commenced. Civil Code § 1722 (a) (1).

If the Seller Misses the Deadline

If the merchandise or service is not delivered or commenced within the specified four-hour period, you can sue in Small Claims Court for lost wages, expenses actually incurred or other actual damages up to $500. An exception to this new law would be for delays caused by unforeseen or unavoidable occurrences beyond the control of the retailer, utility or cable company (such as the delivery truck was in an accident or got caught in a major traffic jam). Civil Code §§ 1722 (a) (2) and (3).

FREIGHT SERVICE

Freight service (anything being shipped from one destination to another) within California is regulated by the California Public Utilities Commission (CPUC). Freight service includes trucks, United Parcel Service (UPS), trains and buses. Freight service between California and any other state is regulated by the U. S. Interstate Commerce Commission (ICC).

Where to Complain

For a California freight service problem related to lost or damaged goods or rate problems, contact CPUC. CPUC has three toll-free phone numbers to assist you:
* to verify the permit status of a freight carrier—(800) 877-8867
* to file a complaint against a freight carrier of household goods—(800) 366-4782
* to file a complaint against a general freight carrier—(800) 894-0444.

You might also want to call one of the 18 CPUC district offices. Check the telephone directory white pages, under State Government.

For any interstate freight service problems, ICC maintains two offices in California:
* 360 East Second Street, Suite 304, Los Angeles, CA 90012, (213) 894-4008
* 211 Main Street, Suite 500, San Francisco, CA 94105, (415) 744-6520.

HEALTH CLUBS

The desire to stay healthy and fit has been a real boon for the health club industry. It has also meant financial losses to consumers who paid for a membership in a health club that either never opened or went out of business. Before joining a health club, consider the following suggestions:
* Visit the club during the hours you intend to use the facilities to see how crowded it is.
* Talk to current members to see if they are satisfied with the club.

- Be wary of fees that are very low—clubs which don't charge enough are the most apt to go out of business.
- Be cautious of clubs that demand a long-term commitment. You might be better off paying month to month, even though it may be more expensive. With a shorter term commitment, you'll lose less money if a club goes out of business or you change your mind.
- Do not be pressured into signing a contract, and get all oral promises in writing.
- Ask if you will have the right to sell your membership to another person. Here is a list of your rights (Civil Code §§ 1812.81 through 1812.89):
- You are entitled to a written copy of your health club contract.
- No contract can require payment or financing for more than three years.
- Your service must begin within six months of the date the contract is signed.
- Your contract must have a three-day right of cancellation.
- To cancel, send written notice postmarked by midnight of the third business day—Sundays and holidays are not counted. Telephoning the club to cancel will not protect your rights.
- To protect yourself, send your cancellation by telegram or certified mail with a signed receipt requested—this is your proof of mailing on time. If you deliver the notice in person, get a signed receipt acknowledging that your cancellation was received in time.
- Once you cancel, the club must refund your money within ten days.
- If a doctor provides a written notice prohibiting you from continuing your membership, the club must refund the balance of unused services or cancel the remaining payments due on an installment contract.
- If you move more than 25 miles away from your club and cannot transfer your membership to a comparable facility, the club must refund the balance of the unused service or cancel the remaining payments due on an installment sales contract. The club may charge a cancellation fee—maximum is $100 ($50 if more than half the contract has expired).

Where to Complain

If you are having a problem—such as you have canceled but haven't gotten your money back, or your doctor insists you stop using the club but the club refuses to let you out of your contract—talk to the manager or owner of the club. If the problem persists, contact your District Attorney's consumer fraud unit, or a radio, TV or newspaper "Action Line." The California Attorney General's office, (800) 952-5225, may be able to help if the club is not complying with the law.

You can also sue in Small Claims Court and request treble (triple) damages to compensate you for money lost.

RESTROOMS

Restrooms in Public Places

In some places where the public congregates—such as sports arenas, convention halls and amusement parks—restrooms are required. Health and Safety Code § 3981. Although shopping centers are not specifically named, public restrooms must be available somewhere in the mall. Toilet seat covers are not required in public restrooms.

Restrooms in Restaurants

Restaurants must provide bathrooms for employees. Also, restaurants greater than 20,000 square feet must provide bathrooms for customers. Smaller restaurants, however, are not required to provide bathrooms for customers. In fact, smaller restaurants are forbidden to allow customers to use their bathroom if the customer must walk through the kitchen to use the facility.

Obviously, many smaller restaurants allow patrons to use the restrooms when they have to walk through the kitchen. (The state is concerned that hot liquid might spill on a customer.) Restaurants built after January 1, 1985, that allow patrons to use restroom facilities, however, must not locate those restrooms in the kitchen area. Health and Safety Code §§ 27626, 27627.3 and 27627.5

Restrooms in Gas Stations

A gas station must have a public restroom, if the station is within 660 feet of an accessible right of way of any interstate or primary highway—almost any highway that is not a country road. Access to restrooms must be provided to any customer who purchases *any* product (including a candy bar from a vending machine).

Exceptions are (Business and Professions Code § 13651):

- stations constructed before 1990 without permanent bathrooms, and
- a restroom that has been vandalized.

Where to Complain

A violation by a gas station is an infraction and may be reported to the District Attorney or the City Attorney. Depending on the county, this law may not be vigorously enforced.

STORAGE

Storage companies that also do moving are regulated by the California Public Utilities Commission. See *Freight Service,* above.

Storage companies that do not also do moving are not regulated. If you have a complaint against one of these companies which can't be resolved face-to-face, consider going to Small Claims Court.

TELEPHONE LONG DISTANCE COSTS

Many companies are competing for your long distance phone service. While prices for many basic services are fairly similar, real savings are possible for some types of service—such as regularly called long distance numbers or calls placed at certain times of the day.

Two organizations can help you compare long distance costs:

- Consumer Action, a nonprofit consumer education and advocacy group, does annual surveys of telephone long distance services. Consumer Action's publications are free; send a self-addressed, stamped, business-size envelope with 52¢ postage to 116 New Montgomery Street, Suite 233, San Francisco, CA 94105, (415) 777-9635.
- Trac is a Washington, DC-based organization that charts long distance companies. For a list of comparisons, send $2 (residential services) or $5 (small business services) to Trac, P.O. Box 12038, Washington, DC 20005, (202) 462-2520.

SALES

AUCTIONS

An auction is a public sale where goods are sold to the highest bidder.

Automobile Auctions

Private Auctions

Private parties hold auto auctions. Beware—unless you know a lot about cars or have a mechanic check under the hood, it's easy to buy a good-looking lemon. At an auction you can usually have the car checked out thoroughly before buying, but you can't test drive it and you can't return the car if it turns out to be a piece of junk.

Although you will be bidding against professional auto dealers, you may be able to get a good deal because most dealers bid fairly low so they can mark the car up for subsequent resale. Many banks hold their own auto auctions for repossessed vehicles. Call local banks for information. Also, check weekend newspaper ads for auto auctions open to the public.

Public Auctions

The California Office of Fleet Administration holds auto auctions once a month in Los Angeles or Sacramento. The cars are high mileage (90,000 miles or more), well-maintained, running vehicles with detailed and reliable service records (such as the last smog check or last oil change). For more information and a schedule of auctions, contact Office of Fleet Administration, 1416 10th Street, 2nd Floor, Sacramento, CA 95814, (916) 657-2318.

California Real Property Auctions

The California Department of Transportation (Caltrans) Office of Right of Way sells real property usually near state highways and freeways. Caltrans either holds auctions or sell options to purchase directly to buyers. For general information, call (916) 654-5413.

To get on to an area mailing list, contact one of the 12 Caltrans district offices (look in the telephone book white pages under State Government Offices—Transportation Department of) in Bishop, Eureka, Fresno, Los Angeles, Marysville, Oakland, Redding, San Bernardino, San Diego, San Luis Obispo, Santa Ana or Stockton.

U.S. Government Auctions

The U.S. Government has regular auctions of surplus property, including autos. For recorded messages of sale dates and locations, contact the General Services Administration (GSA)—in Northern California call (415) 744-5120; in Southern California call (213) 894-3210. Or send for the following free pamphlets:

- "Sale of Federal Surplus Personal Property," GSA, Property Management Division, Washington, DC 20407
- "How to Buy Surplus Personal Property from the Defense Reutilization and Marketing Service," Department of Defense (DOD) Surplus Sales, P.O. Box 1370, Battle Creek, MI 49016.

IRS Auctions

The IRS has recorded messages giving descriptions of real and personal property (including autos) to be auctioned, including the dates and location of the auctions, and minimum bids. The IRS recording also includes information on some real property sales being held in other states, such as Oregon and Nevada. The IRS maintains five "seizure sale hotlines" in California:

- Laguna Nigel—(714) 643-4523
- Los Angeles—(213) 894-5777
- Sacramento—(916) 978-5502
- San Francisco—(415) 556-5021
- San Jose—(408) 291-7252.

⚠️ The IRS sells its "interest" in the property, which means the property may not be free of other liens or mortgages. Before buying property this way, do a title search and buy title insurance.

Other Government Auctions

Many other federal government agencies—such as the FBI, Forest Service, Postal Service, Drug Enforcement Agency and Customs Department—hold personal property (including automobiles) and real property auctions. In addition, state, municipal and other government offices hold auctions. For more information, call the specific agencies.

GET FREE AUCTION INFORMATION

A number of businesses advertise publications that list auctions, often at a cost of anywhere from $30 to $100. Charging anything more than a few dollars for this information is a rip-off. Despite what you may think from listening to radio or TV ads, or reading in local newspaper ads, information on private and public auctions is free and readily available.

Where to Complain

The former regulatory agency in California (the California Auctioneer Commission) was abolished. To complain about a private auction house, contact your local District Attorney's office. To complain about a government auction, you'll have to go through the bureaucratic maze of the agency itself.

DOOR-TO-DOOR SALES

When you buy goods or services purchased for personal, family or household use costing $25 or more (including interest, mailing and other charges) from a door-to-door salesperson, you have a right to cancel by midnight of the third business day following when you signed the contract. The seller must give you written notice of your right to cancel and a cancellation form. If you don't receive it at the time of the sale, you have until midnight of the third business day following when you receive the notice.

To cancel, you must sign, date and mail (certified) or return the Notice of Cancellation form to the seller. Then, the seller must return your money within ten days. If the merchandise is picked up sooner, the seller must refund your money at or before this time. In addition to refunding your money, the seller must pick up the goods within 20 days after your cancellation notice. If the seller does not, you are entitled to keep the merchandise or dispose of it. If you have used the product, you may have to pay for this use. Civil Code § 1689.6.

MERCHANT STAMPS

For years, many merchants offered Blue Chip or S & H Green stamps. Consumers would save stamps in books that could be redeemed for merchandise either at a Blue Chip or S & H Green store, or from a catalog. Green stamps are no longer redeemable. Blue Chip Stamps, although not widely used anymore, can still be redeemed for merchandise or money.

To receive a Blue Chip Stamp redemption catalog, call (800) 824-0655.

REFUNDS FROM MERCHANTS

California law does not require a merchant to give a cash refund or a store credit when a purchase is returned. Many stores, however, do give refunds or store credits.

If a retailer does not give a full cash refund, give a credit refund, allow an equal exchange or any combination of the three to someone who returns the item with proof of purchase within seven days of the purchase, the retailer must conspicuously display that policy:

- on signs posted at each cash register and sales counter
- at each public entrance
- on tags attached to each item, or
- on the retailer's order forms.

If a retailer violates this law, he can be held liable to you for the amount of your purchase if you return, or attempt to return, the purchased goods within 30 days of purchase.

Exceptions are:

- food
- plants and flowers
- perishable goods
- merchandise marked "as is," "no returns accepted" or "all sales final"
- goods used or damaged after purchase
- special order goods received as ordered
- goods not returned with their original package, and
- goods which can't be resold due to health considerations. Civil Code § 1723.

RIGHT OF CANCELLATION (COOLING-OFF PERIOD)

You have the right to cancel certain consumer contracts you enter into, as long as you act quickly—most laws require that you cancel a contract within three days of signing. Even if you are not told of your right to cancel the contract, you can. And if you weren't told of your right, you may have longer than the standard three days to cancel.

Federal Right to Cancel

The Federal Trade Commission has a three-day cooling-off rule which lets you cancel two kinds of contracts, in person or by mail, until midnight of the third business day after the contract was signed. You must be given notice of the right to cancel and a cancellation form when you sign the contract. If you were not given a form, ask the seller to send you one. Your cancellation right extends until the seller sends it to you, even if it takes months.

The contracts you can cancel are:

- door-to-door sales contracts for more than $25, and
- contracts for more than $25 made anywhere other than the seller's normal place of business—for instance, at a sales presentation at a friend's house, hotel or

restaurant, outdoor exhibit, computer show or trade show (public car auctions and craft fairs are exempted from coverage).

After you cancel, the seller must refund your money within ten days. Then, the seller must either pick up the items purchased, or reimburse you within 20 days for your expense of mailing the goods back to the seller. If the seller doesn't come for the goods or make an arrangement for you to mail them back, you can keep them. If you send them back but aren't refunded for your mailing costs, you can sue the seller in Small Claims Court. 16 C.F.R. § 429.1.

Home Loans

The federal Truth in Lending Act lets you cancel a home improvement loan, second mortgage or other loan (except mortgage or deed of trust taken out at the time you acquire the property) where you pledge your principal dwelling (including a mobile home or houseboat you live in, but not a second home or vacation home) as security, until midnight of the third business day after you signed the contract. You must be told of your right to cancel and given a cancellation form when you sign the loan papers.

Congress included this right of cancellation because consumers face the loss of their homes if loans secured by their homes are not repaid.

The three-day period begins after the last of three events occurs:
- delivery of the Truth in Lending disclosure
- delivery of the right-of-rescission notice, or
- consummation of the loan (the time you become obligated on the loan—usually when the note is signed).

The lender cannot disburse any loan funds until the three-day rescission period has ended and the lender is reasonably satisfied that you have not canceled. If you rescind a transaction, and loan funds have been disbursed to you, you must return them. 15 U.S.C. § 1635.

State Right to Cancel

Under California law, you can cancel the following contracts within the times listed:
- dance lessons—180 days; you must pay for lessons received (Civil Code § 1812.54)
- dating service—3 days (Civil Code § 1694.1)
- discount buying services—3 days (Civil Code § 1812.118)
- door-to-door sales—3 days (Civil Code § 1689.6)
- employment counseling—3 days (Civil Code § 1812.511)
- health clubs—3 days (Civil Code § 1812.85)
- home equity sales contracts—5 days (Civil Code § 1695.4)
- home improvement contracts signed in the buyer's home—3 days (Civil Code § 1689.8)
- membership camping—3 days (Civil Code § 1812.303)
- motor vehicle financing from a lender other than the seller at a rate specified in purchase contract—time specified in contract (Civil Code § 2982.9)
- prepaid job listing service firms—48 hours (Civil Code § 1812.504)
- seller-assisted marketing plans—3 days (Civil Code § 1812.208)
- seminar sales—3 days (Civil Code § 1689.20)
- weight loss—3 days (Civil Code § 1694.6).

⚠ Automobile sales contracts for new and used motor vehicles, and contracts to buy appliances, furniture or electronic gear which you signed for at the seller's place of business, do not have a three-day right of cancellation.

How to Count the Days

To accurately count three (or five, or whatever the limit) business days for cancellation, start counting the day after you signed the contract. Saturdays are considered business days, but Sundays and holidays are not. For example, if you signed a contract on Friday, the deadline for cancellation would be midnight on Tuesday—Saturday is the first day, Monday the second, and Tuesday the third.

How to Cancel

You must cancel a contract in writing, and have the cancellation letter postmarked by midnight of the time specified. Certain businesses are notorious for claiming they never received your cancellation notice. Send your cancellation notice by certified mail with a return receipt requested. That's your proof. Instead of writing, you may send a telegram—but be sure you get and keep a record of the exact time and date. If you hand deliver the cancellation notice, get a signed receipt from the business acknowledging receipt. Do not cancel by telephone. It is not considered valid and you have no proof.

CHARITIES

If you are unfamiliar with an organization soliciting a donation, request a copy of its financial statement or annual report. If an organization won't provide the information, do not give it any money. If you make a donation, be sure that a large percentage goes to direct charitable services, not administration, fundraising or education (often a phony gimmick that means fundraising).

More Information

- You can obtain copies of any charitable corporation's federal tax exemption application, which discloses the primary purposes, programs and projected fundraising activities of the organization, together with a narrative justifying the group's eligibility for nonprofit tax-exempt status, supporting documentation and tax exemption determination letter from the IRS at any IRS office by paying a small fee. You can also obtain the organization's annual tax return, which includes detailed financial and program information including income, expenses, assets and liabilities; salaries and expense account money; political activities undertaken; plus transactions entered into with related and non-exempt organizations. See IRS Publication 557 for more information.
- The Council of Better Business Bureaus (BBB) publishes *Standards for Charitable Solicitations* (updated every few months), listing the organizations that generate the largest numbers of inquiries to their Philanthropic Advisory Service. The Council is the national umbrella of all BBBs; it has set acceptable standards for charitable organizations; its guide indicates which organizations meet those standards in areas of public accountability, use of funds, solicitations and informational materials, fundraising practices and governance. For a free copy of the latest guide, contact your local BBB or send a stamped, self-addressed, business-size envelope to: Philanthropic Advisory Service, Council of Better Business Bureaus, Inc., Department 024, Washington, DC 20042-0024.
- The National Charities Information Bureau (NCIB) publishes a report, *Wise Giving Guide*, similar to the one produced by the BBB. Write to NCIB, 19 Union Square West, New York, NY 10003-3395.
- The California Attorney General's office maintains a Registry of Charitable Trusts. You can request information (such as the original filing papers and an annual report) or file a complaint against a nonprofit corporation by contacting the California Attorney General's Office, P.O. Box 903447, Sacramento, CA 94203-4470, (916) 445-2021.

BEWARE OF SOUND-ALIKE CHARITY GROUPS

Check carefully to be sure the organization you support is really the one you think it is. Some charities adopt a sound-alike name of a well-known organization to try to capture givers. The American Cancer Society is legitimate; using those same words in a different order (such as the American Society of Cancer) is meant to confuse you. Also, do not be taken in by a solicitation just because it's from an organization identifying itself with a sympathetic cause, such as the homeless, heart disease, battered women or the environment. Many phony groups use emotion-provoking words to get sympathy and dollars.

Make-a-Wish Foundation

This foundation tries to fulfill a wish for children up to age 18 who have a life threatening illness and may not reach their 18th birthday. Wishes can include requests such as a family trip to Disneyland, a computer or a redecorated bedroom. Money is not available for medical expenses.

There are seven chapters around the state:

- Camarillo—(805) 987-0377
- Fresno—(209) 221-2688
- Irvine—(714) 476-9474
- Los Angeles—(310) 207-3023
- Sacramento—(916) 448-9474
- San Diego—(619) 453-9474
- San Leandro—(510) 352-9474.

FOOD

Contamination

If you find a foreign object in food, or you suspect any packaged food or drink has been contaminated, contact your county Health Department. Ask the office to examine the product. Inform the merchant where you bought the item, write to the manufacturer of the product and contact the U.S. Food and Drug Administration (FDA). (See *Government* chapter.)

Short Weight

Your county Weights and Measures office has responsibility for assuring the accuracy of any food that is weighed, measured or counted. The agency is listed in the telephone book white page's Government section, under County Government Offices.

Meat and Poultry Information

The U.S. Department of Agriculture (USDA) runs the Meat and Poultry Hotline, (800) 535-4555, from 7:00 a.m. to 1:00 p.m. pacific standard time, weekdays. Well-trained home economists can answer your questions about:

- the proper preparing and storing of meat and poultry
- thawing, roasting and stuffing
- how to tell if the meat is safe to eat, and
- how to better understand labels.

You can also report problems to the USDA.

Salt and Sodium Information

If you are concerned about the amount of salt in food, you can call a hotline staffed by registered dieticians who answer questions about salt and sodium. They have a computer-based data information system which lists the sodium content of over 10,000 food items. In addition, they will send out a brochure, recipes and coupons. This service is provided by the Alberta Culver Corp. (Mrs. Dash), Monday to Friday, 6:00 a.m. to 2:00 p.m. pacific standard time at (800) 622-3274.

Truth in Menus

California has a "Truth in Menus" law. The purpose is to eliminate misrepresentations and fraud in restaurant menus. One example is the menu that lists "crabmeat" as an ingredient in a dish, but actually uses an imitation product that is much cheaper. People with severe allergies or restricted diets could be injured or killed through false reliance. Business and Professions Code § 17500; Health and Safety Code §§ 26460 and 26461.

To report a restaurant's misleading menu, contact your local Department of Public Health's Environmental Health Services. Not all counties enforce "Truth in Menus" because they do not have the staff or budget, even though it is state law.

HOW TO WRITE A COMPLAINT LETTER

Throughout this book I frequently recommend that you write a letter when you feel your rights have been infringed. There is a real skill to writing an effective and powerful complaint letter which is likely to bring a quick (and I hope positive) response. Here's how.

- Direct the letter to the person with authority to resolve the problem (president, manager or head of customer service).
- Type your letter (or neatly print) and limit it to one page, if possible.
- Indicate if you have been a long-time, satisfied customer. (Most companies want to keep loyal customers.)
- Identify the problem clearly and reasonably briefly. Be businesslike and refrain from sarcasm or insulting comments.
- State what you want (an apology, a refund or a replacement) and be reasonable.
- Give dates and location of purchase, account numbers, name of product and serial numbers if needed.
- Omit irrelevant information. (Give just the facts.)
- Set a reasonable time for a response.
- Send copies of appropriate documentation. (Keep originals for yourself.)
- Keep copies of all correspondence.
- Give your name, address and daytime phone number.

SAMPLE COMPLAINT LETTER #1

Name of person with authority
Title
Company Name
Address
City, State, Zip Code
Date

Dear (preferably use a person's name, or "customer service manager"):

As a "frequent flyer" with XYZ Airlines (account number), I specifically booked Flight 22 for November 19th to take my family of five (husband and three minor children) to Hawaii for a six-day vacation. On November 16th, one of our children suffered a ruptured appendix and was hospitalized for ten days. This family emergency necessitated that we all cancel the trip. Obviously, my other children couldn't go on their own and my husband and I were at our sick child's bedside. I am aware that these were nonrefundable tickets; however, with a medical emergency in the family (enclosed please find copies of the hospital bill and a letter from our nine-year-old son's doctor), we had no choice but to cancel our holiday plans. I was disappointed that XYZ Airlines has offered to refund only one ticket. I would like you to reconsider that decision and refund all five tickets. My preference is for a cash refund; however, I would be willing to accept five replacement tickets for a future trip.

I look forward to your reply and a satisfactory resolution to this problem, and will wait three weeks before seeking third-party assistance.

Sincerely,
Barbara Kaufman
1234 Main Street
Anyplace, CA 94111
(415) 666-0000

SAMPLE COMPLAINT LETTER #2

Customer Service Manager
ABC Hosiery, Inc.
New York, NY 10021

Dear Customer Service Manager:
Enclosed please find a pair of pantyhose (my favorite brand) that I started to put on this morning right out of the packet. The right leg had a small hole on top of the foot—what a surprise! I decided I would wear them anyway and proceeded to put my foot in the left leg. That was a bigger shock—there was a hole with a run. In all my years of buying pantyhose, I have never seen anything like this. You can see that the pantyhose were not worn, in fact, never got above the knees. I would appreciate a replacement pair or a check for $4.95 (preferably the hose). I hope this is a one-time fluke and not an indication of poor quality control, because these are my first choice for pantyhose.
Thank you for your prompt attention.

Sincerely,
Barbara Kaufman
1234 Main Street
Anyplace, CA 94111
(415) 666-0000

I actually wrote the above letter. In response I received a lovely letter with an apology, an explanation regarding the problem the company was having with one of their manufacturers and two pairs of pantyhose for my inconvenience.

Copyrights, Patents and the Like

COPYRIGHT

Copyright law protects authors, artists, software writers and composers from having others copy their original works. You can obtain registration forms, instructions and circulars containing general copyright information free of charge from the U.S. Copyright Office, Washington, DC 20559, (202) 707-9100. To obtain public information by telephone, call (202) 479-0700.

Registering a copyright costs $20, but government fees do occasionally go up.

Additional Resources

The Copyright Handbook: How to Protect and Use Written Works, by attorney Stephen Fishman (Nolo Press), gives detailed information on copyright registration, use and protection. It is available in libraries and bookstores. For specific information on copyrights for software, see *Software Development: A Legal Guide,* by attorney Stephen Fishman (Nolo Press).

Nolo Press also publishes *Patent, Copyright and Trademark: A Desk Reference to Intellectual Property Law,* by attorneys Stephen Elias and Kate McGrath.

INVENTIONS AND PATENTS

If you have a unique idea for a useful product or method, it may be patentable as an invention. If a patent is granted, you get an exclusive 17-year right to use and commercially exploit the invention. Your first step is to do a patent search to make sure someone else has not previously invented it. (For a fee, you can pay someone else to do the search for you.) To do the search, you can use one of California's five patent depositories:

- Los Angeles Public Library
- San Diego Public Library
- State Library in Sacramento
- U.C. Irvine University Library
- Sunnyvale Patent Information Clearinghouse, 1500 Partridge Avenue, Building 7, Sunnyvale, CA 94087, (408) 730-7290.

If you determine that your idea is patentable, the next step is to file a detailed patent application complete with drawings of your idea.

Additional Resources

Patent It Yourself, by patent attorney David Pressman (Nolo Press), gives detailed information on patents and how to do your own patent search. It is available in libraries and bookstores. *Patent It Yourself* is also available in a software version from Nolo Press.

The best protection for your patent is adequate records. *The Inventor's Notebook,* by Fred Grissom and David Pressman (Nolo Press), helps you document the process of successful independent inventing by providing forms, instructions, references to relevant areas of patent law and more. This book is available in public libraries and bookstores.

Nolo Press also publishes *Patent, Copyright and Trademark: A Desk Reference to Intellectual Property Law*, by attorneys Stephen Elias and Kate McGrath.

MUSIC

The United States Copyright Act has established that writers, composers and publishers own the music they have created. What this means is you cannot legally play a person's music publicly (live, recorded or even playing a radio for customers) without paying for the use of the songwriter's product.

If you play music in your place of business, such as a health club, retail store, restaurant, bar, doctor's office and the like, you must have a music license from either Broadcast Music, Inc. (BMI) or the American Society of Composers, Authors and Publishers (ASCAP). (Many businesses get "caught" playing music without a license by songwriters' friends and relatives who happen to visit a business illegally playing music.) License fees are very modest, but these two nonprofit organizations will most likely sue you if they bill you and you refuse to pay or you refuse to stop playing their members' music publicly. Money collected from these license fees (less expenses) is distributed to affiliated songwriters and music publishers.

For more information, call BMI at (800) 326-4BMI. To reach ASCAP, call (415) 574-6023 or (714) 586-1632.

TRADEMARKS AND SERVICE MARKS

Trademark law is the tool used to decide disputes involving the names and symbols used to identify goods and services in the market place. Names and symbols are called trademarks when they are applied to products, and service marks when they are used to market a service. Trademark law has two goals:

- to prevent businesses from stealing the goodwill that others have generated by creatively naming and distinguishing their services and products in the market place, and
- to prevent customers from being misled by the user of confusingly similar names on products and services.

Additional Resources

Trademark: How to Name a Business and Product, by attorneys Kate McGrath and Stephen Elias, with Sarah Shena (Nolo Press), gives detailed information on trademark use and protection. It is available in libraries and bookstores.

Nolo Press also publishes *Patent, Copyright and Trademark: A Desk Reference to Intellectual Property Law*, by attorneys Stephen Elias and Kate McGrath. ∎

COURTS AND COURT ACTIONS

ARBITRATION AND MEDIATION

Arbitration is a way to resolve a conflict without going to court. An arbitrator—an impartial third party—makes a decision that is legally binding and enforceable.

Mediation is a technique to resolve disputes which depend on the disputants' arriving at their own non-coerced agreement with the help of a mediator. In this respect, it differs from both court and arbitration procedures where a decision is imposed by an arbitrator or judge.

Many people prefer mediation or arbitration over going to court because they are faster, cheaper and less burdened with archaic rules and procedures. Arbitration is commonly used to decide new car warranty disputes, disputes over house purchase contracts and disputes between investors and stockbrokers. Mediation often works in neighborhood and small consumer disputes.

American Arbitration Association

The American Arbitration Association (AAA) is a public service, nonprofit, private organization offering arbitration to business executives, individual employees, trade associations, law firms, unions, management, consumers, farmers and government. AAA arbitrators have specialized knowledge and experience in the particular business, profession or field involved in the case. AAA prepares, and forwards to the disputing parties, a list of suitable arbitrators that includes biographical information. The parties select an arbitrator from this list. There is a fee for their arbitration services which may be split between the parties or negotiated.

The AAA has four offices in California:
- 3055 Wilshire Blvd., 7th Floor, Los Angeles, CA 90010, (213) 383-6516
- 417 Montgomery Street, 5th Floor, San Francisco, CA 94104, (415) 981-3901
- 2601 Main Street, Suite 240, Irvine, CA 92714, (714) 474-5090
- 600 "B" Street, Suite 1450, San Diego, CA 92101, (619) 239-3051.

AAA's New York headquarters, 140 West 51st Street, New York, NY 10020, (212) 484-4000, is the main outlet for brochures, information and a national list of arbitrators.

Automobile Accident Arbitration

Arbitration Forums, Inc., a nonprofit organization, offers an innovative binding arbitration program (as well as a mediation program) to help people who have been injured or whose property has been damaged in an auto accident. Called Accident Arbitration Forum, it's a simple process to help consumers resolve disputes with insurance companies. Participants select the arbitrator from a list of three retired judges who formerly served on the state Supreme Court or Appellate Court. Consumers and insurance companies have the option to be represented by lawyers. The process moves quickly and the costs are reasonable: $150 for each party, plus $150 per hour arbitrator's fee, split between the parties.

Arbitration Forums maintains two offices from which you can request free pamphlets or request arbitration:
- 2300 Clayton Road, Suite 500, Concord, CA 94520, (510) 825-0624 (northern California)
- 5400 Orange Avenue, Suite 115 408, Cypress, CA 90630, (714) 995-3614 (southern California).

The national office is located at 3350 West Busch Blvd., Suite 295, Tampa, FL 33618.

Consumer Arbitration

Many local Better Business Bureaus provide free mediation/arbitration services for disputes between a business and a consumer. For example, a homeowner who is dissatisfied with the workmanship of her custom-made draperies and the drapery company who thinks the homeowner is just a nitpicker are probably good candidates for the BBB mediation or arbitration service. The BBB also provides the authorized third-party dispute resolution program to handle lemon law disputes between consumers and more than a dozen auto manufacturers.

Neighborhood Mediation

Many counties in California offer free mediation services as a method of resolving disputes without going to court. Through the mediation process, the individuals involved in a dispute work out their own solutions with the help of a mediator (a neutral third party). The mediator does not make decisions for the parties involved, but guides them to reaching a fair resolution to such problems as landlord/tenant and neighbor disputes.

Many communities have mediation or neighborhood dispute programs. These programs change frequently, so check your local phone book, a local consumer agency, local government or a Small Claims Court advisor.

Gay/Lesbian Mediation Services

In response to the continuing lack of sensitivity of the court system to the needs of gay men and lesbians, gay men and lesbians have taken it upon themselves to establish mediation programs to help with roommate conflicts, neighbor disputes, landlord-tenant matters, business conflicts, break ups and other problems. The two California programs are:

- Gay and Lesbian Alternative Dispute Resolution, San Francisco, (415) 552-4135
- Gay and Lesbian Mediation Services, Los Angeles, (213) 993-7675.

Child Custody/Visitation Mediation

Before a dispute about child custody or visitation can be heard in a California courtroom (whether part of a divorce or not), the disputing parents must attend mandatory court-sponsored mediation sessions to try to resolve the matter. The Superior Court clerk in each county can provide you with more information.

SMALL CLAIMS COURT

Small Claims Court is the place to go if you have a dispute of up to $5,000 that you cannot resolve any other way. It is a people's court where lawyers cannot represent either side—except for a lawyer suing in his own case or as a representative of a corporation in a few instances. The filing fees and service of process costs are minimal and they can be recovered if you win. After you have finished your presentation, ask the judge to include reimbursement for those costs. You cannot recover personal expenses such as taking time off of work or the cost of paying a babysitter.

Some things to consider before filing:

- You must be legally right and be able to prove it. Just being convinced you are right is not good enough. Having witnesses, pictures, documents or other evidence supporting your position is usually critically important.
- If you win, will you be able to collect? Some people are judgment proof—they have no assets or they hide them. The court does not collect the money for you—that is up to you. To avoid wasting time, it makes sense to figure out before you file if you are ever likely to collect your judgment.
- As the person filing the lawsuit (the plaintiff), if you lose, you do not have a right of appeal, but you do have the right to petition the Small Claims Court to correct a judgment on the grounds that a clerical error or legal error was made. See Appeal of Judgment, below, for an exception.

- The person you are suing (the defendant) can appeal a losing decision to Superior Court. Lawyers are permitted for both sides at an appeal and the case is presented over again.

How to Begin
Before you file in Small Claims Court, write a business-like demand letter to the business or individual with whom you have a dispute, asking for what you believe you are owed and why. Indicate that if your demand is not met, you will sue the person in Small Claims Court. If that does not get results in ten days or so, then prepare for court.

Help in Filing Your Lawsuit
Every county has a free Small Claims Court advisor (by telephone or in person, although in some smaller counties it may be only by phone) to help you file your lawsuit. The advisor can help you determine:
- if you have a good case
- the amount of money to ask for in compensation
- if your suit is filed soon enough to meet the statute of limitations
- who to sue—this can be confusing in cases involving businesses or automobiles
- which is the proper (judicial district) court in which to bring suit—usually you can sue where a defendant lives or does business, where you entered into a contract, where you bought a product or where an auto accident happened
- how best to present your case to convince the judge you are right
- how to collect if you win.

How Much Can You Sue For?
The Small Claims Court limit is $5,000. There are two exceptions:
- No one entity (person or company) can sue for over $2,500 more than two times in one calendar year.
- Guarantors, such as surety bond companies (those who insure others), can only be sued up to $1,500.

Who Can Be Sued?
You will need the proper name and address of the person or unincorporated business you want to sue. If it is a business partnership you should sue all partners. To sue a corporation, you must establish that it's registered in California or doing business here. To sue the state or a county or city, you must first notify them of your claim. Publications listed in Additional Resources, below, explain in more detail.

Time Limits for Suing
The statute of limitations defines how quickly you must file your lawsuit in a California court, not just Small Claims court:
- oral contracts—two years from the date the contract is broken
- written contracts—four years from the date the contract is broken
- personal or real property damage—three years from the date of the damage
- personal injury—one year from the discovery of the injury
- lawsuits against city, county or state government—first, you must file a claim against the agency within six months. When the agency denies your claim, then you can take them to court.

Appeal of Judgment
The defendant in a Small Claims suit can appeal a losing decision to the Superior Court. The plaintiff cannot appeal if he loses his case. The plaintiff can appeal, however, if he loses on a claim of defendant—that is, when the defendant

countersues. Civil Code § 117.8 (b). On appeal, all claims of the parties will be tried over again. Civil Code § 117.10.

Additional Resources

The California Department of Consumer Affairs has published a free booklet on the topic. It is not updated all that frequently, making it difficult to use. But it is better than nothing. Contact your county Small Claims Court advisor or clerk, or send a self-addressed, stamped (52¢ postage), business-size envelope to *Using the Small Claims Court*, P.O. Box 310, Sacramento, CA 95802.

Everybody's Guide to Small Claims Court, by attorney Ralph Warner (Nolo Press) is easily the best source of information about California Small Claims Court. It is particularly good on how to write a demand letter and how to present your case in court, and is available in public libraries and bookstores.

MUNICIPAL COURT

Municipal Court (called justice court in rural areas) can hear disputes involving money or property that don't exceed $25,000, as well as a wide variety of minor criminal cases. Cases worth up to $5,000 can be filed either in either Small Claims Court or Municipal Court. Small Claims Court is faster, cheaper and far easier for a non-lawyer to use than Municipal Court. In Municipal Court, however, the plaintiff (the one bringing the lawsuit) can appeal if she loses. She can't in Small Claims Court.

Municipal Court also has jurisdiction over eviction (unlawful detainer) cases where the whole amount of damages (unpaid rent, damage to the premises and the like) doesn't exceed $25,000.

Municipal Court also can hear actions involving dissolution of partnership, enforcing liens, canceling contracts, issuing injunctions and more. For details, see Code of Civil Procedure § 86.

Additional Resources

Everybody's Guide to Municipal Court, by Judge Roderic Duncan (Nolo Press), explains how to prepare and defend the most common types of contract and personal injury cases in California Municipal Court. It is particularly good on preparing and filing forms, gathering evidence and appearing in court; it is available in libraries and bookstores.

Represent Yourself in Court: How to Prepare and Try a Winning Case, by attorneys Paul Bergman and Sara J. Berman-Barrett (Nolo Press), shows how to handle a civil court case from start to finish. It's the most thorough guide to contested court cases ever published for non-lawyers. It is available in libraries and bookstores.

SUPERIOR COURT

This major California trial court has jurisdiction over monetary claims of over $25,000 and also over serious criminal actions. Most family law cases, including divorce, adoption, guardianship and probate, are heard in Superior Court.

Additional Resources

Represent Yourself in Court: How to Prepare and Try a Winning Case, by attorneys Paul Bergman and Sara J. Berman-Barrett (Nolo Press), shows how to handle a civil court case from start to finish. It's the only guide to contested court cases published for non-lawyers. It is available in libraries and bookstores.

COLLECTION OF COURT JUDGMENT

It surprises many people that when they win a court judgment—no matter what court—the court doesn't collect the money for them. Unfortunately, you are on your own. If your judgment is against a person with a job or considerable property, or a going business, collecting it can be fairly routine if you know how to proceed. Often, this involves authorizing a wage garnishment, placing a lien against real property or attaching a bank account—in the case of a business, going after its cash or other assets.

Judgments are good for ten years and can be renewed for subsequent ten-year periods. Interest on the unpaid debt and the cost of collection can also be recovered. Many judgments that initially seem uncollectable can be collected if you're patient enough. Even if the debtor is temporarily "judgment-proof" (has virtually no assets or money), you can often collect years down the line when the person is back at work, inherits property or is otherwise solvent, with a better rate of interest than if you invested in CDs or various bonds. And it's also possible that the person who owes you money could win something sizable from the lottery.

More Information

The California Department of Consumer Affairs has a publication that you can purchase for $6.45 (including tax and shipping) called *Collecting Your Small Claims Court Judgment.* Make a check or money order payable to the State of California or the Department of General Services. Write the name of the publication on your check and send it to the Department of General Services, Documents and Publications, P.O. Box 1015, North Highlands, CA 95660.

Collect Your Court Judgment, by Scott, Elias and Goldoftas (Nolo Press), provides step-by-step guidance for a broad range of collection possibilities for Small Claims, Municipal Court and Superior Court judgments. This book is available in public libraries and bookstores.

JUDGES/COMMISSION ON JUDICIAL PERFORMANCE

The Commission on Judicial Performance is an independent state constitutional agency that handles complaints against California judges for judicial misconduct or wrongdoing including:
- improper courtroom decorum
- improper influence or conflict of interest
- misusing public property or funds
- obstruction of justice, or
- ticket-fixing.

Anyone can file a complaint. If you are simply unhappy with a judge's ruling, do not bother to contact the Commission; it does not have the authority to review or change legal decisions. To attempt to accomplish that you must promptly file an appeal.

To obtain a pamphlet and complaint form, contact the Commission on Judicial Performance, 101 Howard Street, Suite 300, San Francisco, CA 94105, (415) 904-3650.

JURY DUTY

Jurors are randomly selected from lists of names provided by voter registration and Department of Motor Vehicles (DMV) lists. In many counties you will be "on call" for a week, two-week or ten-day period. No matter how your county runs its jury system, if you are selected for a jury, you must serve until the trial is over.

Employers must allow employees time off to fulfill jury duty obligations and cannot fire an employee for absence due to jury duty. Employers are not required to pay employees for time away from work.

A judge may excuse a potential juror for health reasons or undue hardship (such as possible foreclosure on your home if you are without income). If you are on vacation or have some other reason why you need to postpone service, it is possible to get a deferment to a later date, usually not more than 90 days. Promptly write a letter explaining your problem.

CHANGING YOUR NAME

You can choose almost any new name, legally, without a lawyer, and sometimes can accomplish a name change without going to court. If, however, you go to court for a legal name change, there are some limits. You can't choose a new name to defraud creditors, a name that could be construed as "fighting words" or one that is confusingly similar to that of a famous person.

All the forms, instructions and information needed to legally change your name are in *How to Change Your Name*, by attorneys David Ventura Loeb and David W. Brown (Nolo Press), which is available in libraries and bookstores.

PERSONAL INJURY

It may surprise you to learn that if you or a family member are injured in an accident in which someone else was at fault, you should be able to handle your own injury insurance claim without hiring a lawyer for help. All it takes is basic information about how the accident claims process works, a little organization and a lot of patience.

If the injury is not too serious, but you are unable to reach a fair settlement with the insurer or no coverage applies, you may want to sue in Small Claims Court. Otherwise, you may want to contact an experienced attorney for help. Generally, personal injury attorneys take cases on a contingency fee basis—they typically receive one-third of the settlement—which means they get paid only if they win. In addition, you may have to pay certain out-of-pocket legal costs.

Additional Resources

One book that may be helpful if you want to pursue a personal injury claim on your own is *How to Win Your Personal Injury Claim,* by attorney Joseph L. Matthews (Nolo Press). This step-by-step guide shows how to avoid insurance company run-arounds, evaluate what your claim is worth and obtain a full and fair settlement. It's available in bookstores and libraries. ■

CREDIT, LOANS AND DEBT

CREDIT

Credit is a convenience—you can buy something now and pay for it later. If you don't have ready cash, you can use credit. Credit is a privilege, not a right. Establishing good credit (even if you prefer to pay by cash) may be a necessity to buy large items you may need to finance, such as a car or a home. Credit is also helpful and sometimes necessary to rent a car or guarantee a hotel or motel reservation. Creditors, such as department stores or banks, are interested in your ability and willingness to repay a debt. They usually judge this by checking your credit history. If you apply for a large loan, the credit grantor may also ask for a personal financial statement listing your assets, income and other debts.

Creditors use different factors in deciding whether or not to grant credit. Many creditors use a "credit scoring" system to determine whether you are a good risk. Most major retailers believe the credit scoring system is the most accurate predictor of a consumer's bill-paying reliability. A credit scoring system reviews how promptly you pay your bills, your income, whether you own a home, and how many years you have had your job, and whether you've defaulted on bills in the past or filed for bankruptcy.

Even people with perfect credit-paying histories can be turned down for credit. A creditor may decide that you already have enough credit based on your income, and it does not want to be the creditor who is not paid. Also, some creditors heavily weigh an applicant's age. For example, creditors might hesitate in giving credit to people aged 36-48 because people in this age group often have high expenses—mortgages, car loans, braces for their children's teeth and college tuitions. Those same creditors may score people 61 and over higher because the expenses in this age group are usually much lower.

Establishing Credit

If you have never used credit before, establish a credit history or an economic identity by opening a savings and/or checking account in your name. After a few months, apply for a small line of credit with a department store or local merchant. Another possibility is to apply for a "secured credit card" through a bank or savings and loan. Applying for a secured credit card is also a good strategy if you are trying to rebuild your credit.

If you have no or a poor credit history, but have a steady income and are trying to establish yourself as a good credit risk, make an appointment with the credit manager of a department store . Explain your credit-paying history and ask for a small line of credit. Use that credit and make your payments on time. After six months or a year, request an increased credit limit. Then go to another retailer or credit grantor and try the same tactic. This is a slow process, but it will help you establish good credit.

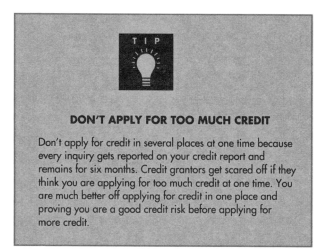

DON'T APPLY FOR TOO MUCH CREDIT

Don't apply for credit in several places at one time because every inquiry gets reported on your credit report and remains for six months. Credit grantors get scared off if they think you are applying for too much credit at one time. You are much better off applying for credit in one place and proving you are a good credit risk before applying for more credit.

Getting a Cosigner

Another way to get credit is to ask someone with an established credit history to cosign your credit application. For the cosigner, it means promising to pay if you do not. If you make your payments on time, you can establish your own good credit history and dispense with the need for a cosigner in the future.

⚠️ Cosigners beware! Not only will you have to pay the debt if the other person does not, but negative information can go on your credit report. For example, an auto repossession can show up on a cosigner's credit history, even if you never drove the car! The Federal Trade Commission requires that co-signers be given a disclosure statement that points out these obligations.

Credit Discrimination

Under the Equal Credit Opportunity Act, it is illegal for creditors to discriminate against applicants on the basis of their sex, race, marital status, national origin, religion, age or because they receive public assistance. This does not mean you are automatically entitled to credit. Creditors can still take into account your income, living expenses, debts and your credit-paying history.

Because California is a "community property" state, a creditor may ask for your marital status if you are applying for a separate account.

CREDIT REPORTING

Credit reporting agencies (called credit bureaus) assemble, store and report bill-paying histories. The three largest in the U.S. are TRW, Equifax and TransUnion. Credit grantors (such as retailers, banks and finance companies) typically report your credit-paying habits to all three credit bureaus. Public records also become part of your file—these include court judgments, tax liens and mechanic's liens, bankruptcies and wage assignments. Creditors, employers and other business people, such as landlords, buy your credit report from the bureaus. Credit bureaus do not make decisions to grant or deny credit—they only store your credit-paying history. Creditors determine whether to grant you credit.

Credit reporting is regulated by the federal Fair Credit Reporting Act. 15 U.S.C. § 1681 and follows, and by several state laws (described below).

Seeing Your Credit Report

If you've been denied credit in the past 60 days, you can obtain a copy of your credit report for free. The creditor who turned you down must give you the name and address of the credit bureau it used. Write to that credit bureau and ask for a copy of your report. The report will contain a sheet with explanations of the codes used in the report. If you have questions, call the bureau and ask for help.

If you have not been turned down for credit, look in the telephone book yellow pages under Credit Reporting Agencies. You'll need to send a letter including your:
- full name, including generations (Jr., Sr., III)
- year or date of birth
- Social Security number
- spouse's name
- telephone number
- current address
- previous addresses and dates there if you've been at your current address fewer than five years, and
- a photocopy of a billing statement, utility bill, driver's license or other document that links your name with your address.

California caps the fee a credit bureau can charge for a copy of your credit report at $8. TRW will send you one free copy a year, on request. Write to TRW Complimentary Report Request, P.O. Box 2350, Chatsworth, CA 91313-2350.

How Long Information Stays in a Credit File

By law, most negative information, such as court judgments, liens and reports that you took more than 30 days to pay a bill, cannot be included in your credit file after seven years. Bankruptcy filings can be included for ten years.

If Information Is Incorrect or Outdated

The Fair Credit Reporting Act gives you the right to dispute anything inaccurate in your file. Write to the credit bureau about anything you disagree with, and the bureau must re-check the disputed item with the source that provided the information. The credit bureau will send you a corrected copy of your credit report.

The credit bureau must change the information if the source reporting it cannot or does not verify it within 30 days. If the creditor says the information is accurate, however, the credit bureau will not remove it from your file. If that happens, you will have to enlist the help of the merchant who reported the negative information. If that doesn't happen, you have the right to add a 100-word statement to your file disputing what has been reported.

DON'T NECESSARILY ADD
A 100-WORD STATEMENT

If you can't get inaccurate, adverse information off your record, you have the right to put a 100-word statement in your file. Doing this isn't always wise, however, for two reasons. First, many credit grantors ignore these statements. Second, many credit bureaus keep these statements for seven years, even if the original negative information has been removed. Consider instead, explaining any disputes to a particular creditor when you apply for credit. If you do put in a statement, link it to a specific item in your credit report and it should come out when that item comes out. Don't just explain away generally bad credit.

There is no central registry of information held by credit bureaus. If inaccurate information is in one bureau's report, it may be in the other bureaus' reports too. If so, you will have to get these records corrected using the same procedure. Recently, Congress has been trying to amend the Fair Credit Reporting Act, which has shaken up major credit grantors. Consequently, some merchants now voluntarily report and correct information with all three credit bureaus so consumers won't have to be responsible for correcting all records themselves. And the credit bureaus have established toll-free phone numbers to take consumer complaints:

- TRW   (800) 392-1122
- Equifax   (800) 685-1111
- TransUnion   (800) 851-2674.

Additional Legal Protections in California

California leads the country with legislation regulating credit bureaus. Here's a summary:

Credit bureaus:

- cannot report an arrest unless it resulted in conviction
- cannot report an eviction action unless it went to judgment and the landlord won the case or the tenant signs an agreement stating that an eviction may be reported to the credit bureaus
- must report the specific type of bankruptcy (Chapter 7, Chapter 11, Chapter 13)
- must specify when an account closed is by you, and
- cannot furnish medical information without your consent. Civil Code § 1785.13. Credit bureaus must provide you with:
- names of all creditors who received copy of your file for the previous six months (two years if file given for employment purposes)
- copy of credit file within five days of receiving your request, and
- telephone disclosure of credit file if you provide proper identification. Civil Code § 1785.15.

If you request a reinvestigation of information in your file, the bureau must provide you with written results of the reinvestigation within five days of completion. If the bureau removes information after you request a reinvestigation, the bureau must maintain reasonable procedures to avoid reinsertion. If the bureau reinserts information because it later verified the information's accuracy, the bureau must notify you in writing within five days of reinserting information. Civil Code § 1785.16.

Creditors must:

- notify credit bureaus when an account is closed by you
- report specific date of any delinquency reported to a credit bureau, and
- complete reinvestigation of your dispute within 30 days. Civil Code § 1785.25.

Creditor must notify you when initially reporting negative information to a bureau before, or within 30 days of, reporting the information. Civil Code § 1785.26.

If you default, the creditor must give notice to any cosigner before or at the time the creditor reports your default to credit bureau. Civil Code § 1799.101.

More Information/Where to Complain

Money Troubles: Legal Strategies to Cope With Your Debts, by attorney Robin Leonard (Nolo Press), is available in public libraries and bookstores, and covers all of this section in much more detail. *Nolo's Law Form Kit: Rebuild Your Credit,* also by Robin Leonard (Nolo Press), contains several suggestions for cleaning up your credit file.

Credit bureaus are overseen by the Federal Trade Commission. (See *Government* chapter.)

CREDIT CARDS

Not all credit cards are created equal. The varieties and selections are quite staggering. When credit card shopping, these are the main features you'll want to compare:

- Annual percentage rate (APR). If you do not pay your bill in full each month, it is going to cost you somewhere between 6% and 21% per year in finance charges (interest) for using a credit card.
- Annual fee. Many credit card companies charge a fee each year for the privilege of using their card. A growing number of credit cards have no annual fee, however, and that can be an attractive option.
- Grace period. This is the number of days you have to pay your balance in full to avoid any finance charges. There is never a grace period if a previous bill is not paid in full. There is never a grace period for cash advances. (One company

charges no interest if the cash advance is paid back in the first month; however, this company charges a fee of 2.5%, up to $10, which generally turns out to be more than the interest would have been.) Some banks issuing credit cards have recently eliminated all grace periods—interest accrues from the time you make the charge, even if you pay your bill in full each month.

- Interest charged from date of purchase or posting. If you carry a balance month to month, you will pay more if your bank charges interest from the purchase date. Some banks don't start charging interest until the charge slip is posted to your account.
- Cash advance transaction fee charged when you use your card to get cash.
- Fees for late payments when you don't pay your bill by the due date.
- Fees for exceeding credit limit. Often your card is rejected for being over your limit; if it's not, you may be charged an extra fee.
- Method used for calculating interest. (See below.)
- Time period from statement billing to due date—that is, the amount of time you have to pay the bill before it is late. The range is 15 to 30 days.
- Credit line available to you. You may start with a low credit line; the bank will probably increase it as you use the card responsibly.
- Affinity. Some credit cards offer extra privileges or help nonprofit organizations. Usually, however, only a small percentage of your purchase is donated while you pay higher than average interest and annual fee. You may be better off getting a credit card with better features and making a donation to the organization on your own.

A GOOD DEAL: CREDIT CARDS THAT PROVIDE FREE AIRLINE MILEAGE

Airline mileage affinity credit cards that provide a free mile for every dollar you spend can be a good deal. If you use your credit card for all purchases, it is amazing how fast mileage builds up. The mileage can be used to get free trips or upgraded seating. For more information, ask various airlines to send you their credit card application. Check annual fees and interest rates to be sure these cards are really your best choice.

Credit Card Interest Calculation

Credit card interest may be calculated using several different methods. These are the most common.

Average Daily Balance

All daily balances are added together and divided by the number of days in the billing cycle to determine the average daily balance. For example, if you pay $950 on your $1,000 bill, you will pay interest not on the unpaid $50, but on the average daily balance of all charges for the previous month.

Adjusted Daily Balance

Some creditors determine the balance by subtracting payments made or credits given during the billing period from the total amount you owe. In this "adjusted balance method," interest is owed only on the outstanding balance at the end of the period—definitely the least costly method.

Previous Balance

Other creditors do not subtract from the balance any payments made during the billing period. This "previous balance method" can cost you more than the other two, because you are charged interest on the amount owed at the beginning of the pay period.

TIP

CHOOSE THE RIGHT CREDIT CARD

If you don't carry a balance from one month to another, consider getting a card with no annual fee or other perks such as air travel privileges. If you carry a monthly or periodic balance, find a card with the lowest interest rate possible.

Secured Credit Cards

If you don't have a credit history or you have a poor credit history, a secured credit card is a good way to establish or re-establish good credit. With a secured credit card, you put a sum of money (such as $1,000) in an interest-bearing account. The deposit institution gives you a MasterCard or VISA with a credit limit below the amount of your deposit (maybe $800), but keeps your savings account as security in case you do not pay your bills.

Finding Issuers of Secured Credit Cards

Consumer Action, a nonprofit consumer advocacy and education organization, provides a free list (annually) of California deposit institutions that issue secured credit cards. To get the list, send a stamped (52¢ postage), self-addressed, business-size envelope to Consumer Action, 116 New Montgomery Street, Suite 223, San Francisco, CA 94105. Specify "secured credit card" on the envelope. Consumer Action also publishes annual comparative studies of checking accounts and credit cards by major California banks. See *Banking* chapter.

Bankcard Holders of America, a nonprofit organization helping bankcard holders become informed consumers, issues a nationwide list of banks offering secured credit cards. The list costs $4 and can be obtained by writing to Bankcard Holders of America, 560 Herndon Parkway, Suite 120, Herndon, VA 22070.

Unsolicited Credit Cards

Federal law prohibits card issuers from sending you credit cards you did not request, although the issuer may send a renewal or substitute card without request. Credit card issuers are allowed to mail you an application for a credit card or solicit you by telephone to see if you want to receive a card—and don't need your signature if you agree by telephone. The card issuer will ask some very specific questions by phone to protect itself in case you later claim that a child, spouse, housekeeper or a boarder gave unauthorized permission to send the card. If you are sent a card you don't want, cut it in half and send it back with a letter saying you don't want it. Don't just ignore it. You will still have an open line of credit.

Credit Card Surcharges

It is illegal for California retailers to charge consumers a surcharge for using a credit card. Retailers can offer a discount on the established price if you pay cash, however. The difference is probably little more than semantics. Civil Code § 1748.1.

Personal Information on a Credit Card Slip

Any California merchant, business or corporation that accepts credit cards is prohibited from asking you to write your phone number on a credit card slip. This rule doesn't apply if you are having merchandise shipped, delivered or installed or for special orders, in which case your address would be necessary. Civil Code § 1747.8.

Anyone who violates this law is subject to a $250 penalty for the first violation and $1,000 penalty for subsequent violations. A civil action may be brought by you, the attorney general or the district attorney or city attorney where the violation occurred. No penalty will be assessed if the merchant shows that the violation was unintentional and was the result of a good faith effort to follow the law.

This is a California law; it's also the law in about 12 other states including Nevada. In the remaining places, merchants can ask for addresses and phone numbers. If so, you may want to explain to merchants that they don't need it. If the merchant correctly processes a credit card transaction, he'll be paid even if the charge exceeds the card's credit limit, so he has no reason to contact the customer. In fact, merchants' agreements with Visa and MasterCard prohibit them from requiring a customer to furnish a phone number when paying with Visa or MasterCard.

Credit Card Billing Errors

The Fair Credit Billing Act requires credit card issuers to correct errors promptly, without any damage to your credit rating. Under the law, a billing error is defined as:

- a charge for something you didn't buy, or a charge made by an unauthorized purchaser using your account
- a charge that is not properly identified on your bill, or for a different amount from the actual purchase price
- a charge for merchandise you refused to accept on delivery or that was not delivered according to agreement
- errors in arithmetic
- failure to reflect a payment or other credit to your account

- failure to mail the billing statement to your current address, provided the creditor received notice of that address at least 20 days before the end of the billing period, or
- an item for which you request additional clarification (a potential error).

If your bill is wrong, write to the creditor within 60 days of the time the first erroneous bill was mailed. Your letter must be sent to the address your lender has given for this purpose. Do not call, write on the bill itself or send your dispute letter along with your payment—no one will see it. Include your name and account number, the amount of the suspected error, and why you believe the bill is in error. If you normally pay your balance in full, pay all other parts of the bill not in dispute. If you normally pay just a portion of your bill each month, make your regular payment. Make a photocopy of all written communications for your records.

The creditor must acknowledge receipt of your letter or resolve the problem within 30 days. Within two billing cycles—not longer than 90 days—either your account must be credited or you must be told why the creditor believes the bill is correct. Under federal law, if your bank does not follow this procedure, it must refund you $50 of the disputed amount (even if you were wrong). Under California law, if the creditor does not correct the bill or tell you why the bill is correct within the two billing cycles or 90 days, you owe nothing of the disputed amount nor any interest, finance or service charges on the debt giving rise to the billing error. Civil Code § 1747.50(b).

During a Billing Dispute

Some creditors will show the amount owed including finance charges, but until the dispute is resolved:

- you do not have to pay the amount in dispute
- the creditor cannot report you or threaten to report you as delinquent to a credit bureau
- the creditor cannot take any action to collect the amount in dispute, but
- the creditor can apply the dollar amount of the disputed item to your credit limit.

If the creditor does not find an error, it must send you an explanation and a prompt statement of what you owe, which may include any finance charges that have accumulated while you were disputing the bill.

Disputes Over Merchandise or Service

If you have a problem with merchandise or a service that you charged on a credit card, and you've attempted in good faith to work out the problem with the seller, you may be able to withhold payment on that disputed amount of your bill. Your bank will try to "charge back" the disputed amount to the merchant. If the merchant disagrees with you, you are out of luck. Even if the bank credited your account temporarily, the charge will be put back on your credit card bill and your bank will tell you to work it out with the merchant.

If you bought merchandise by long distance telephone, your bank is likely to tell you that you can only withhold payment if the purchase exceeded $50 and occurred in your home state or within 100 miles of your billing address (this is federal law). Under California law, however, "any solicitation or communication to sell, oral or written, originating outside of this state, but forwarded to, and received in this state by a buyer who is a resident of this state, shall be deemed to be an offer or agreement to sell in this state." Although it's not clear if this law applies to credit card purchases, most California banks follow this law. Civil Code § 1802.19(b).

Lost or Stolen Credit Cards

Your liability on lost or stolen credit cards is limited under the federal Truth in Lending Act. You must notify your credit card company as soon as you discover the loss or theft of your card—once you notify the company, you do not have to pay any unauthorized charges. In addition, the most you will have to pay for any unauthorized charges before you report your card missing is $50, regardless of the amount charged. And even then, very few lenders charge the $50.

CREDIT CARD PRECAUTIONS

Keep a list of all your credit card numbers in a secure place. If you ever have a problem, you will have all the information at your fingertips. Also, you may want to limit your exposure by not routinely carrying all of your credit cards with you, perhaps just one bank credit card and a gas company card. After all, if you only go to a particular department store four times a year, there is little reason to carry their card every day. It's safer hidden in a secure place at home. Also, never keep gasoline credit cards in your car glove compartment!

Credit Card Protection

Credit card protection is a service marketed to "protect" you from the loss or theft of your credit cards. The scare tactics used by many companies to convince you that you need this protection to avoid liability for thousands of dollars of debt is baloney. As mentioned above, the maximum amount you can be held liable for is $50, and even that is unlikely. And ironically, many of these "protection" services won't reimburse the $50 if your credit card company does charge you. Some protection services offer emergency cash, and claim to cancel all credit cards that are stolen. But do not trust them to do it. It could also be a problem having one source with a list of all your credit card numbers—what a great temptation and opportunity to commit consumer fraud.

Apparently, these credit card protection services are very profitable because so many banks keep getting into the act. One company, however, was sued, and settled for $350,000 for misleading cardholders about the protection offered.

More Information

Consumer Action, a nonprofit consumer advocacy and education organization, does different surveys at different times of the year on bank credit cards. Send a stamped (52¢ postage), self-addressed, business-size envelope to Consumer Action, 116 New Montgomery Street, Suite 223, San Francisco, CA 94105. You can call Consumer Action at (415) 777-9635.

Money Troubles: Legal Strategies to Cope With Your Debts, by attorney Robin Leonard (Nolo Press), is available in public libraries and bookstores, and has much information on credit cards.

HOME EQUITY LOANS

A home equity loan is money you borrow from a bank, savings and loan, credit union or other lender using the equity in your house as security. Normally, money is paid back over a period of months or years. If the money is not paid back, however, the lender can foreclose on your loan and sell your house to recover money still owed. Many homeowners use these loans for major expenses such as home improvements, a college education or large medical bills.

Your home equity credit limit is a percentage (generally 75%) of the appraised value of your home minus the balance owed on the existing mortgage. For example:

Appraised home value	$ 200,000
75% of appraisal	$ 150,000
Minus existing mortgage	$100,000
Possible home equity credit line	$ 50,000

Lenders also consider your ability to repay a home equity loan in calculating your credit limit. This determination is based on your income, the amount of your other debts and financial obligations, as well as your bill-paying (credit) history.

Home Equity Loan Features

Home equity lines generally charge a variable interest rate, rather than a fixed rate. The rate fluctuates up or down tracking a publicly known index, such as the prime rate or a U.S. Treasury bill rate. Basically this means when interest rates in the economy go up or down, yours will too, although there may be a time lag.

When figuring the variable interest rate, lenders will add a margin (profit) to the index value (such as two or more percentage points). For example, if your index rate is 8% and your margin is 2%, you will be paying 10% interest. To compare various home equity plans, you need to know what index and margin each lender uses, how often the index changes and how high it has risen in the past. Variable interest rate plans secured by your home must have a maximum (cap) on how high your loan can go. Most agreements allow the lender to freeze or reduce your credit line when your interest rate reaches the cap.

Home Equity Loan Costs

The costs for setting up a home equity line of credit are similar to those you paid when you purchased your home. The costs may include: an application fee, an appraisal fee, points (one point equals 1% of the credit line), title search and property and title insurance. Some lines of credit include membership or maintenance fees, and some charge a transaction fee every time you use the credit line. It is often possible to avoid some or all of these fees, however, because there is a lot of competition in the marketplace for these loans.

Home Equity Loan Disclosures

The federal Truth in Lending Act requires lenders to disclose the Annual Percentage Rate (APR), miscellaneous charges, repayment terms, and the variable-rate features such as the index and margin used and the maximum (cap) interest rate. Your application fee is fully refundable if the lender does not provide this information. If any terms change—other than a variable rate—before the credit line is opened, the lender must return all fees if you change your mind.

Three-Day Right of Cancellation

The federal Truth in Lending Act gives you three days from the time the account is opened to cancel the line of credit for any reason. All you have to do is inform the lender in writing within the three-day period. The lender must refund all fees including application and appraisal fees, as well as cancel the security interest in your home.

Repaying a Home Equity Loan

You can repay a home equity loan in several ways. For example, you can repay principal and interest monthly over a period of years. Or you may be able to make just interest payments, leaving you with a large (balloon) payment at the end of the agreed upon loan period. Be careful about this type of payment plan—you could lose your home if at the end of the plan you are unable to pay the entire balance that may be owed.

Home Equity Financing Costs Versus the Costs of Other Financing Options

The Annual Percentage Rate (APR) is the cost of credit on a yearly basis expressed as a percentage. Unfortunately, it is not calculated the same way for home equity loans and second mortgages. The APR for a second mortgage includes all additional charges—points, loan fees and other finance charges. The APR for a home equity line is based on the periodic interest rate only—it does not include points, loan fees or other finance charges. In short, using an APR interest figure to compare interest rates for these loans may be deceptive. Despite an APR interest rate on a home equity loan lower than that for a comparable second mortgage, the actual cost to you may not be less. You need to calculate what all those additional points and fees will be to determine the true interest rate comparison.

Before taking out a home equity loan or a second mortgage, do not overlook the possibility of refinancing your existing home mortgage. Refinancing might permit a larger net loan, a lower interest cost and a larger tax deduction.

Where to Complain

If you have a home equity loan problem you cannot resolve with the lender, see Where to Complain in the section on Deposit Institutions in the *Banking* chapter.

FINANCE COMPANIES

Finance companies lend money to consumers. They are probably not the best source of money if you have a choice, as would be the case if you own your own house and qualify for a home equity loan. Finance companies usually charge higher rates than traditional lending institutions.

Finance companies are licensed and regulated by the California Department of Corporations.

AUTOMOBILE FINANCING

Financing a car through an auto dealership is typically more expensive than financing through a bank or credit union. Check out your financing possibilities before you go car shopping; you'll be in a better position to know which is the best deal.

If Financing Is Denied

If you have taken possession of an automobile but the dealer cannot get financing for you, the contract is null and void. You must return the new car but you are entitled to get your deposit back as well as your trade-in. If the trade-in has been sold, you are entitled to the fair market value or the price listed in the contract, whichever is higher.

In addition, a seller cannot change the financing or payment terms after you take possession of a vehicle. It is an unfair or deceptive practice to try to do so, and you need not agree to new financing terms. Many dealers, however, have added to their sales contracts a "rescission agreement," which means if you can't get financing, the seller can rescind the contract. It's not clear whether the law prevails over the rescission clause. Civil Code § 2982(h).

CREDIT, LOANS AND DEBT

⚠️ If financing falls through or isn't available on the terms promised, you do not need to sign another contract no matter how long you have been driving the car, unless you voluntarily agree to the new terms. Civil Code § 2982.

Paying Off a Loan Early—Rule of 78

If you take out an auto loan and you do not pay off the loan early, you will pay the amount of interest and principal listed in the contract. But what if you pay off your auto loan early? Most auto contracts include the following statement: "Prepayment refund: Any refund for prepayment will be calculated either according to the Rule of 78, or according to the sum of the Periodic Balance Method." Most auto financers use the Rule of 78.

The Rule of 78, also called "the sum of the digits," apportions the ratio of principal to interest payments so that more interest is paid early in the loan; the ratio reverses in later months. The number 78 is the sum of a year's worth of months: 12 plus 11 plus 10, etc., equals 78. On a one-year loan, the bank allocates 12/78ths of the first month's payment to interest, 11/78ths of the second month's payment, and so on. What this really means is if you prepay the loan in the first few months, the Rule of 78 could cost you about 10% more in interest. By making more interest due toward the beginning of the loan's life, lenders assure themselves of making money on the loan. If you prepay the loan after a few years, the difference will be minimal, perhaps just a few cents or a few dollars. The Rule of 78 has been outlawed in most states as being anti-consumer. In California, it cannot be used on loans longer than 62 months.

CONSUMER CREDIT COUNSELING SERVICE (CCCS)

Consumer Credit Counseling Service (CCCS) is a nonprofit organization sponsored by creditors such as department stores, credit card companies and banks, and overseen by volunteer creditors and consumer advocates. CCCS can produce a decent result for free or a low price.

To use CCCS to help you pay your debts, you must have some disposable income. A CCCS counselor contacts your creditors to let them know that you've sought CCCS assistance and need more time to pay. Based on your income and debts, the counselor, with your creditors, decides on how much you pay. You then make one or two direct payments each month to CCCS, which in turn pays your creditors. A CCCS counselor can often get wage garnishments revoked and late charges dropped. For example, Citicorp waives minimum payment and late charges—and may freeze interest assessments—for customers undergoing CCCS credit counseling.

CCCS may charge you a monthly fee for setting up a repayment plan. CCCS also helps people make monthly budgets, and charges a one-time fee of about $20. If you can't afford the fee, CCCS will waive it.

CCCS has offices in most counties. Look in the phone book to find the one nearest you, or call (800) 388-2227.

Participating in a CCCS plan is somewhat similar to filing for Chapter 13 bankruptcy. Working with CCCS has one advantage—no bankruptcy will appear on your credit record. A CCCS or "Debt Counseling Service" notation may be placed on your credit report by your creditors. But it's up to the creditors—and very few report that you've sought CCCS assistance. Most just bring your accounts—and report you as—current.

But CCCS also has two major disadvantages when compared to Chapter 13 bankruptcy. First, if you miss a payment, Chapter 13 protects you from creditors who would start collection actions. A CCCS plan has no such protection, and any one creditor can pull the plug on your CCCS plan. Also, a CCCS plan usually requires that your debts be paid in full. In Chapter 13 bankruptcy, you're only required to pledge your disposable income to pay the value of your non-exempt property, which can mean that you pay only a small fraction of your unsecured debts.

BEWARE CREDIT REPAIR CLINICS

Do not believe ads that promise to remove negative information and bankruptcies from your credit report. These slick operators will try to charge you hundreds of dollars for things you can do yourself for free. Accurate information cannot be removed, but you can correct inaccurate information yourself by writing to the credit bureaus and disputing the wrong information. In the past, credit repair clinics had some success by overwhelming credit bureaus with verification requests designed to force them to remove information pending verification. This tactic now usually fails because credit reporting bureaus can legally ignore requests that they deem frivolous.

BILL COLLECTORS (COLLECTION AGENCIES)

If you pay your bills, you probably won't ever be bothered by the collections department of a creditor or a collection agency. If you don't pay your bills, creditors will begin collection efforts. They will first try to collect in-house; if unsuccessful, they will turn to a collection agency. A collection agency regularly collects debts for others. If you are contacted by a collection agency, the Fair Debt Collection Practices Act contains regulations designed to see that you are treated fairly, although it does not let you off the hook for money you owe.

If you can't pay your bills because of illness, unemployment or some other problem, contact your creditors immediately and try to work out a reasonable payment schedule. Don't wait until a creditor's collection department or a collection agency comes after you. If you are having trouble working out a payment plan with a creditor or a collection agency, and you are employed, consider contacting Consumer Credit Counseling Services (CCCS) for help in working out a payment schedule with creditors.

Before most creditors can go after your wages, bank accounts or real property, they must get a court judgment. (Exceptions are for child support, spousal support, student loans and back taxes.) If a creditor takes you to court, you could end up paying court costs, and sometimes attorney's fees, on top of the debt. If possible, it is better to work out a payment plan with the original creditor or collection agency before being taken to court.

Fair Debt Collection Practices—What's Legal?

The following restrictions apply to collection agencies under federal law and to all bill collectors—collection agencies and original creditors—under California law:

- You may be contacted by person, mail, telephone (between 8:00 a.m. and 9:00 p.m.) or telegram.
- If you have an attorney, the collector can only contact the attorney.
- A collector may contact third parties, such as parents or friends, but only to try to locate you.
- Collectors may charge interest on the bills they collect, but the interest must be broken out separately from the principal amount. Federal law allows interest to be charged if it was called for in the original contract or if it is allowed by state law. California law allows interest to be charged even if it wasn't in the original contract.
- Collectors usually start by demanding payment in full; they do not have to accept partial payments. Many collection agencies will accept reasonable payments only if the original creditor agrees and they believe you will keep to the schedule. If you miss payments, the collection agency may revoke the arrangement and demand the full amount.
- Many collectors make their first contact by phone. Within five days of the initial contact, collectors must send you written notice of the amount owed and to whom you owe the money. You must also be told what to do if you do not believe you owe the money.
- If you request written verification of the debt within 30 days of the initial contact by the agency, collectors must stop collection activities until they have supplied this information.
- You can stop collection agencies from contacting you by requesting (in writing) no further contact. After receiving such a letter, the agency must stop further phone calls, letters and other contacts, except it may notify you of some specific legal action it is taking, such as filing a lawsuit. This is federal law only and does not apply to original creditors.

Fair Debt Collection Practices—What's Illegal?

Like the above list, the following prohibited activities apply to collection agencies under federal law and to all bill collectors—collection agencies and original creditors—under California law:

- failing to state the agency's name, address, telephone number; the amount of money owed; the amount of interest; the creditor's name; date; the name and address of the regulatory agency
- harassing, threatening, abusing or oppressing you, such as using the telephone repeatedly to harass someone
- using obscene or profane language
- using documents that look like government or legal forms
- using aliases or pretending to be a government official
- threatening to include you on a "deadbeat list" of people who do not pay their bills
- attempting or collecting more than is owed
- threatening to ruin your credit
- failing to correct your credit report which contains mistakes
- failing to provide proof of the debt if you dispute the debt or the amount
- contacting you at work if the collector knows your employer prohibits it
- falsely threatening to take you to court or garnish wages (unless the action is actually intended), and
- continuing to contact you after you tell the collector (from a collection agency) to stop.

Additional California Debt Collection Law

California law allows original creditors and bill collectors to contact an employer for the following reasons only: to verify the debtor's employment and location; to set up wage garnishment after winning a judgment in court; and to verify medical insurance for medical debts. Collectors cannot discuss the debt with the debtor's employer or contact relatives except to locate the debtor. Civil Code §§ 1788.2. and 1788.12.

More Information/Where to Complain

Money Troubles: Legal Strategies to Cope With Your Debts, by attorney Robin Leonard (Nolo Press), is available in public libraries and bookstores, and has extensive information on liens, wage attachments, student loans, repossessions and other debt problems.

The Federal Trade Commission accepts complaints about collection agencies. Although the FTC doesn't handle individual complaints, if it gets a number of complaints about the same company, it will investigate.

REPOSSESSIONS

If you pledge an item as security for a loan, or as part of a purchase contract where you agree to pay on time, and you fail to pay as promised, the creditor has the legal right to repossess the property. How and when this can occur depends on the type of property involved.

Personal Property

A creditor or repossessor cannot enter your home and take your furniture or any other possessions to satisfy a debt, without first suing you, winning a court judgment and obtaining authorization from the court, unless you give the creditor permission to do so. You are under no obligation to give this permission, but if you don't and the creditor sues, attorney's fees and court costs will normally be added to the amount you already owe.

Motor Vehicles

If you fail to make required payments, a creditor or repossessor can repossess a motor vehicle (car, truck, motor home or motorcycle) without a court order or notice to you if it's out in a public place, such as a street or parking lot. Repossessors cannot enter your garage. This will be disclosed in your loan agreement.

Can You Get a Repossessed Car Back?

If your car has been repossessed, you have the right to retrieve the car by paying all overdue amounts of money owed plus all the repossession costs and fees—which can be pretty hefty. You can't get the car back if you:

- gave false information on your credit application
- tried to hide the car out of state or elsewhere to avoid repossession
- have reduced the value of the vehicle by not taking care of it properly
- used the car for criminal purposes, or
- acted violently against the seller of the car.

If You Can't Pay What's Owed

If you do not have the money to pay all the overdue costs, the car will be sold, probably for far less money than it is worth. You must be given 15 days' notice of the time and place of a public sale of your car. You can show up and bid on the car. Unfortunately for you, if the amount the seller gets is less than what you owe—and it will be—the seller can come after you for the difference (called a deficiency judgment). And most deficiency judgments are huge!

WAGE GARNISHMENT

A wage garnishment is an interception of a portion of your wages to satisfy a court judgment. For creditors with a court judgment, it is often the most effective way to collect unpaid bills. Both federal and California law limit the amount that can be taken—usually 25%—from any one paycheck. (50% can be taken to satisfy child support or an alimony order.) You may be able to reduce that amount if you can show that you absolutely need more than 75% of your wages to live on. Your employer can give you the form that explains how to claim this exemption. The law prohibits you from being fired because of a garnishment for one debt, no matter how many times money is taken from your check.

Federal employees used to be exempt from all wage garnishment laws. Beginning April 4, 1994, however, federal employees are subject to the same wage garnishment laws as all other employees. 5 U.S.C. § 5520a.

More Information

Collect Your Court Judgment, by Scott, Elias and Goldoftas (Nolo Press), covers the advantages, disadvantages and the "how tos" of wage garnishment. It is available in bookstores and libraries.

Money Troubles: Legal Strategies to Cope With Your Debts, by attorney Robin Leonard (Nolo Press), is available in public libraries and bookstores, and has extensive information on wage attachments.

BANKRUPTCY

Bankruptcy is a legal proceeding which relieves you from paying your debts. In exchange, you may have to give some property to the bankruptcy court to pay your creditors. During the bankruptcy case, your creditors can't collect what you owe except that secured creditors (auto loans, furniture loans and mortgage holders) are entitled to have the secured item (auto, furniture or house) returned as a condition of wiping out their debt. When the bankruptcy is over, creditors are barred forever from trying to collect, unless a particular debt is not erased (discharged) during your bankruptcy case. See below for a list of non-dischargeable debts.

Kinds of Bankruptcies

Chapter 7 bankruptcy is the most common type, and is sometimes called straight bankruptcy. Debtors, both individual and business, ask the court to erase their debts. In exchange, debtors must give up all of their non-exempt property (defined below), which is used by the bankruptcy trustee to pay the creditors on a pro-rata basis.

Chapter 11 allows businesses or organizations with enormous amounts of debt to reorganize in order to pay off their bills under the protection of the bankruptcy court. You do not give up any property during the case, and creditors are prohibited from trying to collect outstanding debts. The reason for this action is to allow the business to cut expenses while trying to increase profits, so that everyone will benefit if the reorganization is successful. Unfortunately, Chapter 11 often doesn't succeed, due to the condition of the business when it files or to the amount of attorneys' fees that are collected from the assets of the business.

Chapter 12 is for family farmers. It lets them reorganize their farm businesses and pay off their debts under the supervision of the bankruptcy court.

Chapter 13 is sometimes called the wage earner plan, and only individuals may qualify. Under this plan, you must use all of your monthly disposable income for a minimum of three years (in some cases as long as five years) to pay the bankruptcy trustee (the person appointed by the court to oversee your case). The trustee then pays the creditors, who must receive as much as they would have had you filed for a Chapter 7 bankruptcy.

Exempt Property

When you file a Chapter 7 bankruptcy, you may claim certain assets as exempt—that is, unavailable to be taken and sold by the trustee to pay your creditors. In California, you can choose between two different sets of exemptions, although you cannot mix them. As a general rule, homeowners opt for System 1, non-homeowners select System 2.

Exemptions/System 1
- Homestead equity (fair market value, less what you owe):
    — $50,000 for a single (non-disabled) person
    — $75,000 for families
    — $100,000 age 65 or older, or mentally/physically disabled
    — $100,000 age 55 or older, single, with earnings under $15,000, or married with earnings under $20,000
- Insurance: disability or health benefits; life insurance proceeds, unmatured life insurance to $4,000 loan value
- Pensions: private and public retirement benefits
- Personal property: appliances, furnishings, clothing and food needed; bank deposits from Social Security to $500; burial plot; health aids; jewelry, heirlooms and art to $2,500; motor vehicles to $1,200
- Public benefits: aid to blind, aged, disabled, AFDC; unemployment benefits; workers' compensation
- Tools of trade: tools, materials, uniforms, books, equipment, vessel, motor vehicle to $2,500 value
- Wages: 75% of wages paid within 30 days of filing.

Exemptions/System 2
- Homestead: equity to $7,500
- Insurance: disability benefits; life insurance proceeds needed for support of family; unmatured life insurance contract accruals to $4,000
- Alimony, child support needed for support of family
- Pensions: ERISA, qualified benefits needed for support
- Personal property: animals, crops, appliances, furnishings, household goods, books, musical instruments and clothing to $200 per item; burial plot to $7,500, in lieu of homestead; health aids; jewelry to $500; one motor vehicle to $1,200
- Public benefits: crime victims' compensation; public assistance; Social Security; unemployment compensation; veterans' benefits
- Tools of trade: books and tools to $750
- Wild card: $7,900 in any property, less any amount claimed for homestead or burial exemption.

Non-Dischargeable Debts

You still owe these debts after bankruptcy:
- debts you do not list in your bankruptcy papers and where the creditor hasn't otherwise learned of your bankruptcy
- most recent student loans where payment first became due less than seven years ago
- most recent federal, state and local taxes
- child support and alimony
- fines and penalties imposed for breaking the law
- debts for personal injury or death caused by your intoxicated driving
- debts incurred on a fraudulent basis, including using a credit card when you know you cannot pay

- debts from willful or malicious injury to another person or property
- debts from embezzlement, larceny or breach of trust
- credit purchase of $500 of more for luxury goods or services within 40 days of the bankruptcy filing, and
- loans or cash advances of $1,000 or more within 20 days of the bankruptcy filing.

Some of the debts on this list, such as child support and alimony, can never be discharged. Others are dischargeable unless the creditor objects. *How to File for Bankruptcy* (described below) contains a detailed explanation of this point.

Additional Resources

How to File for Bankruptcy, by Elias, Renauer and Leonard (Nolo Press), contains a detailed explanation of how Chapter 7 bankruptcy works, as well as do-it-yourself forms. *Nolo's Law Form Kit: Personal Bankruptcy,* by Elias, Renauer, Leonard and Goldoftas, is a stream-lined bankruptcy kit with all the forms and instructions necessary to file a straight-forward Chapter 7 bankruptcy. Both are available in libraries and bookstores. ■

EDUCATION

EDUCATION

The California Department of Education oversees the educational policies established by the State Board of Education for public and private schools, kindergarten through 12th grade, adult education and private postsecondary institutions (technological, vocational or professional instruction). The Department's main office is located at 721 Capitol Mall, Sacramento, CA 95814, (916) 657-2451.

Where to Complain

If you have a complaint about a public school, bring it to the school administrators. If you do not get satisfactory results, contact the school board.

To complain about a private school's adult education program, contact the Department of Education's Adult Education Field Services at (916) 322-2175. You can also write to the Services at the Department of Education address listed above.

To complain about a vocational, professional or technological school, contact the Private Postsecondary & Vocational Educational Council, 1027 10th St., 4th Floor, Sacramento, CA 95814, (916) 327-9481. Many state and federal laws has been passed in the last few years regulating trade schools. If you've been defrauded—you haven't received the education, training or job opportunities promised—be sure to complain loud and clear.

STUDENT FINANCIAL AID

The federal government has been helping students with higher education costs for nearly 50 years. The largest number of student loans made are Guaranteed Student Loans, which have been called Stafford Loans since the fall of 1987.

A Stafford Loan is not the only way to fund a college education. Colleges often lend money in the form of loans created and funded by the federal government. These loans include:

- National Direct Student Loans (NDSL), now called Perkins Loans
- Parental Loans for Students (PLUS)
- Supplemental Loans for Students (SLS)
- Health Professions Student Loans (HPSL), and
- Health Education Assistance Loans (HEAL).

Repayment of all of these loans—including Stafford Loans—is guaranteed by the federal government. Your bank or school lends you money for your college or graduate school education. You do not have to start repaying until six to nine months after you graduate or drop out of school, and even then you may be able to defer payment in some situations.

In addition, many colleges offer work-study to students, and make grants and loans from private or university sources. Some state universities make loans from state funds. And local organizations (such as your town's Garden Club), professional organizations, nonprofit companies and large corporations award scholarships and make grants to students for their education.

Resources If You Are Looking for Student Financial Aid

The following are helpful resources for finding college scholarships, grants and loans:

- *California Student Financial Aid Programs* describes different financial aid programs. For a free copy, contact the California Student Aid Commission, P.O. Box 510845, Sacramento, CA 94245-0845, (916) 445-0880. *California Student Financial Aid Workbook*, also published by the California Student Aid Commission, explains federal and state grants and loans, who qualifies, how financial need is determined and how the family's share is determined, and has valuable listings of additional resources. This book is available through your high school or college.
- *The Student Guide*, published by the U.S. Department of Education. Call the Federal Student Aid Information Center, (800) 333-INFO, from 6:00 a.m. to 2:30 p.m. weekdays.
- *Need A Lift?*, published annually by the American Legion Education Program for $1. This handy guide lists educational opportunities, careers, loans, scholarships and employment information. Write to: Emblem Sales, *Need a Lift?*, P.O. Box 1050, Indianapolis, IN 46206.
- *Paying Less for College*, published annually by Peterson's Guides in Princeton, NJ, describes over $28 billion dollars in financial aid available for undergraduate study. Available in bookstores.
- *Complete College Financing Guide*, published by Barrons, explains scholarships, low-interest tuition loans and other strategies for affording college costs.
- Contact the school you are interested in and ask about student aid.

Student Loan Problems

If you have a question or a problem concerning repaying a student loan, you should first take it up with the holder of your loan. This could be any of the following:

- the bank or school that made the loan

- a company on the secondary market, which is a place banks sell non-defaulted loans they decide not to collect themselves
- a loan servicer, which "services" the loan—receives payments—for the lender or secondary market company that bought the loan from the lender
- a guaranty agency, which pays the lender or secondary market company that bought the loan from the lender if you default
- Department of Education (DOE), which tries to collect defaulted loans turned over by a guaranty agency, or
- a collection agency, which may have contracted with a guaranty agency or the Department of Education to try to collect a defaulted loan.

If this fails to solve your problem, help may be available from:

- The Student Loan Marketing Association (Sallie Mae), 1050 Thomas Jefferson Street NW, Washington, DC 20007, (800) 292-6868. Sallie Mae, a federally chartered corporation, is the major loan servicer of student loans. Sallie Mae services about 40% of Stafford Loans.
- The California Student Aid Commission, P.O. Box 510845, Sacramento, CA 94245-0845, (916) 445-0880. Have your Social Security number handy. The Commission can help you with only certain types of problems—such as the holder of your loan has not given you credit for payments made. If you have defaulted on a student loan, call the Commission's repayment program, (800) 36PAYIT.
- The U.S. Department of Education, Student Financial Assistance, 50 United Nations Plaza, San Francisco, CA 94102, (415) 556-8382. The Department of Education cannot forgive student loans, but it may be able to set up a repayment plan if you are in default.

When the Holder of Your Loan Gets Aggressive

If you've seriously defaulted on your student loan, the holder of the loan will probably take agressive steps to collect, including:

- Asking the IRS or Franchise Tax Board to intercept any tax refunds due you. Only the Department of Education or a collection agency hired by the Department of Education can request a tax intercept.
- Suing you. There is *no time limit* on a lawsuit to collect a student loan. Even if you took out a loan in 1965 (the first year student loans were made), you can be sued if you haven't yet paid in full. And the holder of the loan can tack on interest for all the years.

Additional Resources

Money Troubles: Legal Strategies to Cope With Your Debts, by attorney Robin Leonard (Nolo Press), has a chapter on student loans that covers canceling loans, deferring payments, negotiating with the college, bank or government, having a tax refund intercepted, having your wages garnished, getting sued on a loan and filing for bankruptcy to eliminate your student loan. It's available in bookstores and libraries. ■

EMPLOYMENT

CROSS-REFERENCES

DISCRIMINATION IN EMPLOYMENT

The California Department of Fair Employment and Housing (DFEH) may pursue a complaint regarding discrimination in employment if it is based on race, religion, national origin or ancestry, physical handicap, sex, age (40 and over) or marital status, or for anyone who's been cured of cancer.

The federal Equal Employment Opportunity Commission (EEOC) also has jurisdiction in cases of employment discrimination. It may pursue complaints about employers, employment agencies and labor organizations that discriminate because of race or national origin, sex, religion, pregnancy and age discrimination for people between 40-70 years of age. It may also investigate unequal wages between men and women doing the same job for the same employer.

Complaints of sexual harassment on the job, which is a recognized form of employment discrimination, may be filed with either the DFEH or the nearest EEOC office.

Both of these agencies are notoriously overburdened and take action on only a small percentage of complaints filed. What is most likely to happen is that you will be issued a Right to Sue Letter—usually within two months of filing your complaint. The Letter gives you legal authority to bring a private lawsuit alleging discrimination.

More Information/Where to Complain

For more information on sexual harassment, take a look at *Sexual Harassment on the Job: What It Is and How to Stop It*, by William Petrocelli and Barbara Kate Repa (Nolo Press). It describes what harassment is and gives strategies for ending it. It also includes guidance to employers who want to create a policy against sexual harassment. It's available in libraries and bookstores.

The California Department of Fair Employment and Housing headquarters is located at 2014 T Street, Suite 210, Sacramento, CA 95814, (916) 445-9918. It also has district offices all over the state and can be found in the phone book white pages under the Government section, State of California.

The EEOC has district offices in Fresno, Los Angeles, Oakland, San Diego, San Francisco and San Jose. Check the phone book white pages under United States Government Offices.

EMPLOYEE RIGHTS

California employees have a number of legal rights. Here are some of the most important ones:
- Minimum wage is $4.25 per hour.
- Minimum wage for minors under age 18 is $3.80 per hour.

- Overtime pay must be one-and-a-half times the rate of pay for hours exceeding eight in one day or 40 in one week.
- Workers' compensation coverage is required of all California employers.
- Pay statements must itemize all deductions.
- Paydays must be at least twice a month—once a month for executive, professional or administrative employees.
- You must be given meal periods of at least 30 minutes for every five hours worked, if the total work day is at least six hours.
- You must be given a rest period of at least ten minutes for each four hours worked.
- If you quit your job without notice, you must be paid within 72 hours.
- If you are fired, you must be paid immediately.

Benefits

California does not require employers to pay benefits, such as vacation, sick leave or sick pay. If the employer offers or promises benefits, however, then the employer must fulfill that obligation. Also, if an employer offers these benefits to some employees, the employer must make them available to all employees.

Compensatory Time Off Versus Overtime Pay

Some employers offer employees compensatory time off from work—comp time—in place of cash payments for overtime. But there are very strict rules controlling how compensatory time may be earned and taken. In California, compensatory time off is permitted only if all five of the following requirements are met:

1. The employee must voluntarily request, in writing, that he or she wants time off in lieu of overtime compensation—before the overtime is worked.
2. The time off must be taken by the end of the pay period following the pay period in which the overtime is earned.
3. The time off must be given at an applicable overtime rate—usually 1 1/2 times the normal rate of pay.
4. The time off must be given during the employee's normal work time.
5. The employer must keep records that accurately reflect the overtime earned and taken as compensatory time off.

Regulations on paying overtime differ depending on the type of work performed and are found in the Industrial Welfare Commission Orders. The applicable one must be posted in your workplace.

In actual practice, by mutual agreement between employee and employer, comp time is often taken at a much later date than the current pay period and isn't always comparable to time-and-a-half. This is fine as long as no one complains. If an employee files a wage dispute with the California Labor Commissioner over comp time not being the equivalent of time and a half (even if the employee agreed to lower comp time terms), however, the employer will be held liable for making up back wages owed the employee.

Pregnancy Leave

Employers are required to give a four-month unpaid leave of absence for pregnancy, childbirth or related medical conditions. Employees must also be allowed to use any accumulated vacation and sick leave as additional time off. An employer must reinstate the pregnant employee to her former job or a similar job, with no loss of seniority, wages and fringe benefits. While a pregnant employee is at work, she must be treated the same as any other employee with a disability—that is, given modified tasks, alternate work assignments or disability leave if such accommodations are made to other disabled employees. The California Department of Fair Employment and Housing has jurisdiction over pregnancy-related discrimination complaints.

If You've Been Fired

If you have been fired and you believe you were discriminated against, that a long-term contract was violated or that you were singled out for any other unfair reason, you may want to see a labor law attorney to find out whether you have grounds for a wrongful termination lawsuit. A half-hour consultation will cost approximately $25-$30. Because most labor law attorneys now specialize in representing employers—that's where the most money can be found—it may be difficult to find a lawyer willing to handle an employee's complaint. If you are having a hard time finding a lawyer willing to evaluate your situation, contact the National Employment Lawyers Association, (415) 397-6335.

More Information/Where to Complain

Two Nolo Press publications contain a vast amount of information to help workers through their employment concerns: *Your Rights in the Workplace*, by Barbara Kate Repa, and *Sexual Harassment on the Job: What It Is and How to Stop It*, by William Petrocelli and Barbara Kate Repa.

If you have a complaint about your wages or hours—for example, you are required to work overtime but you are not paid extra—contact the Labor Commission. Look in the telephone book white pages, Government section (State of California), Department of Industrial Relations—Labor Standards Enforcement or Labor Commission.

If you have a discrimination complaint (such as you are being sexually harassed at work or denied a promotion because you are pregnant), contact the California Department of Fair Employment and Housing, with headquarters located at 2014 T Street, Suite 210, Sacramento, CA 95814, (916) 445-9918, or one of the district offices located in Bakersfield, Fresno, Los Angeles, Oakland, San Bernardino, San Diego, San Francisco, San Jose, Santa Ana and Ventura. The office nearest you can be found in the telephone book white pages, Government section (State of California).

If you're an employer wanting more information, I suggest *The Employer's Legal Handbook*, by Fred S. Steingold (Nolo Press).

PENSIONS

A pension is a plan established or maintained by an employer, a union or other employee organization, or fraternal organization, which provides retirement income to employees. Not all companies have pension plans, nor are they required to. Most pension plans require employees to meet certain eligibility requirements such as age or length of employment before they can benefit from the plan. To benefit from most pension plans, you must work for an employer for a specified number of years, at which point the pension "vests" (short-term employees usually don't get pension benefits). Once you become vested—that is, have met all requirements to get the pension, such as working 25 years—you can lose or leave the job and still maintain your legal right to all pension benefits. You may not be able to collect the benefits until retirement age, however, depending on your plan.

ERISA

The Employee Retirement Income Security Act (ERISA), administered by the U.S. Department of Labor and the Internal Revenue Service (IRS), protects the interests of workers and beneficiaries who depend on benefits from employee pension and welfare plans. No federal or state laws guarantee anyone a pension; however, if one is offered, your employer is required under ERISA to provide a written description of the pension plan. Ask the pension plan administrator for a summary plan description and the official plan document. These will explain the rules and vesting. If your plan is subject to ERISA, you must be given a statement listing the amount of benefits you have earned, if you request it. If you leave your job, your employer must automatically provide a statement showing your vested benefits.

How Pensions Work

To understand how your plan operates, you need to understand how your pension is funded and distributed. Most pension plans are either a defined benefit plan or an individual account (defined contribution) plan.

A *Defined Benefit Plan* determines in advance the amount of pension benefits you will receive when you retire, based on your earnings and length of employment. It is usually funded by the employer without employee contributions. This is the only type of plan insured by the government's Pension Benefit Guaranty Corporation, which provides termination insurance for pension plans.

An *Individual Account Plan/Defined Contribution Plan* has a fixed contribution amount by both the employer and the employee, but the actual amount of benefits you will receive at retirement is unknown. The value of the pension will depend on how well the money was invested during your working years.

Integrated Plans are integrated with your Social Security retirement benefits, which means your pension benefits will be reduced by some percentage of, or all of, your Social Security check. The rules and percentages of various integrated plans vary widely. Check with your plan administrator to find out if, and how much, your pension will be reduced through integration with your Social Security benefits. This type of plan has become popular with employers because it's relatively cheap to fund, but it's not usually as favorable to employees as are the other type plans.

Government Pension Insurance

Pension Benefit Guaranty Corporation (PBGC) is a public, nonprofit insurance fund that provides coverage against bankrupt vested, defined benefit plans pension funds. Other benefits, such as disability, health coverage and death benefits, aren't usually covered. If you have a question about termination of benefits because of failure of your pension plan, call or write the Pension Benefit Guaranty Corporation, 2020 K Street NW, Washington, DC 20006, (202) 778-8800.

More Information/Where to Complain

U.S. Department of Labor, Pension and Welfare Benefits Administration, Office of Program Services, 200 Constitution Avenue NW, Room N5625, Washington, DC 20210, (202) 219-6999.

U.S. Department of Labor, Pension and Welfare Benefits Administration, 71 Stevenson, Suite 915, Box 190250, San Francisco, CA 94119, (415) 744-6700. Have your plan in hand if you call. Unless your question is routine, this office will usually refer you to the Washington, DC, office.

Internal Revenue Service, Employee Plans Division, 1111 Constitution Avenue NW, Washington, DC 20224, (202) 622-6720, or contact your local IRS office listed in the phone book white pages, Government section.

For answers to a wide range of private pension questions (not government pensions), call or write the Pension Rights Center, 918 16th Street NW, Suite 704, Washington, DC 20006, (202) 296-3776. This private, nonprofit organization will do a preliminary review of your case. If you need legal advice, it will refer you to a lawyer in your area that specializes in pension rights. The Center publishes numerous books and pamphlets covering common topics, including pension rights of divorcing couples, military personnel, widows and widowers.

Social Security, Medicare and Pensions: The Sourcebook for Older Americans, by Joseph L. Matthews and Dorothy Matthews Berman (Nolo Press), is available in libraries and bookstores.

Divorce and Money: How to Make the Best Financial Decisions During Divorce, by Woodhouse, Felton-Collins, with Blakeman (Nolo Press), contains extensive information on pension rights for pension holders and their spouses going through a divorce.

The Older Women's League (OWL) is an organization that lobbies for women's pension rights. The League was instrumental in getting group health insurance continuation coverage (COBRA) into federal law. In addition, this organization worked to make sure wives were protected with pension and retirement benefits by requiring companies to obtain wives' signatures (not just the husband's) on distribution payments. In the past, too many husbands opted for larger payments while they were alive (without ever discussing this with their wives), which then left widows with no income after their husbands died. OWL's main office is at 666 11th Street NW, Suite 700, Washington, DC 20001, (202) 783-6686.

SOCIAL SECURITY

Social Security is a combination of federal programs designed to pay benefits to workers and their dependents. Benefits are paid based on the worker's average wage in jobs covered by Social Security over her working life. The three basic categories of benefits under Social Security are:

- Retirement Benefits. You may choose to begin receiving your retirement benefits any time after you reach age 62, but the amount of benefits goes up for each year you wait to retire.
- Dependents' and Survivors' Benefits. If you're the spouse of a retired or disabled worker, or the surviving spouse of a deceased worker who would have qualified for retirement or disability benefits, you and your children may be entitled to benefits based on the worker's earning record. You may also be eligible for these benefits if you're 62 or older and divorced—if your marriage to the worker lasted at least ten years, you've been divorced at least two years and have not remarried.
- Disability Benefits. See Supplemental Security Income, below.

Who Is Eligible for Benefits

The specific requirements within each program vary. To qualify for all benefits, however, you must have worked in "covered employment" for a sufficient number of years, which differs depending on when you reach age 62, become disabled or die. Any job or self-employment from which Social Security taxes are reported is covered employment.

You must have accumulated enough "work credits" from covered employment to reach insured status. Work credits are measured in quarter-years (January through March is the first quarter of each year, April through June is the second, and so on). You receive credit for every quarter in which you earned more than the required minimum amount of money in covered employment. The number of work credits you need depends on the benefit you're applying for and your age when you apply.

If you're eligible for benefits, the amount you will receive is determined by the history of all your reported earnings in covered employment since you began working. The amount of your benefits will depend on your average reported income.

Spouses and unmarried children up to certain age limits are also eligible for benefits.

Call the Social Security Administration (SSA) for details, (800) 772-1213, Monday through Friday from 7:00 a.m. to 7:00 p.m.

If the SSA turns down your request for benefits, you will be told about the Administration's extensive appeal procedure. In essence, it permits you to:

- file a reconsideration request

- if it's rejected, file an appeal
- if it's denied, have a hearing before an administrative law judge
- if you lose, file an appeal with the Appeals Council, and
- if you lose, file a lawsuit in civil court.

Supplemental Security Income

Supplemental Security Income (SSI) is a joint federal-state program intended to guarantee a minimum income to elderly, blind and disabled people.

Who Is Eligible for Benefits

To be eligible for SSI, you must meet these three requirements:

1. You must be 65 or over, blind or disabled. You're considered blind if your vision is no better than 20/200 or your field of vision is limited to 20 degrees or less, even with corrective lenses. You're considered disabled if you have a physical or mental impairment that prevents you from doing any substantial work and that is expected to last at least 12 months or to result in death.

2. Your monthly income must be less than $719 for an individual blind person, $645 for an individual elderly or disabled person or $514 for a disabled minor. (Income limits for married couples are higher.) Any income you earn in wages or self-employment, and any money you receive from investments, Social Security benefits, pensions, annuities, royalties, gifts, rents or interest on savings, regular food and housing provided by others is counted against the SSI limits.

Some things don't count as income for SSI purposes, including:

- the first $20 per month you receive from any source (except other public assistance based on need)
- the first $65 per month of your earned income (wages or self-employment)
- one-half of all your earned income over $65 a month
- irregular or infrequent earned income (such as from a one-time only job) if such income isn't more than $10 a month
- irregular or infrequent unearned income (such as a gift or dividend on an investment) up to $20 per month
- food stamps or housing assistance from a federal housing program run by a state or local government agency, and
- some work-related expenses for blind or disabled people paid for through public assistance.

3. Your assets, not counting your home and car, must not be worth more than $2,000 ($3,000 for a married couple). Some items are excepted, including:

- your automobile, up to a current market value of $4,500—if you use your car for work, or to get to and from a job or regular medical treatment, or it is specially equipped to transport a handicapped person, the value of your car isn't counted, no matter how much it's worth
- your personal property and household goods up to a total current or equity value of $2,000; wedding and engagement rings aren't counted, regardless of their value
- property essential to self-support, such as tools or machines used in your trade, and
- life insurance policies with a total face value of $1,500 or less per person, burial policies, or term life insurance policies with no cash surrender value, as well as a burial plot for each spouse.

Spouses and unmarried children up to certain age limits are also eligible for benefits.

Amount of Benefits

The maximum federal SSI payment is the same as the monthly income limits for eligibility. These maximum benefit amounts, though, are reduced by any income you make as follows:

- Your benefit check will be reduced by one dollar for every two dollars you earn in current wages or self-employment over $65 a month.
- Your payment will be reduced dollar for dollar by the amount of unearned income you receive over $20 a month; such income includes your Social Security benefits, pensions, annuities, interest on savings, dividends or any money from investments or property you own.
- Your SSI payment will be reduced by one-third if you live in a friend or relative's home and receive food or clothing there.

How to Apply for SSI Benefits

Apply for SSI benefits at your local Social Security office. After you complete the necessary paperwork, it will take from four to eight weeks to receive your first regular monthly SSI check. Call the Social Security Administration for details, (800) 772-1213, Monday through Friday from 7:00 a.m. to 7:00 p.m.

Verifying Social Security Retirement Benefits

You can request a free statement of your earnings covered by Social Security. This statement shows your Social Security earnings history, tells you how much you have paid in Social Security taxes, estimates your future Social Security benefits and provides some general information about the program. Call the Social Security office's toll-free number, (800) 772-1213, and follow the instructions given by the automated telephone service. After you send in the completed form, it takes up to six weeks to receive the information. It is a good idea to verify this record every few years to make sure Social Security has accurately credited your Social Security account. In case an error has been made, you can get it corrected before retirement.

When a Social Security Recipient Dies

A person must live for an entire month to be entitled to Social Security benefits for that month. For example, a Social Security recipient dies on October 31. On November 3, her Social Security check for the previous October is sent to her or automatically deposited into her bank account. When SSA learns that she did not live for the entire month of October, it will demand repayment from her heirs or automatically withdraw the money from her bank account. This may take several months.

To Whom Must You Give Your Social Security Number?

Any time any government agency asks for your Social Security number, the agency is required to tell you whether giving your number is mandatory, the agency's authority for requesting your number, how the agency intends to use your number and the consequences of your failing to give your number. Welfare, tax and motor vehicle departments are excepted from this rule.

Many other organizations—such as credit grantors, insurance companies, universities, schools and hospitals—commonly ask for your Social Security number. If you don't supply it, they may withhold their service. Also, employers and financial institutions need your Social Security number (or Taxpayer Identification number) to report your income (wages or receipts of an independent contractor and interest on deposit accounts) to the IRS.

More Information

To obtain a copy of "What to Do When They Ask for Your Social Security Number," contact Chris Hibbert at 1195 Andre Avenue, Mountain View, CA 94040, (415) 968-6319.

FREE INFORMATION FROM SOCIAL SECURITY

Don't pay a fee to anyone who offers to obtain your Social Security benefits statement, Social Security numbers for your children or a new Social Security card when you get married. Because you can obtain this information free from Social Security—and only you can legally fill out the application forms—it makes no sense to deal with one of the companies that send out mailers offering their services for a fee.

Children and Social Security Numbers

If you want to open a savings account in a minor's name, or if you want to claim your children as a tax exemption with the IRS, children one year old and over must have a Social Security number. To obtain Social Security cards, parents must provide two original documents (photocopies are not valid) verifying the child's age and identity. Acceptable documents are a birth certificate, vaccination certificate or valid passport. Call the number listed below if you do not have any of these documents. Parents may present the documents at a Social Security office or mail them (registered mail) along with a two-page application, which can be obtained by calling (800) 772-1213. The Social Security Administration promises to mail the child's card within ten days, and to return the identification documents.

Additional Resources

The Social Security Administration maintains a toll-free number for easy access to information, although be prepared to spend some time on the telephone wading through its recorded messages. Call the Social Security Administration, (800) 772-1213, 7:00 a.m. to 7:00 p.m., Monday through Friday.

UNIONS

Labor unions are organizations that deal collectively with employers on behalf of employees. Their best-known role is negotiating group employment contracts for members. But unions also often perform other workplace chores, such as lobbying for legislation that benefits their members and sponsoring skill training programs.

Some labor unions also operate benefit programs such as vacation plans, healthcare insurance, pensions and programs that provide members with discounts on various types of personal needs, such as eyeglasses and prescriptions drugs.

Most unions are operated by a paid staff of professional organizers, negotiators and administrators, with some help from members who volunteer their time. In general, the money to pay unions' staffs and expenses comes from dues paid by their members—which typically total about $40 per member per month.

Labor unions got the legal right to represent employees in their relationships with their employers in 1935, when the National Labor Relations Act (NLRA) was passed. That federal Act also created the National Labor Relations Board (NLRB) to police the relationships among employees, their unions and their employers. The NLRA requires most employers and unions to negotiate fairly with each other until they agree to a contract that spells out the terms and conditions of employment for the workers who are members of the union. The NLRB enforces this requirement by using mediators, administrative law judges, investigators and others.

The basic union building block under the NLRA is the bargaining unit—a group of employees who perform similar work, share a work area and who could logically be assumed to have shared interests in such issues as pay rates, hours of work and workplace conditions.

Your Right to Unionize

The National Labor Relations Act guarantees employees the right to create, join and participate in a labor union without being unfairly intimidated or punished by their employers.

Generally, the courts have ruled that Section 7 of the NLRA gives employees the right to:

- discuss union membership and read and distribute literature concerning it during non-work time in non-work areas, such as an employee lounge
- sign a card asking your employer to recognize your union and bargain with it; to sign petitions and grievances concerning employment terms and conditions; and to ask your co-workers to sign petitions and grievances, and
- display your pro-union sentiments by wearing message-bearing items, such as hats, pins and T-shirts, on the job.

The courts have also ruled, in general, that Section 8 of the NLRA means that an employer may not:

- grant or promise employees a promotion, pay raise, a desirable work assignment or other special favors if they oppose unionizing efforts
- dismiss, harass, reassign or otherwise punish or discipline employees—or threaten to—if they support unionization, or
- close down a worksite or transfer work or reduce benefits to pressure employers not to support unionization.

How to Unionize

What typically occurs when a group of employees wish to campaign for unionization of their jobs is that they contact a union they think would be interested and propose the idea.

Unions are usually listed in the yellow pages of your local telephone directory under Labor Organizations. Don't let their names discourage you. It's not unusual nowadays for meatpackers to belong to the United Steel Workers, for example, or for office workers to belong to the Teamsters union that originally represented freight drivers. The only practical way to determine which unions might be interested in unionizing your workplace is to call and ask.

Your Right to De-Unionize

What if your bargaining unit is unionized, but you don't think union membership is serving your best interests? Just as it gives them the right to unionize, the NLRA give employees the right to withdraw from union membership.

There are two basic ways to de-unionize:

1. Conduct a campaign among the members of your bargaining unit to get them to petition the NLRB to conduct a de-certification election. If you're able to bring about an election, you'll probably also have to campaign hard against the union for the votes of other members of the bargaining unit.

2. Resign your individual membership. The courts have ruled that informing your employer that you want check-off deductions for union dues and fees stopped is not sufficient to quit a union; you must advise the union in writing of your decision to quit.

Limitations on Unions

The NLRA also prohibits unions from interfering with your right to reject or change union membership. Unions may not:

- restrain or coerce employees from exercising their rights under the NLRA—this includes the violence and threats of violence that some unions use against people who reject union membership
- cause or encourage an employer to discriminate against an employee or group of employees because of their de-unionization activities
- interfere in any way with an employee's right to freely express opinions on union membership
- fail or refuse to bargain in good faith with an employer on behalf of a bargaining unit that has designated the union as its bargaining agent, even if the union and the bargaining unit are at odds, or
- prevent you from going to work by using such tactics as mass picketing.

More Information/Where to Complain

The National Labor Relations Board has more information about your rights as a union member. It also handles complaints against unions. There are five regional offices in California:

- 811 Wilshire Boulevard, 11th Floor, Los Angeles, CA 90017-2803, (213) 894-5200
- 11000 Wilshire Boulevard, 12th Floor, Los Angeles, CA 90024, (310) 575-7351
- 555 W. Beech Street, Suite 302, San Diego, CA 92101, (619) 557-6184
- 901 Market Street, Suite 400, San Francisco, CA 94103, (415) 744-6810
- 1301 Clay Street, Suite 300, Oakland, CA 94612, (510) 273-7200.

WORKERS' COMPENSATION INSURANCE

Workers' Compensation Insurance provides benefits to you for an injury (physical or mental) or illness resulting from the job. Almost all California employers—federal employees have coverage through the U.S. Department of Labor—are required to provide and pay for workers' compensation insurance. The worker receives benefits from the employer's workers' compensation insurance company whether the injury is the fault of the worker or the employer.

Employers are required to provide a claim form to their injured employees upon notification of an injury. In addition, insurance carriers must begin payment of benefits within 14 days of notification of the injury if the employee is off work or hospitalized for more than three days as a result of the injury.

Types of Benefits

Workers' compensation provides several types of assistance:

- medical benefit (all medical costs are paid by the insurance company or your employer)
- temporary and permanent disability payments—the weekly rate is usually based on two-thirds of your gross weekly pay, with a maximum weekly payment of $336 for injuries occurring on or after January 1, 1991; maximums will increase to $406 (July 1, 1994), $448 (July 1, 1995) and $490 (July 1, 1996)
- vocational rehabilitation—to retrain the worker for another type of work
- cost of transportation (within limits) for medical treatment or rehabilitation, and
- death benefits—may be payable to qualified surviving dependents.

If Your Employer Does Not Have Workers' Compensation Insurance

Your employer violates the law by not having workers' compensation insurance. You may be eligible for benefits from the Uninsured Employers Fund of the State Department of Industrial Relations (which can be found in the telephone book white pages under Government Offices).

If Your Employer Is Self-Insured

If your employer self-insures (pays benefits without buying coverage from an insurance company—some companies believe this is more economical), your benefits will be the same as those provided by an insurance company.

What Doctor Must You Use?

Generally, you must be treated by the company doctor or company's recommended physician or clinic for the first 30 days after the injury, unless you have notified the company in writing prior to the injury of the name and address of the doctor who has your medical records. If you see your own doctor, your employer has the right to have you examined by its medical provider as well. If so, you can go directly to that doctor. If your employer does not refer you to a doctor, or if you are still receiving medical treatment after 30 days, you then have the right to choose your own doctor.

If the Insurance Company Won't Pay

If the insurance company is stalling on paying benefits, the problem can be partially and temporarily solved by applying for State Disability Insurance (SDI). Although SDI does not normally pay for job-related injuries (it covers loss of pay for non-job-related disabilities), it must pay if you file a workers' compensation claim and the insurance carrier has not paid you. (You must file a form entitled "Application for Adjudication of Claim," with a case number given by the clerk, at any office of the Division of Industrial Accidents.) SDI gets its money back from the insurance company if you are found eligible for workers' compensation. If your injury is ultimately found to be not work-related, you are eligible for SDI and will have already started receiving your benefits.

If the Insurance Company Stops Paying

The insurance company usually stops paying because it receives a new medical report from a doctor indicating further benefits are unnecessary. If you believe you are still injured, this is the time to see a lawyer if you haven't already done so.

Do You Need a Lawyer?

Workers' compensation disputes regarding denied or limited benefits may be resolved by litigation before the Workers' Compensation Appeals Board. Doctors' reports are usually the key evidence regarding the duration or the extent of the disability.

Workers' compensation lawyers get paid only when there is a settlement or litigation victory. Many attorneys take on large caseloads in order to compensate for relatively low fees (about 10% of the settlement or award) and are sometimes too busy to provide much personal contact. If you feel your lawyer is not doing anything, you could be right, but it could be that no doctor will support your claim. You have the right to change lawyers, usually without cost. Consult with another lawyer if you are dissatisfied; if you decide to switch, the prior lawyer must forward your file on request.

Finding a Workers' Compensation Lawyer

You may want to consider hiring a lawyer the State Bar of California has designated as a "certified legal specialist" for a workers' compensation case. Attorneys do not have to be Bar-certified to handle workers' comp cases, and many who are well-qualified have chosen not to become certified. If you don't have a good referral, however, hiring a specialist may be a good way to find competent legal representation. For a list of specialists, contact the Board of Legal Specialization, State Bar of California, 555 Franklin Street, San Francisco, CA 94102-4498, (415) 561-8265.

More Information/Where to Complain

How to Handle Your Worker's Compensation Claim, by Christopher Ball (Nolo Press), shows how to file a claim, receive the benefits you are entitled to, get appropriate medical care and negotiate a settlement. Look for it in libraries and bookstores.

If you are dissatisfied with the way your workers' compensation claim was handled by the Division of Industrial Accidents, you can appeal to or request a hearing by the Workers' Compensation Appeals Board.

The Division of Industrial Accidents has 22 offices; each one has an Information and Assistance Officer, a Rehabilitation Consultant and a Workers' Compensation Appeals Board. The offices are in Bakersfield, Eureka, Fresno, Long Beach, Los Angeles, Norwalk, Oakland, Pomona, Redding, Sacramento, Salinas, San Bernardino, San Diego, San Francisco, San Jose, Santa Ana, Santa Barbara, Santa Rosa, Stockton, Van Nuys, Ventura and West Los Angeles. Look in the phone book white pages under State Government Offices, Department of Industrial Relations (Division of) Industrial Accidents. If you cannot find the office nearest you, call (800) 736-7401 for information and assistance. This number also has good recorded information.

Federal Employees

If you are a federal employee or are covered by federal legislation, you need to contact the U.S. Department of Labor, Office of Workers' Compensation Programs, 71 Stevenson Street, San Francisco, CA 94105, (415) 744-6610. ■

GOVERNMENT

GOVERNMENT AGENCIES

Census Bureau

The Census Bureau conducts the federal "census" that is done every ten years. All citizens are legally required to answer the census questionnaire. The population count for your area determines how many seats in the U.S. Congress and state legislature will be allocated. Billions of dollars are distributed for hospitals, schools, day care, senior centers and other community needs based in part on population and housing information. Businesses use the information for employment and expansion plans.

You may be concerned that agencies, such as Welfare, Immigration, the FBI, the IRS, the courts or the military will have access to your census questionnaire. Federal law, however, prohibits census data from being used for any purpose other than the compilation of statistics.

Census Bureau "Survey"
Every month, the Census Bureau surveys 70,000 households selected by address, not by name. (If you move, you are not followed.) The four areas about which residents are questioned are:

- employment or unemployment of each household member
- total income for residents at the address
- consumer expenditures—the figures for the basis of the Consumer Price Index, inflation rate and Social Security adjustments, and
- crime—both reported and unreported.

The Census Bureau survey is the basis for the national unemployment figures announced monthly by the government. Each survey (which is done during the week in which the 19th of the month falls) takes place over four months—the first survey is in-person. It is followed by three months of phone surveys. The address then goes out of the sample pool for eight months, but returns when the cycle starts again the next year.

Consumer Product Safety Commission (CPSC)

The Consumer Product Safety Commission is a federal agency that regulates and establishes safety standards for household and recreational products. CPSC investigates injuries associated with consumer products and welcomes questions and complaints from the public. It is charged with reducing unreasonable risks of injury associated with consumer products used in the home, school and in public places.

More Information/Where to Complain

Consumer Reports magazine is always interested in hearing from consumers that have product defect information.

Also, CPSC has many free fact sheets, brochures and pamphlets covering diverse topics such as:

- bicycles
- carbon monoxide
- cribs
- electrical safety
- fire safety
- high chairs
- kitchen ranges
- lead in paint
- power mowers
- senior citizen safety
- smoke detectors, and
- toys.

For copies or a list of publications, or to report a hazardous product or product-related injury, contact CPSC at one of the following:

- 600 Harrison Street, Room 245, San Francisco, CA 94107, (415) 744-2966
- 4929 Wilshire Boulevard, Suite 320, Los Angeles, CA 90010, (213) 251-7464.

In addition, to hear recorded information about hazardous products, call (800) 638-CPSC. To request a publications list, write to CPSC, Publications List, Washington, DC 20207.

Department of Motor Vehicles (DMV)

The Department of Motor Vehicles (DMV) licenses and regulates new and used automobile dealers, auto salespeople, leasing companies selling used cars and driving schools. DMV also registers motor vehicles and vessels, licenses drivers and issues California ID cards. DMV can be located by looking in the Government listings of your telephone book white pages.

Federal Trade Commission (FTC)

The Federal Trade Commission is a federal agency that regulates deceptive and misleading business practices and administers consumer protection laws. It does not handle individual complaints but is nevertheless interested in hearing from consumers. If the FTC gets enough complaints about a particular company or practice, it will investigate.

The FTC has jurisdiction in the following areas:

- advertising
- product labeling
- door-to-door sales

- debt collection
- credit reporting, and
- warranties (except motor vehicles).

The FTC focuses on problems of national concern, although it might investigate a problem that occurs just in California or refer the complaint to local law enforcement.

More Information/Where to Complain

The FTC maintains two offices in California:

- 11000 Wilshire Boulevard, Suite 13209, Los Angeles, CA 90024, (310) 575-7575
- 901 Market Street, Suite 570, San Francisco, CA 94103, (415) 744-7920.

You can file a complaint at either office. You can also obtain a list of the FTC's free publications, which includes the following:

- Automatic Debit Scams
- Auto Service Contracts
- Building a Better Credit Record
- Businessperson's Guide to Federal Warranty Law—although written for a businessperson, this booklet has much information to benefit consumers
- Buying a Used Car
- Buying and Borrowing: Cash In on the Facts
- Car Ads: Low Interest Loans and Other Offers
- Choosing and Using Credit Cards
- Consumer Guide to Vehicle Leasing
- Contest Cons
- Cosigning a Loan
- Credit and Charge Card Fraud
- Credit and Older Americans
- Credit Billing Errors? Use FCBA—Fair Credit Billing Act
- Credit Practices Rule
- Credit Repair Scams
- Dance Studios
- Door-to-Door Sales
- Electronic Banking
- Equal Credit Opportunity
- Escrow Accounts for Home Mortgages
- Fair Credit Billing
- Fair Credit Reporting
- Fair Debt Collection
- Fix Your Own Credit Problems and Save Money
- Franchise and Business Opportunities
- "Gas-Saving" Products
- General Motors Consumer Mediation/Arbitration Program
- Getting a Loan: Your Home as Security
- Health Spas: Exercise Your Rights
- Home Equity Credit Lines
- How to Write a Wrong: Complain Effectively and Get Results
- Investing by Phone
- Layaway Purchase Plans
- Lost or Stolen: Credit and ATM Cards
- Mortgage Money Guide: Creative Financing for Home Buyers

- Rain Checks
- Real Estate Brokers
- Refinancing Your Home
- Scoring for Credit
- Second Mortgage Financing
- Service Contracts
- Shopping by Mail
- Shopping by Phone and Mail
- Solving Credit Problems
- Telephone Investment Fraud
- Timeshare Tips
- Unordered Merchandise
- Using Ads to Shop for Home Financing
- Utility Credit
- Vehicle Repossession
- Warranties
- Women and Credit Histories
- Work-at-Home Schemes.

Food and Drug Administration (FDA)

The Food and Drug Administration (FDA) is a federal agency with jurisdiction over the quality, safety and side effects of:

- foods (except meat and poultry—they are under the jurisdiction of the U.S. Department of Agriculture)
- drugs and medical devices
- cosmetics
- animal feeds
- medications, vaccines and blood plasma, and
- radiological devices involving health (such as microwave ovens and color TVs).

You can file a complaint with the FDA Consumer Complaint Coordinator around the state:

- Calexico—(619) 357-4609
- Canoga Park—(818) 904-6325
- Fresno—(209) 487-5305
- Irvine—(714) 836-2377
- Los Angeles—(213) 252-7877
- Sacramento—(916) 551-1086
- San Bernardino—(714) 383-5885
- San Diego—(619) 557-5659
- San Francisco—(415) 556-1435
- San Jose—(408) 291-7548
- Santa Barbara—(805) 687-7098
- Stockton—(209) 946-6306
- Terminal Island—(310) 514-6112.

Postal Service

Dropping a piece of mail in a mailbox is something we all take for granted. What we often forget, however, is the importance of following some simple rules—such as including a delivery address, a return address and the correct amount of postage. You will get the best possible service if you clearly print or write the address (better yet, type) and use common abbreviations and zip codes.

When There's a Street Address and a P.O. Box

Many businesses have both a street address and a post office box. If you want to visit the business, use the street address. If you want to write to the business, use the P.O. Box—the business will get your mail sooner.

If you include both addresses on an envelope, delivery will be made to the address written directly above the city. *Example:* PollyAnna, P.O. Box 45, 99999 Main Street, San Francisco, CA 94000, will be delivered to 99999 Main Street. On the other hand, PollyAnna, 99999 Main Street, P.O. Box 45, San Francisco, CA 94000, will be delivered to P.O. Box 45.

Obtaining the Address of a Post Office Boxholder

The Postal Service will provide the recorded name and address of the holder of a post office box being used for business purposes just for the asking. The Post Office, however, will not normally reveal the name and home address of a private individual who is not using the box for business purposes with some exceptions. A boxholder's name and address will be furnished in the case of a lawsuit to:

- a person legally empowered to serve legal papers
- the attorney for the party on whose behalf service of legal papers is being made, or
- a party to a lawsuit who is representing himself without an attorney. Postal Service Administrative Support Manual § 352.44d.

When You Move

If you complete a change-of-address form, the Post Office will forward your mail for 12 months. From the 13th to 18th months, the Post Office will return mail to the sender with your forwarding address noted. After 18 months, letters are simply returned to the sender.

If a person or business you are looking for has filed a change-of-address, you can get that information by filling out a request form and paying a small fee. The Post Office keeps change-of-address cards for one year. Your name will be kept on file and is available to the person you are looking for if she asks the post office for a list of people who requested her change of address information.

Undeliverable Mail

Undeliverable mail is returned to the sender, if the sender included a return address. If she didn't, the mail is sent to the "undeliverable mail department" where the mail is opened. Anything of intrinsic value, such as a check, is returned to the sender—assuming there is an address. The rest is burned under tight security.

Sometimes, the sender includes with the mailing: "Postmaster: If Undeliverable, Please Handle In Accordance With USPS Reg.#694." This means that the Post Office can throw away undeliverable junk mail.

Certificate of Mailing

For a small fee you can purchase a "Certificate of Mailing" from the Post Office. It is merely a receipt proving you mailed a specific item on a specified day. Unlike certified or registered mail, it does not provide proof of delivery and the Post Office does not keep a record.

Certified Mail

Certified mail provides you with a mailing receipt, and a record of delivery is kept at the recipient's Post Office. You can also obtain a return receipt for proof of delivery. Certified mail is not available for international mail. For valuable or irreplaceable items, registered mail provides the most protection. Also, you will probably want to purchase insurance.

Registered Mail

Registered mail is the most secure service the Post Office offers; it incorporates a system of receipts to monitor registered articles from point of acceptance to delivery. Irreplaceable items, regardless of value, and anything worth over $400 should be sent by registered mail. You can purchase postal insurance to cover articles sent by registered mail valued up to $25,000.

Insured Mail

You can insure valuable items sent First, Third and Fourth Class up to $400. You can get a return receipt as proof of delivery for any mail insured for more than $20. Keep your postal receipt; you'll need it if you file a claim for lost mail that has been insured. Also, you will need to prove the value of the insured item with purchase receipts or by completing a form indicating the value of the contents.

Paying Bills by Mail

When paying bills by mail, allow a few extra days for the mail to be delivered. Your payments must normally be received by the creditor by the due date, not by the postmark. Most creditors will charge late fees even though you claim the Post Office is to blame for the delay. *Exceptions:* Postmark deadlines are acceptable for the IRS, Franchise Tax Board and certain contracts with a three-day right of cancellation.

Mail Fraud

When a postal inspector suspects that a mailing contains false or fraudulent materials, he can apply to a court to obtain an order to intercept the company's incoming mail (usually containing checks sent by unsuspecting consumers). Unfortunately, investigation and subsequent action often takes a long time, which means many consumers lose money in the meantime. In many instances, the fraudulent business has long since been closed down by the time a postal inspection occurs.

If you suspect mail fraud, or receive illegal mail such as chain letters, send the items to the Chief Postal Inspector, Western Region, 850 Cherry Street, San Bruno, CA 94098-0100.

Pornographic Mail

You can stop receiving sexually oriented mailings by filling out Form 2201, Application for Listing Pursuant to 39 U.S.C. 3010, at your local post office. You can also stop what you consider erotically arousing or sexually provocative advertisements by filling out Form 2150, Notice for Prohibitory Order Against Sender of Pandering Advertisements in the Mail, at your post office.

Chain Letters

Chain letters (called that because they go on endlessly), which instruct you to send money (or something else of value) to a number of named people, dropping the last name on the list and adding your own instead, are illegal. A typical chain letter begins with a phony name—three widely used names are Dave Rhodes, Edward L. Green, and Philip Brown—telling you that he was heavily in debt until he made $50,000 by sending out chain letters. Even chain letters that claim to sell a valid service and quote a postal regulation still violate the law.

CHAIN LETTERS ARE NONSENSE

Don't waste your time or money on chain letters—you are extremely unlikely to profit from them. Besides being illegal, the cost of postage, photocopying and buying mailing lists will probably cost you more than you will get back. I have regularly heard from consumers who spent anywhere from $50 to $100 and never got one response.

California Public Utilities Commission

The California Public Utilities Commission (CPUC) is an independent state agency which regulates the rates and services of privately owned utilities, including companies that supply gas, natural gas, electricity, telephones and water. Most electric, gas and telephone companies in California, including PG&E and Pacific Bell, are privately owned. The CPUC does not have jurisdiction over municipal or district-owned utilities unless so required by the Legislature.

CPUC also regulates the rates and services of privately owned freight and passenger transportation systems operating within the state, which include buses, limousines, trains and trucks. CPUC does not have jurisdiction over municipal or district-owned transportation systems unless so required by the Legislature.

More Information/Where to Complain

To complain about an energy or telephone company, call (800) 649-7570, Monday through Friday between 10 a.m. and 3 p.m. Your call will be directed to your local CPUC office. To complain about a freight transportation company, turn to the *Consumer Rights* chapter's section on Freight Services.

TURN (Toward Utility Rate Normalization) is a watchdog organization that closely monitors utility rates and really fights for consumers' interests. You can contact TURN at 625 Polk Street, Suite 403, San Francisco, CA 94102, (415) 929-8876.

Weights and Measures

Every county in California has an office of Weights and Measures which has jurisdiction over any commodity that is weighed, measured or counted. Weights and Measures is responsible for ensuring the accuracy of the weights and measures of such commodities as food, medicine and gasoline. Weights and Measures also makes sure the laundry scales are accurate where you take your clothing in for cleaning. If you think some commodity has been short-weighted, or inaccurately counted, contact your local Weights and Measures Office and it will investigate. Check the telephone book white pages under County Government listings.

BIRTH CERTIFICATES

To obtain a copy of your own or your child's California birth certificate, contact the County office of Vital Statistics or Birth Records Section, or the Recorder's office in the county where the birth occurred. You may also obtain a certified certificate from the California Registrar of Vital Statistics, Department of Health Services, 304 S Street, P.O. Box 730241, Sacramento, CA 95814-0241, (916) 445-2684. It costs $12 and takes about 6-12 weeks to get a certified birth certificate. You'll need to provide the following:

- full birth name
- birth date
- city or county of birth
- father's name, and
- mother's maiden name.

For an additional $5, you can fax your request to (800) 858-5553. Include the above information as well as your Visa or MasterCard number, the card's expiration date, your daytime phone number and your return address.

This information applies to California births only. You need to contact Birth Records or Vital Statistics departments in other states if you were born elsewhere.

New Birth Certificates

A new birth certificate may be issued and the old one sealed and made available only with a court order if:

- no father is named on the original certificate and both parents want to acknowledge paternity
- the correct father's name is listed, but the child has a different last name listed
- a court-ordered paternity decree is obtained
- a child is legally adopted
- a birth certificate contains a derogatory, demeaning or colloquial racial description, or
- a person undergoes a sex-change operation and obtains a court order for a new birth certificate.

If a California birth certificate contains errors or has omissions, the state will add an official attachment showing a name change, but will not issue a new birth certificate.

To amend or obtain a new California birth certificate, contact the California Registrar of Vital Statistics at the address listed above. The cost is $19.

Adoption

Adopted children usually have their names changed as part of the adoption order. A new birth certificate is then automatically issued for the child exclusively in the name of the new parents (unless they object). Health and Safety Code § 10430. As of 1993, same-sex parents who are adopting a child (or the same-sex partner of a biological parent who is adopting her partner's child) may have both names listed as parents on the birth certificate.

Following an adoption and issuance of a new birth certificate, the old birth certificate and all records pertaining to the change are sealed and can be opened for inspection only by court order. Health and Safety Code §§ 10439, 10450.5 and 10456.5.

No Birth Certificate

If you can't find your birth certificate and the state won't issue a replacement, contact the Bureau of the Census, Personal Census Search Unit, P.O. Box 1545, Jeffersonville, IN 47131, (812) 285-5314. Ask for Form BC600—Application for Search of Census Records. Return the completed form to the same place with a check for $40. The Census Bureau will search its records for evidence of you. If the Bureau finds you, you will be sent a record showing the state of your birth if you were born before 1960, and/or your birth date. Most agencies will accept this record in lieu of your birth certificate.

More Information

How to Change Your Name (California only), by attorneys David Ventura Loeb and David W. Brown (Nolo Press), is available in public libraries and bookstores.

County Courthouse Book, by Elizabeth Bentley (Genealogical Publishing Co.), lists location, address and phone number for birth records in most counties in the U.S. This book is available in many libraries.

MARRIAGE

California requires that people who want to marry be:

- of the opposite sex. Some lesbian and gay couples go through religious marriage or commitment ceremonies, but the resulting relationship is not recognized by the state, even if the marriage was performed in a country where same-sex marriage is legal (such as Denmark or Norway).

- at least 18 years old. People under 18 need the consent of a parent or guardian and of a Superior Court judge, who probably will require marriage counseling. Civil Code §§ 4101-4102.

- sufficiently unrelated to each other. Parents and children, grandparents and grandchildren, brothers and sisters (including half siblings), and uncles and nieces or aunts and nephews cannot marry each other. Civil Code § 4400. First cousins can marry each other in California, although these marriages are banned in many states.

- sane and mentally capable of consent. Insane and severely mentally retarded persons can't marry. Because it is difficult to tell when someone is or isn't insane, a person experiencing a lucid interval between periods of insanity can legally marry. That a person has been mentally ill in the past is no bar to marriage.

- sober. The county clerk can deny a marriage license to a person who has been drinking or is obviously under the influence of a drug. Civil Code § 4201.

- physically able to consummate the marriage. In theory, each party to a marriage must have the physical ability to have sexual intercourse, even if the woman is past child-bearing age. (This requirement is not enforced.)

- unmarried. You can be married to only one person at a time. Civil Code § 4100. To get married, you must have the following:

- a license. Both spouses must visit the county clerk's office to buy a license before marrying. You must give the clerk a physician's statement, no more than 30 days old, saying that neither has communicable syphilis, and that both have been offered an HIV test. Also, the woman, unless she is over 50 or surgically sterilized, must present a doctor's note stating whether or not she is immune to German measles (rubella).

- a ceremony. You must participate in some form of ceremony, performed by an active or retired judge, commissioner or assistant commissioner, or by a priest, minister or rabbi of any religion.

- a witness. You need one witness other than the person conducting the ceremony.

Confidential Marriages

Couples who wish to avoid the licensing and blood test requirements may choose a confidential marriage. To be eligible, a couple must have lived together for a period of time established by the county, and must both be 18 or older. You can get a confidential marriage from the county clerk or from a notary public who is licensed to perform such marriages. In either case, you must pay a fee and file a marriage certificate. Ask the county clerk for details. Civil Code § 4213.

More Information

Nolo Press publishes two books containing information on marriage:

- *California Marriage and Divorce Law*, by Ralph Warner, Toni Ihara and Stephen Elias
- *Nolo's Pocket Guide to Family Law*, by Robin Leonard and Stephen Elias.

VETERANS

If you want to know what benefits a U.S. Armed Forces veteran is entitled to, or if you have a problem of red tape with the Veteran's Administration (VA), *The Veteran's Guide to Benefits*, by Ralph Roberts (Signet Book), covers all the information needed. In addition to answering eligibility and entitlement questions, it lists VA Centers, State Veterans Affairs Offices, Vet Centers and Veterans organizations.

Vietnam Veterans

Two organizations are available to assist Vietnam veterans.

- Veterans of the Vietnam War will do anything it can for the Vietnam veteran. You can call 24 hours a day, seven days a week, toll-free at (800) VIETNAM.
- Vietnam Veterans of America is a nonprofit group providing information and referrals for questions about claims and benefits, Agent Orange, post-traumatic stress disorder and other matters. Call (800) 424-7275.

BONDS

Municipal governments (state, city, county and town) issue bonds to pay for projects, such as schools, highways and sewers. The federal government, through the U.S. Treasury, issues bonds to pay for a variety of federal government activities. A few private corporations sell bonds to finance operating expenses, expansion and modernization.

A bond is a debt security—a promise to pay by the issuer. By contrast, when you buy stock you own a piece of a company—that is, you gain equity in the company. A person who invests in bonds loans money to the government or private entity, in exchange for interest payments. Good quality bonds can be an excellent investment. It's important to understand, however, that a bond is only as good as the governmental agency or corporation issuing it. So-called junk bonds are issued by corporations who already have a heavy debt load. They pay a higher than normal rate of interest, but will be worth little or nothing if the corporation goes bankrupt.

How Bondholders Make Money

While stock dividends rise or fall depending on company profits, bond interest payments are usually regular fixed amounts. Some bond certificates come with detachable coupons which the investor sends in to collect the interest payment. Bonds with coupons are called "bearer" bonds (the owner's name is not on them) and are owned by whoever "bears" (possesses) them. By contrast, most bonds are registered in an individual's name and do not have coupons. The issuer of these "non-coupon" bonds automatically sends the interest payments to the registered owner.

Lost Federal Government Bonds

For a duplicate federal government bond (at no charge) write to Bureau of Public Debt, Savings Bond Information Office, 200 3rd Street, Parkersburg, WV 26106, (304) 480-6112. Include the following:

- the name on the bond
- Social Security number
- serial number, if known
- amount of the bond, and
- approximate date of purchase.

Lost Corporate Bonds

Replacing lost corporate bonds isn't easy. Start with the brokerage house which sold you the bond. It can advise you where to write for a replacement—often the bond's transfer agent. You may have to put up a "surety bond" (similar to an insurance policy providing the corporation security against loss if the original bond is cashed in) in order to get a replacement certificate. Insurance companies issue surety bonds, and can be found in the telephone book yellow pages under Bonds (Surety and Fidelity).

Zero Coupon Bonds

A zero coupon bond is a bond sold at a big discount from its face or pay-off value. For example, a bond that will pay $1,000 in ten years might sell for $350 today. The bond does not pay current interest, but instead interest builds up in the value of the bond. (Many other bonds pay interest twice a year.) When the bond matures, the issuer pays off at face value. Each year, the investor must report as taxable income the interest he would have received, even though she will not receive the interest until the bond's maturity. The only exception is if the investor purchased tax-free zero coupon bonds, such as municipal zero coupon bonds.

FREEDOM OF INFORMATION ACT

The Freedom of Information Act is a federal law establishing the public's right to obtain federal records with some exceptions, such as data gathered from the Census Bureau, national security information and the like. For example, you have the right to obtain someone else's forwarding address from the U.S. Postal Service.

Additional Resources

A step-by-step guide, *Using the Freedom of Information Act,* by Allan Adler and Ann Profozich, is available for $2.50 from the American Civil Liberties Union, 1663 Mission Street, San Francisco, CA 94103.

Paper Trails: A Guide to Public Records in California, by Barbara T. Newcombe, is published by the Center for Investigative Reporting and the California Newspaper Publishers Association.

GOVERNMENT GRANTS

The most comprehensive source of information on government grants is the *Catalog of Federal Domestic Assistance,* published by the Executive Office of the President with the Office of Management and Budget, part of the General Services Administration (GSA). The various branches of government list grants available, eligibility requirements, uses of grants, restrictions on using government grants and filing dates. The *Catalog* also spells out the appeals procedure if your grant application is denied. This enormous (six-inch thick) book is available in many public libraries. Its loose-leaf format makes it easy to photocopy the pages you need.

UNCLAIMED PROPERTY

Each year, billions of dollars of valuable financial assets are lost or abandoned. Often, this happens when a person dies or becomes incompetent and leaves poor records.

Lost, Forgotten or Abandoned Personal Property

What happens to valuable financial assets that have been forgotten, such as old bank accounts or insurance policies? What if you are convinced your now-deceased father had some stocks, bonds or savings accounts, but you just cannot find them?

In California, property such as the following must be turned over to the State Controller if there has been no customer contact for more than three years:

- checking and savings accounts
- thrift certificates
- certificates of deposit
- wages
- pensions
- gift certificates
- common stocks
- bonds
- dividends
- money orders
- traveler's checks
- cashier's checks
- insurance policies, and
- safe-deposit boxes and keys.

The state holds the property in perpetuity, paying 5% interest compounded annually (since approximately 1977).

Claiming Property

To obtain property in the hands of the state, you will have to submit an unclaimed property form providing your full name, address, Social Security number and your signature to the State Controller's Office. If your claim is based on the will of a deceased person, or by right of intestate succession in the absence of a will, you must provide information to establish the deceased person's ownership. The search for, and payment of, money takes eight to 12 weeks.

For information or an unclaimed property form, contact the State Controller's Office, Division of Unclaimed Property, P.O. Box 942850, Sacramento, CA 94250-5873, (800) 992-4647. This office can provide you with state agency addresses in the other 49 states if you want to check on unclaimed property outside of California.

GREETINGS FROM THE PRESIDENT

A nice thing you can do for elderly friends or relatives is to surprise them with a greeting card from the President of the United States. This is available for people celebrating their 80th birthday or more, and couples celebrating their 50th anniversary or more. All you have to do is send the name and address of the recipient(s) and the special occasion date to: Greetings Office, The White House, Washington, DC 20500. Make your request at least four weeks in advance. ■

Healthcare

TOPICS

Medical Information Bureau (MIB)
Access to MIB Records
Seeing Your File
MEDICAL DIRECTIVES
Obtaining a Medical Directive Form
NURSING HOMES
More Information/Where to Complain

CROSS-REFERENCES

Consumer Rights—Products—Contact Lenses and Eyeglasses
Consumer Rights—Services—Health Clubs
Employment—Workers' Compensation Insurance
Insurance—Insurance, Generally
Insurance—State Disability Insurance
Safety and Hazards—Poisoning
Service Providers—Chiropractors
Service Providers—Dentists
Service Providers—Doctors
Service Providers—Osteopaths
Service Providers—Pharmacists

HEALTH INFORMATION

Planetree Health Resource Center, a consumer health library containing a wide range of health and medical information, is open free to the public. You can do your own research (librarians at Planetree will help you), or you can pay a fee and have the Planetree librarians research your health question for you. This is especially helpful if you have a very specific medical question—the librarians will search a large information database and send you a personalized, in-depth packet concerning that problem.

For recorded information about Planetree, call (415) 923-3680. For a free brochure or to speak with a librarian, call or write Planetree Health Resource Center, 2040 Webster Street, San Francisco, CA 94115, (415) 923-3681. Planetree is open Tuesday, Thursday, Friday and Saturday, 11 a.m. to 5 p.m., and Wednesday, 11 a.m. to 7 p.m.

HEALTH INSURANCE COUNSELING FOR SENIORS

Each county in California has a free service called the Health Insurance Counseling and Advocacy Program (HICAP) for senior citizens, funded through grants from the California Department of Aging. Trained volunteers, under the supervision of experts, will do the following:
- help you understand Medicare and health insurance coverage
- help you evaluate and compare supplemental health insurance (Medi-gap policies)
- give information about different types of coverage
- help you file Medicare and supplemental insurance claims, and
- help you set up a recordkeeping system.

Appointments are recommended. To find HICAP, contact your area agency on aging, any senior center, a senior information and referral line listed in your phone book, or the California Department of Aging, HICAP, 1600 K Street, Sacramento, CA 95814, (916) 323-7315.

Many senior citizen centers provide individualized health counseling that's even better than what HICAP provides.

HEALTH INSURANCE

Many types of health insurance are offered in California; some are purchased individually but most are coordinated and offered by employers—although employees often have to pay a share of the costs. The California Department of Insurance licenses and regulates the companies and agents selling health insurance in the state.

Federal Rules Covering Health Insurance

The federal government, under the Employee Retirement Income Security Act (ERISA) protects the interests of workers and beneficiaries who depend on benefits from employee pension and welfare plans. ERISA requires employers or unions to provide a summary plan description of the health insurance coverage. If a claim is denied, an employee must be given a reason and also must be given the right to appeal the decision. If these requirements have not been followed, you can file a complaint with the U.S. Department of Labor. Self-insured programs do not fall under the jurisdiction of the California Department of Insurance, nor the Department of Corporations.

Types of Health Insurance

Individual Coverage

Individual insurance coverage, purchased by many self-employed consumers and those not covered by employer-sponsored group plans, often are more costly than participating in a group plan. As an individual, you can choose any insurance company which offers individual coverage (many don't), and if you change jobs, you will not lose your coverage. One exception may be if your new job is more hazardous, requiring additional or extraordinary coverage. Depending on the particulars of your policy, the insurance company pays or reimburses you for all or part of the medical services received, minus the deductible. As an individual, you deal directly with the insurance company, not a group administrator, as is often the case with a group health plan. Either you or your doctor must file claim forms with the insurance company before being reimbursed.

Group Coverage

If you can participate in a group health plan through your employer, union or professional association, your premiums will usually be less than with an individual policy. In a group plan, the eligibility and benefits and the amount of the premium you must pay is determined by the employer, association or other group. There are no set standards as to what type of insurance a group must offer. Some groups pay the entire premium for your insurance coverage. Some groups share the expense with you; others require you to pay the entire cost. If your group coverage is through your job and you change or lose your job, you lose your group coverage. A federal law—the Consolidated Omnibus Budget Reconciliation Act (COBRA)—allows you to continue group health insurance coverage temporarily.

Self-Insured/Self-Funded Group Insurance

Some employers—generally those with 500 or more employees—and some unions pay healthcare costs themselves rather than pay an insurance company for coverage. Many groups find this self-insured or self-funded insurance option to be more economical. Often, these employers and unions pay third-party administrators to manage their program—to pay claims and deal with complaints.

Health Maintenance Organizations (HMOs)

HMOs are membership organizations comprised of hospitals, doctors and other medical personnel which provide many prepaid health services. Either you or your group pay a monthly fee whether or not you use any available medical services. Because these are not fee-for-service operations, generally there are only nominal charges for any medical service you receive, and no claim forms to fill out. Many HMOs have stopped accepting individual members; they accept only groups for memberships. In order to have services covered, members must use the HMO facilities and doctors—except for emergencies or for pre-approved special services not provided by the HMO.

Reviewing an Insurance Policy

You are allowed to review a health insurance policy for 30 days after receipt of the policy or certificate. During that time you may cancel the policy without any obligation.

INSURANCE APPLICATIONS AND HONESTY

It pays to answer questions honestly on applications for health insurance. If you file a claim for treatment for a condition you did not previously reveal, the insurance company—after checking out your medical history—may deny your claim based on the false information given on your application. The company is also free to cancel your policy.

Deductibles

The deductible is the amount you must pay out of your own pocket before your insurance company will pay any claims. For example, if you have a $700 medical bill and your annual deductible is $500, you are responsible for paying the first $500, and your health insurance company would pay the balance or the portion of the balance specified in your policy—unless it claims the bill is higher than what is considered "reasonable and customary." (See below.) If you continue to have more medical bills throughout the year, you will not have to pay the deductible again until the beginning of the next policy year. Generally, the higher the deductible, the less the insurance costs. As with auto collision and comprehensive insurance, it may be cheaper in the long run to have a higher deductible and pay the first few hundred dollars of medical bills yourself than to have a lower deductible and higher premiums.

"Reasonable and Customary" Payments

If your insurance company thinks your medical bills are too high, it will not pay the bill in full; it will only pay an amount considered "reasonable and customary" —

determined by the prevailing rates in your area. Most county medical societies have a committee to review disputes with doctors and insurance companies. This peer review committee might intercede to get the total cost of your bill reduced.

If you want to be spared from future surprises from your insurance company later, ask your doctor what the cost will be for a particular procedure, and then ask your insurance company if it covers the cost. If your insurance company advises you that your doctor's fees are much higher than what other doctors in the area charge, consider shopping for a less expensive doctor. Another possible way to avoid this problem may be to join an HMO (see above), in which one monthly fee covers most medical services.

Time of Payments

The California Insurance Code requires health insurers to pay medical claims within 30 days. Unfortunately, there is no penalty for noncompliance.

Group Plans: When You Lose Coverage

If you lose or change your job or your group health plan is eliminated, you have two possible choices for getting insurance—COBRA coverage or a conversion plan.

COBRA Coverage

Under a federal law called the Consolidated Omnibus Budget Reconciliation Act (COBRA), temporary group health insurance can be continued at group rates for certain unemployed workers, spouses and dependents who are laid off, fired or quit. The law applies to private employers with 20 or more workers and to state and local government health plans. It includes employer health plans that are self-insured or provide coverage through Health Maintenance Organizations (HMOs). Federal government and church-related employers are excluded. COBRA premiums, which are the same as the group rate, must be paid by the insured, not the former employer. The employer can charge an administrative fee.

Eligibility

People who are covered by a group health insurance plan through an employer can continue the coverage if they have lost their coverage due to the death, divorce or retirement of a spouse, or because they are no longer employed or they don't work enough hours to qualify for the employer's plan. Those eligible for COBRA coverage include:

- widows, divorced spouses and Medicare-ineligible spouses of retired workers, and
- employees who are laid off or terminated (unless they have been terminated for gross misconduct) or have reduced hours.
  Dependent children of qualified COBRA recipients are also covered.

How Coverage Begins

Employers must give employees and their spouses written notice when COBRA plan eligibility begins. The plan administrator will send an Election Form to the person requesting continuation coverage. You will have 60 days to make your election. You have 45 days after the election deadline to pay the premiums for retroactive coverage.

How Long Coverage Lasts

In cases of death or divorce, spouses and dependent children may continue COBRA coverage for up to three years. For job loss or reduced hours, the employee, spouse and dependent children may continue COBRA coverage for up to 18 months.

An individual who is considered to be disabled by the Social Security Administration when he or she qualifies for COBRA benefits may be eligible to extend coverage for an additional 11 months—29 months total. That individual must notify the plan administrator before the end of the 18 months of COBRA coverage of the intention to continue coverage. Documentation of eligibility for Social Security Disability Insurance may be required. The plan administrator is allowed to increase premiums up to 150% during the extra 11 months.

COBRA coverage ends if:
- you fail to pay the premiums
- the employer ceases to provide group health insurance for all employees
- you become covered by another group health plan
- you become eligible for Medicare benefits, or
- you qualified for an 11-month extension based on disability, but your disability no longer exists.

When you run out of COBRA eligibility, you may have the right to convert from a group health plan to an individual policy with the same insurance company without having to qualify medically. Verify this by reading your group certificate. Generally, this individual coverage will not be as extensive and will be more expensive. If you have health problems and have difficulty getting other insurance coverage, however, consider accepting the conversion plan until you are able to secure better coverage elsewhere.

Conversion Plans

Conversion plans may be available whether you use COBRA in the interim, or you go directly from a group to an individual plan. A conversion means you have the right to convert from a group health plan to an individual policy with the same insurance company without having to qualify medically.

⚠️ **Pre-Existing Conditions.** Whether you take out new insurance or change insurance from individual or group coverage, most insurance companies will not cover a pre-existing illness or health problem—that is, one for which you had prior treatment for a waiting period of six months to a year. In some cases, a waiver or rider is attached to your policy eliminating coverage for that pre-existing condition.

THE BEST TIME TO CHANGE COVERAGE IF YOU HAVE A SERIOUS CONDITION

If you have a serious medical condition, it's usually a poor idea to change insurance coverage. If you do change, wait until an employer's open enrollment period, or until the employer changes insurance plans, when coverage for pre-existing conditions is usually not restricted.

Double Coverage for Married People

Many married couples have double insurance coverage. The following rule usually determines which company is responsible for coverage: The plan that covers the employee who required medical treatment is considered the "primary carrier" (the one that pays the largest share of the expense), and the spouse's plan is the "secondary carrier" (responsible for the balance of covered charges that the first policy doesn't pay). Total benefits paid under both policies cannot exceed 100% of the medical cost.

If the healthcare is for children or other dependents of a named person with double coverage, many insurers determine which is the primary carrier based upon which spouse's birthday occurs earlier in the calendar year. The plan of the spouse with the later birthday becomes the secondary carrier.

More Information/Where to Complain

The California Health Insurance Guarantee Association exists to pay claims of impaired or insolvent health insurance companies. In addition, the Association will provide consumers covered by insolvent companies with the continuation of health coverage up to certain limits—either by making available substitute coverage from another insurer or providing coverage itself for a limited time—from 30 days to one year. There are a number of exceptions and restrictions. For more information, call the California Department of Insurance. Insurers will recoup the cost of this "guaranty fund" through a surcharge on premiums paid by policyholders.

Health insurance companies: Call the California Department of Insurance's toll-free line, (800) 927-HELP. Workers there may be able to get your insurance company to process a claim faster or to convince a company to pay a claim it has denied. The Department also publishes a free brochure that explains health insurance information.

Health Maintenance Organizations (HMOs): Call the California Department of Corporations, (213) 736-3104. It will send you the appropriate complaint forms and filing information.

Self-insured employer or union plans not with insurance companies: Call the U.S. Department of Labor, Office of Pension and Welfare Benefits, listed in the telephone book white pages under United States Government Offices.

COBRA: Contact the U. S. Department of Labor, Pension and Welfare Benefits, Division of Technical Assistance and Inquiries, 200 Constitution Avenue NW, Room N5658, Washington, DC 20210, (202) 219-6999.

MEDICARE AND MEDI-CAL

Medicare

Medicare is a federal program designed to help senior and some disabled Americans pay for medical costs. The program is divided into two parts: Part A is hospital insurance; Part B is medical insurance.

Part A: Hospital Insurance

You are automatically entitled to Part A coverage if you are:

- 65 or older and eligible for Social Security retirement benefits or for Railroad Retirement benefits
- under 65 and have been entitled to Social Security disability benefits for 24 months, or
- a person with a spouse or dependent who has permanent kidney failure.

If you're 65 or over but not automatically eligible for Part A insurance, you can still enroll in the Medicare hospital insurance program. You must pay a monthly premium of at least $156; the premium increases by 10% for each year after your

65th birthday during which you're not enrolled. You will also have to pay an initial hospital insurance deductible of about $650, which increases every year.

Part A hospital insurance pays a portion of hospital and in-patient treatment costs. Only treatment that is medically reasonable and necessary, however, is covered. The hospital or skilled nursing facility must be approved by Medicare and accept Medicare payment, and the specific care and treatment you receive must be prescribed by a doctor.

Among the specific things Part A Insurance pays for are:

- a semi-private room (two to four beds per room) and all your meals, including any special, medically required diets
- regular nursing services
- special care units, such as intensive care, coronary care or a private hospital room if medically necessary
- drugs, medical supplies and appliances furnished by the facility (casts, splints, wheelchairs)
- hospital lab tests, X-rays and radiation treatment billed by the hospital
- operating and recovery room costs
- rehabilitation services while you're in the hospital or nursing facility, and
- part-time skilled nursing care and physical therapy and speech therapy provided in your home.

Part A Insurance does not pay for:

- television, radio or telephone in your hospital room
- private duty nurses
- a private room, unless medically necessary, or
- the first three pints of blood you receive, unless you make arrangements for their replacement.

Part B: Medical Insurance

Part B Medical Insurance pays some of the costs of treatment by your doctor either in or out of the hospital, and some medical expenses incurred outside the hospital.

Anyone who is age 65 or older and a U.S. citizen or five-year resident is eligible. If you want Part B medical insurance, you must enroll in the program and pay a monthly premium. This premium is adjusted each year based on the cost of living.

Part B insurance pays only a fraction of most people's medical bills. Many major medical expenses are not covered. For treatment that is covered, Medicare pays only 80% of what it considers to be a reasonable charge for the doctor's services—which may be much less than the doctor charged you.

Part B insurance pays for:

- doctors' services, including surgery, provided at a hospital, at the doctor's office or at home
- mammograms and PAP smears for women
- medical services provided by nurses, surgical assistants, or laboratory or X-ray technicians
- services provided by pathologists or radiologists while you're an in-patient at a hospital
- out-patient hospital treatment, such as emergency room or clinic charges, X-rays and injections
- an ambulance, if required for a trip to or from a hospital or skilled nursing facility
- drugs or other medicine administered to you at the hospital or doctor's office
- medical equipment and supplies, such as splints, casts, prosthetic devices, body braces, heart pacemakers, corrective lenses after a cataract operation, oxygen equipment, wheelchairs and hospital beds

- some kinds of oral surgery
- some of the cost of out-patient physical and speech therapy
- manual manipulation of out-of-place vertebrae by a chiropractor, and
- part-time skilled nursing care, and physical therapy and speech therapy provided in your home.

Medicare Part B medical insurance does not pay for:

- routine physical examinations
- treatment that isn't medically necessary, including some elective and most cosmetic surgery and virtually all alternative forms of medical care, such as acupuncture, acupressure and homeopathy
- vaccinations and immunizations
- drugs—prescription or not—which you can administer or take yourself at home;
- routine eye or hearing examinations, eyeglasses, contact lenses (except after a cataract operation) or hearing aids
- general dental work, and
- routine foot care.

Medi-Cal

Medi-Cal (called Medicaid outside of California) is a program established by the federal government and administered by the state that helps pay medical costs for qualified, needy people. For low-income seniors, Medi-Cal covers some of the medical costs for which Medicare does not pay.

Eligibility

To apply for Medi-Cal, you must fall into one of these categories:

- have children under 21 years old living in your home
- be under 21 yourself
- be 65 or over
- have a disability or be blind
- be pregnant
- be a refugee living in the U.S. less than a year, or
- currently be living in a skilled nursing facility.

Only those who have limited resources qualify for Medi-Cal. One person can have assets worth up to $2,000, two people can have assets worth up to $3,000, three people can have assets worth up to $3,150 and so on. There is no income limitation for eligibility, but people who make more than these amounts may be required to pay for some of the costs of care.

Generally, Medi-Cal won't consider the income or assets of your children or any other relatives in deciding your eligibility, unless you receive regular financial support from a relative. If you live with your spouse, his or her income and assets will be counted as your income. Different rules apply if your husband or wife is in a nursing facility.

To apply for Medi-Cal, you or your representative must file a written application in person at the local office of the State Department of Social Services.

Medi-Cal Benefits

Medi-Cal covers the following medical services:

- in-patient hospital or skilled nursing facility care
- out-patient hospital or clinic services
- independent laboratory and X-ray services
- physicians' services
- home healthcare services

- transportation (ambulance, if necessary) to and from the place you receive medical services
- state-licensed practitioner's care (chiropractor, optometrist, podiatrist, acupuncturist)
- eyeglasses
- dental care
- prosthetic devices
- prescribed drugs
- physical, speech and occupational therapy
- private-duty nursing
- diagnostic, preventive, screening and rehabilitative services, and
- in-patient psychiatric care for those 65 and over.

In addition, Medi-Cal will pay some of the costs not covered by Medicare, including:

- the in-patient hospital insurance deductible that Medicare doesn't pay
- the Medicare medical insurance deductible
- the 20% of the "reasonable charges" that Medicare medical insurance doesn't pay of doctor bills and other out-patient care, and
- the monthly premium charged for Medicare medical insurance.

Coverage

The care or service must be prescribed by a doctor and provided by a doctor or facility that participates in Medi-Cal. Also, in-patient services must be approved as medically necessary by the facility. And Medi-Cal coverage for certain medical services must be approved by a Medi-Cal consultant before you receive them.

Hospitals, doctors and other providers of medical care that accept Medi-Cal patients must accept Medi-Cal's payment as payment in full. If you're eligible for both Medicare and Medi-Cal, and you're treated by a medical facility or doctor that accepts Medi-Cal patients, the treating physician must accept the total amount that Medicare determines is reasonable. You cannot be billed for any extra amounts for the covered services.

More Information/Where to Complain

The Medicare Handbook, a free booklet, includes information on Medicare benefits, what Medicare does not pay for, your right of appeal and much more. It is published every year with updated information, and is available at any Social Security office or by calling (800) 772-1213.

Social Security, Medicare and Pensions: The Sourcebook for Older Americans, by Joseph L. Matthews and Dorothy Matthews Berman (Nolo Press).

Working your way through the Medicare system can be like finding your way through a maze. To help the 3.2 million Medicare beneficiaries in California find their way through the system, a nonprofit peer review organization, California Medical Review, has a toll-free Medicare hotline, (800) 841-1602. You can ask questions about Medicare billing, register concerns about the quality of care received while in the hospital, request information on beneficiaries' rights or get a referral to other senior advocacy agencies.

To report fraudulent billing of Medicare or to report that a physician, hospital or healthcare provider has performed a service not medically necessary or appropriate, contact the following:

- The California Department of Aging, 1600 K Street, Sacramento, CA 95814, (916) 322-5290
- The Medicare Fraud and Abuse Hotline, toll-free, (800) 368-5779, between 7:00 a.m. and 1:00 p.m., pacific standard time

- The Department of Health and Human Services, Office of the Inspector General, at one of its California locations:

  — Symphony Towers, 750 B Street, Suite 1020, San Diego, CA 92101, (619) 557-6057

  — 50 United Nations Plaza, Room 174, San Francisco, CA 94102, (415) 556-8880

  — 600 West Santa Ana Blvd., Suite 805, Santa Ana, CA 92701, (714) 836-2371.

MEDICAL RECORDS

You or your designated representative has the right to inspect and/or copy your medical records, upon presentation of a written request to a California healthcare provider. Healthcare providers include licensed health facilities, clinics, home health agencies, physicians, surgeons, podiatrists, dentists, optometrists and chiropractors. Health and Safety Code § 25251.

Within five days of the request, the healthcare provider must permit inspection of your patient records—that is, any kind of record kept by a doctor, hospital or other healthcare provider relating to your past and/or current health diagnosis and condition as well as treatment provided or proposed. You are not entitled to receive copies of confidential information given to one provider by another or given to a provider by someone other than you. In addition, the healthcare provider may withhold access to the records if the provider believes it would have a detrimental effect or adverse consequences for you to see the records. Health and Safety Code § 25250.

If copies are requested in writing, the provider must do so within 15 days. The provider may charge for payment of reasonable clerical costs. However, the law allows a healthcare provider to prepare a written summary instead of the actual records (within ten days of written request). If the medical record is unusually long or if the patient has been discharged from a hospital in the last ten days, then the provider has 30 days to comply.

Where to Complain

Any healthcare provider who violates this law is guilty of unprofessional conduct. The provider is subject to disciplinary action (including suspension or revocation of a license or certificate) by the licensing agency, such as the Medical Board of California or the Board of Dental Examiners. (See chapter on *Service Providers* for addresses and phone numbers of medical professional licensing agencies.)

Medical Information Bureau (MIB)

The MIB is a nonprofit membership organization sponsored by life, health and disability insurance companies. It operates an information bureau containing the health histories of millions of Americans. MIB files contain physical and medical data requested by insurance companies from a person who applies for coverage. MIB's members use the files to check the medical background of current and potential customers, in much the same way as a credit grantor uses a credit bureau to see what kind of a risk you present. The files are also used to look for medical fraud.

Access to MIB Records

When you apply for medical insurance or obtain medical care, you usually sign a "blanket waiver" or "general consent form" agreeing to let the insurance company see your medical records or let the medical provider release your records to government agencies, insurance companies and employers.

Government agencies request your medical records to verify claims made through Medicare, Medi-Cal, Social Security Disability and Workers' Compensation. Insurance companies require you to release your records before they will issue a policy or make payment under an existing policy. Insurance companies may share your medical information with other insurance companies through the MIB.

Seeing Your File

Federal law gives you the right to see and correct (if necessary) your MIB records with a written request. The MIB does not have a file on everyone. But if your medical information is on file, you may want to make sure it is correct. In the past, information in your medical file would only be disclosed to your physician. Now, you can obtain a free copy by writing or calling the Medical Information Bureau, P.O. Box 105, Essex Station, Boston, MA 02112, (617) 426-3660. First ask for a copy of the Request for Disclosure of MIB Record Information form. Then complete it and return it to MIB.

MEDICAL DIRECTIVES

The increasing use of life-sustaining medical technology over the last decades has raised fears in many of us that our lives may be artificially prolonged against our wishes. The right to die with dignity, and without the tremendous agony and expense for both patient and family caused by prolonging lives artificially, has been addressed now by the U.S. Supreme Court, the federal government and the state legislature.

This individual right also protects against the situation where doctors might wish to provide a patient with less extensive care than he or she would like. For example, a doctor may be unwilling to try experimental treatments or maintain long-term treatments on a patient who he or she feels has slim chances of recovering.

California was the first state to pass laws authorizing individuals to create simple documents that allow them to set out wishes concerning life-prolonging medical care. The documents are called a Declaration—formerly known as a Living Will—and a Durable Power of Attorney for Healthcare. It is important to note that your instructions regarding life-prolonging medical care take effect only when you are diagnosed to have a terminal condition or to be in a permanent coma and cannot communicate with medical personnel.

The basic difference between the two types of document is simple. The Declaration is a statement made by you directly to medical personnel which spells out the medical care you do or do not wish to receive if you become terminally ill and incapacitated. It is presented directly to your doctor and the hospital or other medical provider, and becomes a part of your official medical record, legally binding the doctor or hospital to follow your wishes. It acts as a contract with the treating doctor, who must either honor the wishes for medical care that you have expressed—or transfer you to another doctor or facility that will honor them.

In a Durable Power of Attorney for Healthcare, you can appoint someone else to oversee your doctors, to make sure they provide you with the kind of medical care you wish to receive. The person you appoint is called an attorney-in-fact. Your attorney-in-fact then has the power to ensure that wishes regarding medical treatment are followed by doctors and hospitals. It is also a good idea to appoint a second person as a backup or replacement attorney-in-fact, to act if your first choice is unable or unwilling to serve. Many people in good health create a Durable Power of Attorney for Healthcare so that an attorney-in-fact is named, in the event the person becomes injured or incapacitated and is no longer able to make healthcare decisions.

To make an informed decision about which procedures you do and do not want, as well as about others which might pertain to your particular medical condition, it may be a good idea to discuss your medical directive with your physician. He or she can explain the medical procedures more fully and can discuss the options with you. You will also find out whether your doctor has any medical or moral objections to following your wishes. If he or she does object and will not agree to follow your wishes regardless of those objections, you may want to consider changing doctors.

Obtaining a Medical Directive Form

In most instances, you do not need to consult a lawyer to prepare a Declaration or Durable Power of Attorney for Healthcare. The forms are usually quite simple and can be obtained, free or for a nominal fee, from a number of sources.

• Contact a local hospital. Most will give you the forms free—and many have Patient Representatives on staff who will help you in filling them out.

• Nolo Press has developed an easy-to-use software program, called *WillMaker*, that helps you prepare and update a medical directive for any state. It comes with a manual providing necessary background information, and leads you step-by-step through the process.

• The white pages in most telephone directories have a listing for Senior Referral and Information. This number refers people to various agencies, groups and other sources of assistance for seniors, including medical directive forms and help in filling them out.

• The national nonprofit organization Choice in Dying (formerly the Society for the Right to Die) is one of the nation's oldest patients' advocacy groups. It welcomes donations, but will provide information on current laws on medical directives and can provide forms. Send a stamped, self-addressed envelope, along with your request for information on California's medical directive laws to: Choice in Dying, 200 Varick Street, New York, NY 10014-4810, (212) 366-5540.

NURSING HOMES

The suggestion of putting someone you love in a nursing home is often difficult to face for many older people and their families. Even so, nursing homes obviously serve a necessary and useful role in our society. Often, once the need for a nursing home is beyond dispute, the main task is to find the best one available at an affordable price. Nursing homes are licensed and certified by the California Department of Health Services, which has offices throughout the state. For information on licensing and standards in nursing homes, contact the California Department of Health Services, Licensing and Certification, 1800 3rd Street, Suite 200, Sacramento, CA 95814, (916) 445-2070. For other information, contact the Director's Office of the Department of Health Services, 714 P Street, Room 1253, Sacramento, CA 95814, (916) 657-1425.

More Information/Where to Complain

The California Association of Homes for the Aging publishes annually a membership directory of nonprofit retirement communities that covers independent living facilities, intermediate care facilities, skilled nursing facilities and continuing care facilities. To obtain a copy, send a check for $10 to Attn: Lock Box Department 98-61, P.O. Box 45256, San Francisco, CA 94145.

For information on nursing facility insurance, contact: Health Insurance Association of America, Consumer Information Service, 1025 Connecticut Avenue NW, Suite 1200, Washington, DC 20036, (202) 223-7780; hotline (800) 942-4242.

Beat the Nursing Home Trap: A Consumer's Guide to Choosing and Financing Long-Term Care, by Joseph L. Matthews (Nolo Press), is available in public libraries and bookstores.

Every county in the state is required, by the Department of Aging, to have a Nursing Home Ombudsman to help resolve problems regarding patient abuse, dietary considerations, medical care and other concerns. Every nursing home should have the local Ombudsman's phone number posted publicly. A hotline is available, 24 hours a day, seven days a week, for residents of long-term care facilities, at (800) 231-4024. ■

Insurance

INSURANCE, GENERALLY

Insurance is a part of most peoples' lives. Whether it's car, life, health, disability, renter's, homeowner's, or workers' compensation, the basic idea is the same. If a person suffers a loss covered by insurance, he is entitled to recover according to the policy terms.

The California Department of Insurance licenses and regulates insurance companies and people who work in the insurance field, including agents and brokers. The Department also sets rates for disability, automobile assigned risk insurance and minimum rates for workers' compensation insurance. Most insurance rates are set by companies themselves and are monitored by the Department. Different companies may charge substantially different rates for similar policies.

Sellers of Insurance

Insurance may be sold by any of the following people:

- a direct writing agent—an employee of an insurance company (such as State Farm or Allstate) who may only sell that company's policies
- an independent agent—represents and sells the insurance policies for several companies, or
- a broker—represents you (in theory at least) and will look for insurance policies that meet your needs by contacting companies on your behalf.

More Information/Where to Complain

The American Council of Life Insurance has an Insurance Hotline, (800) 942-4242. These people can answer general questions about life, health, automobile, homeowner's and renter's insurance.

Under California law, insurance policies must be interpreted considering the reasonable expectations of the insured. In disputes about claims, any vagueness, uncertainty or ambiguous language in the policy must be interpreted in your favor and against the insurance company (because it wrote the policy). In addition, the sections of the policy that define "coverage"—what the insurance company will pay—must be interpreted broadly, and policy "exclusions"—what the company claims is not covered by the policy—must be interpreted narrowly.

If your insurance company denies a claim, talk to the claims adjuster. Ask which clause, paragraph endorsement or section of the policy was the basis for the denial. If you disagree, let the insurance company know that you will file a complaint with the California Department of Insurance for an unfair claims settlement practice. If the company is concerned about having a complaint registered against it, it might reconsider your claim. A radio, TV or newspaper "Action Line" may also be helpful in getting an insurance company to reconsider. If a lot of money is at stake, you may want to seek the advice of a public adjuster or an attorney.

The California Department of Insurance has a toll-free number, (800) 927-4357. You can call it to ask questions or file a complaint. You can also request brochures on auto insurance and automobile extended warranties. Many people criticize the Department. It can often be effective, however, in getting consumers a speedier response or more money from their insurance company than they would have obtained on their own.

LIFE INSURANCE

Life insurance provides the beneficiaries you name with a pre-established amount of money if you die during the policy term. In addition, some types of policies also amount to investment accounts—you get money back at the end of the policy term if you are still alive. In purchasing life insurance, your primary concern should be to determine how much money your dependents will need when you die. If you can afford it, your policy should provide enough income for your family's living expenses, including children's education and other debts, less money you will receive from Social Security, private death benefits, investments and other family resources.

If you request life insurance, you have ten days from the day you receive the policy to review it and decide if you want to purchase it. If you die after the year's premium is paid, your heirs do not get a partial refund—there is no provision in life insurance policies for refund of premium.

The three basic types of life insurance are whole, term and endowment. Annuities offer a variation on the theme of life insurance.

Whole Life Insurance

Whole life (also called straight life or ordinary life) provides life insurance if you die, plus a savings feature if you live. In short, the premiums you pay build up a cash value which you get at the end of the policy term. In the meantime, that cash value can be used as collateral for a loan or can be borrowed against at the interest rate shown in the policy. If you are young, premiums on whole life will be considerably higher than ones for the same coverage on a term insurance policy. Typically, with whole life you pay more in the early years but less in the later years of the policy. Some companies offer variations—such as very low payments for a few years with a graduated payment increase built-in. Two particular variations of whole life—universal life and variable life—are very popular.

Universal Life

With a universal life policy, part of your premium pays for your insurance and administrative costs, and the rest is placed in an interest-bearing account (often at competitive rates), which becomes the cash value of your policy. With a universal life policy, you can borrow or withdraw money from this account, vary the amount and timing of premium payments, or increase or decrease the death benefit.

Variable Life

A variable life policy lets you choose the type of investment (one of the insurance companies' investment accounts) in which the the cash value of the policy is invested, such as stocks, bonds, mutual funds, money market accounts or mortgages. A high rate of return in the investments will raise the death benefits, while a low rate of return will cause the death benefits to go down.

Term Life Insurance

Term life provides a set amount of coverage if you die while the policy is in force. It has no savings or investment features and can't be borrowed against—that is, it has no cash value. If you have a limited amount of money to spend on insurance, term insurance gives you the most coverage for the cheapest price. As you get older, term insurance becomes more expensive. Many consumer activists think term insurance is the best buy, especially when you are young.

Endowment Insurance

Endowment insurance pays a set amount of money when you die or if you live to be a certain specified age. You can use an endowment policy to accumulate retirement money to be paid in a lump sum or in installments when you stop working. But this feature is subject to ever-changing tax laws, so speak to a tax advisor before assuming an endowment policy will help you with your retirement. Even though the premiums are high, the cash values are also high, which is why endowment insurance pays a smaller death benefit than does a whole or term policy.

Annuities

Annuities, often purchased for retirement needs, provide money for the insured person while she is alive. Many companies offer group annuities as fringe benefits, with payments beginning at retirement. Individuals can also purchase annuities with a variety of benefits, such as payments made monthly or payments for a specified period of time. Under many policies, if the insured dies, benefits continue for a spouse or named beneficiary.

Missing Life Insurance Policies

Occasionally, a surviving family is sure a deceased person had insurance, but can't find the policy. If you are in this situation, call the Insurance Hotline, a division of the American Council of Life Insurance, at (800) 942-4242. The person you speak to will tell you all the information the organization needs to do your search and will send you a form to fill out. When you return the form, the Council will ask cooperating insurance companies to check their records. The investigation will take at least three months. If an insurance company locates a policy, it will contact you directly. If you do not hear from any insurance company, it means no company found a policy. Once you send your form to the American Council of Life Insurance, you won't hear from the organization again.

Government Policies

The National Personnel Records Center in St. Louis, Missouri, accepts written requests for copies of personnel or medical records (including issued life insurance policies) for former military (completely discharged with no further military obligations) and civilian government personnel. You must call the Center and leave your request on an answering machine. The Center will send you a form on which you can make your request. Here are the phone numbers:

* Civilian personnel—(314) 425-5761
* Army—(314) 538-4261
* Navy—(314) 538-4141
* Marines—(314) 538-4141
* Coast Guard—(314) 538-4141
* Air Force—(314) 538-4243.

More Information/Where to Complain

How to Buy the Right Policy From the Right Company at the Right Price, written by the editors of Consumer Reports Books with Trudy Lieberman.

The American Council of Life Insurance has an Insurance Hotline, (800) 942-4242. These people can answer general questions about life insurance. The California Department of Insurance also has a toll-free number, (800) 927-4357. Call to ask questions or file a complaint.

STATE DISABILITY INSURANCE

California's State Disability Insurance program (SDI) provides income when you lose wages due to sickness or injury not related to the job. Most California workers are covered by SDI, which is paid entirely by workers through payroll deductions. The California Unemployment Insurance Code defines "disability" as any physical or mental injury or illness, including elective surgery, pregnancy and childbirth, AIDS or alcoholism, that keeps you from doing your regular work. Benefits normally begin after a seven-day waiting period of disability, or the first day of hospitalization or treatment at an approved medical facility.

You may apply for State Disability by mail or in person at any Employment Development Department (EDD) branch office. You must mail your claim within 49 days from the first day you are disabled. If a form is late and you believe you have a good excuse, include an explanation of the reasons with the form. Benefits are based on wages paid during a specific 12-month base period (the minimum base period earnings you need to qualify is $300), which is figured using the date your claim begins. The base period is not the last 12 months before your claim begins, however, so if your income has fluctuated, obtain specific rules from EDD and carefully consider when to start your claim. If you want your claim to begin at a later date than when your disability began, include that request with your claim form.

The minimum weekly benefit is $40 and the maximum is $250 for up to one year. If you have a total disability which you expect to last more than a year, contact the Social Security Administration at (800) 772-1213.

Pregnancy Disability

Pregnancy disability is determined in the same way as any other disability—which means you are entitled to disability benefits when you cannot do your regular or customary work. The usual disability period for a normal pregnancy is up to four weeks before the expected delivery date and up to six weeks after the actual delivery date, but may be longer if complications or other medical conditions exist or if delivery is done by Caesarean section. Pregnancy disability claims should not be submitted until the date the doctor certifies you are disabled.

How to Apply

Your employer, hospital or doctor may have the necessary claim forms. If not, you can get a claim form from any EDD office (commonly called the unemployment office) by calling, writing or asking in person. EDD offices are listed in the white pages of the telephone book under State Government. You will need to ask your doctor to fill out the "Doctor's Certificate" portion.

If Disability Benefits Are Denied

You are entitled to an explanation of why your benefits were reduced or denied. Request an explanation by writing to the State Disability office (at the EDD office where you applied for benefits); be sure to include your name and Social Security number. If you are not satisfied with the explanation given, you are entitled to a hearing before an administrative law judge. And if you are still dissatisfied, you may go to the Appeals Board and, subsequently, to the courts. ■

MOTOR VEHICLES

AUTOMOBILE PURCHASES

New Cars

Buying a new car takes a lot of time, energy and patience. Be sure you are happy with your purchase—there is no "cooling off" period; that is, you have no right to cancel or change your mind when you buy a vehicle. In fact, because so many consumers think they have a few days to change their mind after purchasing a car, every new car contract must include the following, which you are required to initial:

California law does not provide for a "cooling off" or other cancellation period for vehicle sales. Therefore, you cannot later cancel this contract simply because you change your mind, decide the vehicle costs too much, or wish you had acquired a different vehicle. After you sign below, you may only cancel this contract with the agreement of the seller or for legal cause, such as fraud.

To shop smart, do some homework first. The following are two excellent resources available in many public libraries:

- *Edmund's New Car Prices*, published every six months by Edmund Publications. This tells you the dealer's cost of any car, as well as the dealer's cost of every accessory on the car. There is an "American Automobile" edition and a "Import Automobile" edition.

- *The Complete Car Cost Guide*, published each February by IntelliChoice, Inc., (800) 227-2665 (sold directly by IntelliChoice for $45 or found in the public library), gives the dealer's cost, as well as what the car will cost over a five-year period, such as the cost of repairs, maintenance, insurance and expected resale value. It also ranks the best and the worst vehicles in several different categories.

Armed with either book, you'll be in a great position to negotiate with a car dealer.

If a Car Was Damaged Before the Purchase

If a car dealer knows of any "material" damage to a new or previously unregistered vehicle that's been subsequently repaired, he must notify the buyer(s) in writing before entering into a contract. "Material" damage means:

- damage of components which are bolted or attached to the vehicle, such as bumpers, tires and glass, replaced with identical new, original manufacturer's components, if repairs exceed 10% of the manufacturer's suggested retail price (MSRP)
- damage of components not bolted or attached to the vehicle, exceeding 3% of the MSRP or $500, whichever is greater (except to components listed)
- damage to the frame or drive train
- damage occurring in connection with the theft of the entire vehicle, or
- damage to the suspension, requiring repairs other than wheel balancing or alignment.

For any damage (not just material damage) the dealer is unaware of at the time of making the contract, the dealer must give notification prior to delivery, if the vehicle is not repaired.

The law also prohibits dealers from responding to consumer inquiries in an untrue or misleading manner. Vehicle Code § 9990 and following.

DON'T PICK UP A NEW CAR AT NIGHT

Never take delivery of a new vehicle at night if you can avoid it. Even though it may be inconvenient to take time off during the day, you'll be able to look the car over carefully in the daylight. At night, even in good artificial light, it's hard to see nicks and dents. Also, you'll miss subtle changes in paint that may be a tip-off that the car was damaged in transit, requiring repainting.

Used Cars

Buying a used car is a tricky business. Never, never buy a used car without having a trusted, independent mechanic or a diagnostic clinic check it out first. As with the purchase of new vehicles, you have no right to cancel or change your mind when you buy a used car.

For a used car to be sold legally, horn, lights, windshield wipers, tires and brakes must be in working order. Also, the smog equipment must be intact. It is illegal to sell a car with smog equipment that has been disconnected or tampered with. Sellers of a used car must provide buyers with the title to the car and an original smog certificate that is no more than 90 days old.

The Federal Trade Commission requires all dealers selling used cars to post a large sticker in the car window stating whether the car is being sold "as is" or with a warranty. Most used car dealers sell vehicles "as is." If you get a written warranty, you automatically get an implied warranty that the car is fit for driving.

Private parties do not have to post stickers—which means that for all intents and purposes, you buy the car "as is" with no warranty. Nevertheless, if you relied on the seller's "positive statements" about the car, such as it was only driven to the supermarket by a little old lady, and then discover the car was used for hot-rod racing and is falling apart, you may be successful in suing the seller in Small Claims Court for the cost of repairs or rescission (cancellation) of the contract. To make your case, be sure you have a witness or written documentation to the seller's misleading claims. See *Everybody's Guide to Small Claims Court*, written by attorney Ralph Warner (Nolo Press), available in libraries and bookstores.

Demonstrator Cars

New car dealers' demonstrator cars are legally considered used cars—even if the dealer gives you a new car warranty. The only exception is for "lemon law" purposes. Then, a demonstrator car sold with a manufacturer's new car warranty is considered a new vehicle. See Vehicle Code § 665 (defines "used vehicle"), 13 California Regulatory Code § 404.20(c) (defines "demonstrator vehicle") and Civil Code § 1793.2 (e)(4)(B).

Additional Resources—New and Used Vehicles

- Jack Gillis (public affairs director for Consumer Federation of America, formerly of the U.S. Department of Transportation), has written two books published annually by Harper & Row. *The Car Book* covers safety, maintenance and insurance information for new cars. It also includes unpublished government data on new car complaints. *The Used Car Book* includes unpublished government data on used car complaints.

- *Consumer Reports* magazine publishes an "Annual Auto Issue" every April. If you don't subscribe, check your public library or newsstand. Also, for a fee, Consumers Union will send you a computer printout of the actual dealer's cost for any auto, including the dealer's cost of each accessory. For more information on how to order this computer printout called "Consumer Reports Auto Price Service" see any April issue of the magazine.

- *Consumer Reports* "Buying Guide" issue, which covers repair records and rates used cars, is a good predictor of what is likely to be wrong with a particular used car.

- Several paperback books, available in bookstores and libraries, written by former automobile salesmen, although a few years old, are real eye-openers: *Don't Get Taken Every Time,* by Remar Sutton (Penguin Books), *How to Outsmart the New Car Salesman,* by Gary Carr (Collier Books, Macmillan Publishing Company) and *The Car Buyer's Art—How to Beat the Salesman at His Own Game,* by Darrell Parrish (Book Express).

- *Edmund's Used Car Prices* is issued quarterly; it's readily available on newsstands and contains price information on used cars.

- *The Kelly Blue Book,* used by all auto dealers, is available at your bank, library or any California State Automobile Association (CSAA) office. It too contains price information on used cars.

Extended Warranties or Service Contracts

All new cars come with a written warranty covering needed repairs and adjustments over specific lengths of time and mileage. When you buy a new car, dealers will try to sell you an extended service contract. Read the contract for yourself; don't rely on the salesperson's verbal representations of what's covered. Too many salespeople claim these service contracts cover everything—not true.

⚠️ Extended service contracts are high-profit items for the dealership, which means they are likely to push you to buy one. Studies show that a consumer is likely to pay more for the coverage than will ever be recovered; however, some car buyers feel the added security is worth the relatively high cost. Under California law, extended service contracts sold after January 1, 1991, cannot duplicate coverage offered by the manufacturer's express warranty (the one that comes with the car). An extended service contract may run concurrently with or overlap an express warranty, however, if the service contract covers items or costs not covered by the express warranty, or the service contract provides replacement of the product when the express warranty only provides repair. Unfortunately, if you bought an extended service contract before January 1, 1991, your service contract coverage started at the same time as the warranty that came with the car. If your car had a three-year warranty and you bought a five-year extended warranty, the extended contract will cover only years four and five. Civil Code § 1794.41.

Are Extended Service Contracts Worth the Price?

That's a decision you'll have to make yourself. Extended service contracts will not cover everything that can go wrong on your car. Find out what is covered to see if it's worth the asking price and remember that the prices quoted are negotiable. The average new car has 15,000 parts, so a long list isn't necessarily great because many parts are not covered. Check the exclusions. Generally, an exclusion will be for damage that was the result of an uncovered part. If a major engine component is damaged by a part that is not covered, you probably won't be covered. For example, many service contracts exclude coverage for seals, gaskets and hoses. If an engine is damaged because a worn seal allowed a sudden oil leak to seep through, many service contracts won't pay for the engine repair. Even if a covered part breaks, you may have to prove you have properly maintained the car (including proper fluid levels) with records of your routine maintenance. Without that, you may have a hard time collecting.

Some extended service contracts have a deductible or require a fee every time you use it. Some may not completely cover towing or rental car expenses. In addition, you may have to pay a transfer fee if you sell the car, so these contracts can be a poor deal if you trade in your cars often.

Independent Versus Manufacturer's Extended Service Contracts
Many dealers push service contracts sold by independent companies rather than the manufacturer's own extended contract because there is more profit in selling independent ones. Unfortunately, companies offering these contracts aren't always reliable.

Independent extended service contracts:
- are only as good as the companies that write them—many of these companies go out of business without making good on their commitments
- often require pre-approval (by calling their 800 number) before authorizing any work to be done on your car—sometimes they insist on inspecting the car before authorizing repairs, which could delay getting the repairs done promptly, or
- often require you to pay for the work before they reimburse you.

In my experience, there are fewer problems with extended service contracts written by car manufacturers than those offered by independent companies. Manufacturers typically do not require prior authorization to have repairs made, nor do they expect to be paid for the work before reimbursing you. In addition, the manufacturer is less likely to go out of business.

Canceling an Extended Service Contract
The dealer must notify you (in writing) of your right to cancel your extended service contract and receive a refund. Your cancellation must be in writing and sent to the person specified in the contract—either the dealer or an administrator (often used by independent companies). Civil Code § 1794.41. The amount of your refund depends on how fast you cancel.
- If you cancel within 60 days after receiving the contract (30 days for a used car), you are entitled to a full refund if you have not filed any claim under the extended warranty.
- If you cancel within 60 days (30 days for a used car) and you have filed a claim under the extended warranty, you are entitled to a partial refund based on elapsed time or mileage specified in the contract.
- If you cancel after 60 days (or 30 days for used cars), you are entitled to a partial refund (based on elapsed time or mileage), regardless of whether you have filed a claim under the extended warranty. The dealer may hold back a $25 fee.

Where to Complain
If you are having a problem with an independent company's extended service contract—for example, the company is stalling on paying for covered repairs or the

company has gone out of business—contact the underwriter (insurance company) listed in the contract. If the underwriter doesn't respond to your problem, contact the California Department of Insurance at (800) 927-4357.

If you are having a problem with a manufacturer's extended service contract, contact the California New Motor Vehicle Board at 1507 21st Street, Suite 330, Sacramento, CA 95814, (916) 445-1888.

AUTOMOBILE LEASING

People often ask whether leasing (as opposed to buying) a motor vehicle makes sense. Auto leasing will ultimately cost more money than buying a car outright, but for many people it works well because most lease transactions require no down payment. It also works well for people who like driving new cars all the time. You can lease a car for a few years and then turn it back in and lease another. Day-to-day expenses should be about the same whether you buy or lease, because most leases hold you responsible for maintaining and insuring the car just as if you owned it.

There are two types of leases—open-end and closed-end.

Closed-End Lease

Virtually all auto leases are closed-end. With a closed-end lease, your monthly payments will be higher than with an open-end lease, but when the lease term is up, you give back the car and walk away owing nothing more. This assumes that you return the car undamaged, with no more than normal wear, and within the specified miles allowed under the lease. If you and the dealer dispute the value of the returned auto, under the Consumer Leasing Act you have the right to have an independent appraisal at your expense by someone approved by both of you.

⚠️ Most "approved" auto appraisers do most of their work for auto companies, which means you may not get an objective appraisal. This can be a serious problem since you are legally bound by the appraisal.

Open-End Lease

Few leases are open-end. They have lower monthly payments than closed-end leases, but there is a catch. If, at the end of your lease term, the car is worth less than the "estimated residual value" specified in your contract, you will owe the difference. And you will be required to pay it in one large balloon payment.

There is one exception. If the difference is more than three times what a monthly payment was, the amount owed is considered unreasonable. To recover the excess, the lessor must sue you and, even if successful, must pay your attorney's fees. This is what has lead to the virtual abandonment of open-end leases.

Where to Complain

The Department of Motor Vehicles (see below) handles complaints against leasing companies. If the company has violated the law, DMV may be able to help. If you just made a bad deal, DMV can't do much. A complaint form is available and can be filed at any DMV field office.

AUTOMOBILE INSURANCE

Liability Insurance Required by the State

California law requires all drivers to be financially responsible (able to pay) for damage caused by owning or operating an automobile up to the following amounts:

- bodily injury $15,000 per person/$30,000 per accident, and
- property damage of $5,000 per accident.

Some drivers comply by buying the minimum amount of liability auto insurance. Some drivers (mostly businesses) comply by putting up a bond with the state through the DMV. The bond consists of a $35,000 deposit made with a financial institution that turns over the passbook to the DMV. For more details, contact the DMV for a packet of information: DMV, Financial Responsibility, P.O. Box 942884, Sacramento, CA 94284-0001.

The required liability insurance protects you from the following types of potential risks up to the policy dollar limit:

- bodily injury liability insurance—injuries you cause to someone else while operating a motor vehicle, and
- property damage liability insurance—damage you caused to someone else's property, including another car, a street light, a telephone pole or a building, while operating a motor vehicle.

Other Suggested Types of Coverage

You may wish to consider these other automobile insurance coverage:

- Medical payments insurance—covers you, your family and other passengers injured in an accident, whether in your car or someone else's, up to the limits of your policy. If you have your own comprehensive health insurance, you may not need this coverage; however, it offers protection for other passengers.
- Uninsured motorists protection—covers bodily injuries (to you and other passengers in your car or someone else's car) caused by an uninsured or a hit-and-run driver. It also covers you if you are struck by an uninsured motorist while walking. Uninsured motorist property damage covers damage to your car if you can identify the uninsured car owner or driver or the vehicle license plate number. If you have collision, you do not need the uninsured motorist property damage coverage.
- Collision insurance—covers damage to your car in an accident involving another vehicle, another object (such as a wall or telephone pole) or as a result of turning over. Your insurance company pays to fix the damage (or the value of the car if it's totaled), less the amount of your deductible no matter who is at fault. Collision does not cover injuries or damage to others. Collision is required by lenders as a condition of obtaining a car loan. If a car you own outright is very old and has very little resale value, you may not want to pay for collision.
- Comprehensive physical damage insurance—covers loss resulting from fire, theft, vandalism or malicious mischief, glass breakage, windstorms or hail, water, floods, riots, explosions, earthquakes, falling objects, or a collision with an animal or bird. Comprehensive coverage does not apply to an accident involving another vehicle or object.

Collision and Comprehensive Insurance Deductibles

Collision and comprehensive insurance rarely pay 100% of a loss. You almost always have to pay a deductible amount. The insurance company then pays the amount over the deductible up to the policy limit. For example, if you have a $200 deductible and an accident caused $1,000 damage to your car, you would pay the first $200; the insurance company would pay $800. If the accident involved another vehicle (and the other driver was at fault), your insurance company should try to collect the entire $1,000 from the other driver's insurance company. If it does, you will get your $200 deductible back.

GET A HIGHER-DEDUCTIBLE
TO SAVE PREMIUM DOLLARS

The higher your deductible, the lower your premium (insurance payment) will be. Since I believe the main reason for having insurance protection is to cover you for a major loss, it makes good economic sense to keep a high deductible ($500-$1,000 or more). Yes, you will have to pay for any damage to your car up to the deductible, but the trade-off of lower premiums while maintaining good insurance coverage for major damage will save you money in the long run. Also, if you pay more for a lower deductible and make several small claims, your insurance company may not renew your policy.

Insurance Required by a Lender

If you are financing the purchase of a vehicle, your lender—be it a bank, savings and loan, credit union or finance company—will require you to have "physical damage coverage," including collision and comprehensive insurance. If you do not provide the lender with proof of insurance, the lender will purchase it for you and add the cost to your monthly payments. This insurance will be more expensive than you can buy on your own and will only cover the lender's ownership interest—not yours. Also, the lender's policy will not include liability coverage, so you will be breaking the law unless you purchase it separately.

If You Can't Find Auto Insurance

If you have a hard time finding auto insurance coverage, you can buy the required liability coverage through the California Assigned Risk Plan, a program designed to provide insurance for high-risk drivers. All auto insurers in California must take their pro rata share of high-risk drivers. Any licensed agent can help you with the application. You can call the plan directly at (800) 622-0954.

Policy Rates

Proposition 103 went into effect a few years ago. Its purpose is to help drivers pay fair and reasonable amounts for insurance. Under the law, insurance companies must determine automobile insurance rates and premiums using the following criteria, listed in order of importance:

- your driving record
- the number of miles you drive each year
- the number of years you have been driving, and
- other standards adopted by the Department of Insurance.

GET ENOUGH AUTO LIABILITY COVERAGE

With today's high medical costs, it's a good idea to purchase more than the required minimum liability coverage. If you get into an even moderately serious accident for which you are at fault, you'll likely face a claim for more than $15,000 per person/$30,000 per accident. If you don't have enough insurance to cover it, you'll be responsible to pay out of your own pocket which could wipe out your savings or force you to sell other assets. The good news is that the cost of additional liability coverage is often quite reasonable.

Also, your insurance carrier must offer you a "good driver" discount if:
- you have been licensed to drive for at least three years, and
- during the past three years, you have not had more than one violation point count against you.

The good driver discount is automatic for anyone who has been licensed to drive in California for the past three years. If you have been licensed to drive in another state or Canada for the past 18 months and meet the other good driver discount qualifications, argue to your insurance company that you are entitled to the discount. It's unlikely that your insurance company will offer you the discount—don't be afraid to ask about it or to even press for it.

If you qualify for the good driver discount, the rate charged to you must be at least 20% less than the rate would have been.

Policy Renewals

An insurance company may choose not to renew your policy based on your claims and/or driving record. Many insurance companies will not renew policies if drivers make too many claims. What constitutes "too many" depends on the company.

Premium Increases at Renewal Time

At renewal time, an insurance company will examine your claims record. If you—or other drivers—have made too many claims on your policy under which you were at fault, your premium probably will be increased. In addition, there is likely to be an increase if you have one or more moving violations.

The law prohibits an insurance company from increasing auto insurance premiums based on an accident in which you were not at fault. Insurance Code § 491.

Premium Increases Mid-Term

Insurance companies can change the rate during the first 60 days of verifying the rate and underwriting (determining the risk) of a new policy. After that time, they cannot change the premium even if they made an error.

Canceling an Insurance Policy

You have no grace period—additional time period to pay a premium beyond the due date—to pay auto insurance premiums. If the insurance company does not receive your payment by the due date, it can cancel the policy.

In addition, an insurance company which originally insured you may reject your application for coverage within the first 60 days, but it must give you at least ten days' notice. Generally, after 60 days, the only reasons an insurance company can cancel your policy are if:

* you fail to pay premiums
* you give false information on your application
* you commit fraud, or
* there is a major change in your risk to the insurance company—such as your driver's license gets suspended or revoked.

For failure to pay your premiums, the company must give you or the lienholder/lender ten days' notice of cancellation. For all other reasons, the company must give you or the lienholder/lender 20 days' notice prior to canceling.

If an insurance company cancels your policy, you will receive a pro-rata refund (the dollar amount for the time not covered). If you cancel the policy early, you are entitled to a partial refund. Most insurance companies, however, will refund less than the pro-rata share. Insurance companies view your voluntary cancellation as creating a "short-term" policy for which they are entitled to charge a higher premium "short-term rate" than a longer-term rate. Yes, in English, this amounts to a penalty for cancellation.

When Does a Policy Expire?

Policies expire at 12:01 a.m. (in the middle of the night) on the date payment is due. This should be so stated in the policy.

Making a Claim When Your Car Is Damaged

An insurance company cannot dictate which repair shop you must use. When your car is damaged, you take it to the repair facility of your choice, where the company's adjuster will inspect the damage and negotiate with the body shop to pay to fix your car. If you don't know where to go, you can ask the insurance company for names of repair shops it has a relationship with—this can help get the repairs done with the least possible inconvenience and delay to you. Always make sure any body shop is reliable and guarantees the work; ask the insurance company if it will back that guarantee. Get all promises in writing. Body shops that belong to the California Auto Body Association have committed themselves to upholding high standards of work.

Once your car is at a repair shop, find out in advance what must be done to release your car after the repairs have been made. Will the repair shop give you the car back without payment from the insurance company? Or, will you have to wait until the insurance company gets around to paying the body shop before your car is released? If so, call the company and make sure the check is cut promptly. Also, find out how your insurance company and body shop will handle or respond to hidden damage, or damage not immediately evident until the body shop starts to work on your car. Often, such problems have to await further inspection and approval by the company's claims adjuster, causing you delay and frustration.

Making a Claim When Your Car Is Totaled

If you have collision insurance and your insurance company indicates that your car has been "totaled" (the cost to repair the damage exceeds the value of the car), the company should offer you its fair market value. The same is true if an accident was someone else's fault and her insurance company is paying. Fair market value is what it takes to purchase a comparable vehicle (a vehicle of the same year and make, with like features and mileage). If your car has recently been repaired or reconditioned, its fair market value may be slightly more than the average value for a car of the same make and model.

If you feel the insurance company's offer is too low, you will need to establish that your car has a higher value. The *Kelly Blue Book* is one source of valuation information. This book, considered the auto dealer's "bible," is in libraries, banks, auto dealerships and California State Automobile Association (CSAA) offices. Many people, however, consider its prices 10% to 15% lower than prices on the open market. So also check the newspaper classified ads to see if you can find an equivalent vehicle being advertised for sale at a higher price than you've been offered. (The Sunday *Los Angeles Times* has one of the largest automobile classified sections in the country. But car prices tend to be a little lower in Southern California than in other parts of the state, so check local papers—if you're not in the southern part of the state—as well.) If you can produce photographs of your car in good condition and service and repair records to show how well you maintained it, you will help your case, especially if you recently made major repairs.

Making a Claim If You Must Rent a Car

If the accident was your fault, and you have rental car coverage in your policy (most policies provide this coverage), your insurance company will pay for a rental car. Usually, however, you have a dollar and time limit which often results in the company paying less than you need to rent even a modest rental car.

If the accident was the fault of the other driver, the other driver's insurance company has a responsibility to pay all "abnormal" transportation expenses reasonably incurred while your car is being repaired. It's your responsibility to get your car fixed promptly given the circumstances. You may have to fight to get reimbursement of a rental car, as many companies try not to pay. If you let the other driver's company know that you will take it to Small Claims Court over this issue, it probably will give in.

If Your Insurance Company Becomes Insolvent

California law requires a special surcharge on all auto, homeowners' and property insurance policies. The money collected from this surcharge is put into a "guaranty fund" to cover the cost of claims, up to $500,000 including the cost of legal defense, for any insured person whose company becomes insolvent.

More Information/Where to Complain

The California Department of Insurance licenses and regulates auto insurance companies and their agents. Call its toll-free number to ask questions or file a complaint at (800) 927-HELP. Although many people criticize the Department, often it can be effective in getting consumers a speedier response or more money from their insurance company than they can get on their own. If you feel your insurance company is giving you the run-around or is offering an unsatisfactory settlement, tell your insurance company you plan to file a complaint with the Department of Insurance and/or a radio, TV or newspaper "Action Line"—that may be enough of a threat to get better cooperation from your company. The Department of Insurance has free brochures on auto insurance and extended automobile service contracts.

AUTOMOBILE REPAIRS

The Department of Consumer Affairs, Bureau of Automotive Repair (BAR) licenses and regulates automobile repair facilities. Mechanics must give a written estimate for repair work and get your consent (over the telephone is sufficient) before proceeding with any additional work. Auto repair shops must provide an invoice itemizing the work done and the parts supplied. You are also entitled to receive all replaced parts, but you must ask for them when you bring your car in for service.

If you have a complaint or a dispute with a mechanic, call BAR at (800) 952-5210. BAR will send you a complaint form. A BAR representative will try to help you get any dispute resolved. If the mechanic or repair shop has violated the law, BAR can take necessary action.

Botched automobile repairs are the bane of all car owners. If you have a repeated problem with getting your car repaired, talk to the owner of the dealership. If the owner is not available, discuss the problem with the manager. If the dealership can't fix your car, ask to have the manufacturer's representative inspect the car. If you're still not successful, a consumer hotline with a radio, TV station or newspaper might be able to get the problem resolved. If that fails, invoke the lemon law procedure.

If Your Car Is a Lemon

The intent of the "new car lemon law" is to protect buyers of new cars that have serious problems which can't be fixed. It sounds better on paper than in reality. The lemon law applies to new motor vehicles purchased (or leased for more than four months) for personal or family use only. It does not apply to motor homes, motorcycles or off-road vehicles.

Here is how the lemon law works: If, during the first 12 months or first 12,000 miles of the car's warranty period, a defect covered by the warranty that substantially reduces the use, value or safety of the car can't be fixed, you are presumed to be entitled to a refund or replacement. If, during the car's warranty period (but after the first 12 months or first 12,000 miles, assuming your warranty period is longer), a defect covered by the warranty that substantially reduces the use, value or safety of the car can't be fixed, you may be entitled to a refund or replacement—but you are not automatically presumed to be entitled. To invoke the lemon law presumption, either of the following must be true:

- The dealer attempts to repair the defect at least three times and the manufacturer attempts a repair at least once.
- The vehicle is out of service for any combination of defects for more than 30 days during the 12 month/12,000 mile period, not counting delays beyond the control of the dealer and the manufacturer.

To get a new vehicle or a refund, you must get a favorable ruling from a third-party arbitration program, such as the Ford or Chrysler Consumer Appeals Board, the American Automobile Association or the Better Business Bureau, which is the authorized lemon law arbitrator for more than a dozen manufacturers including General Motors. Even if your car is truly a lemon, the outcome of arbitration may not be a new car; however, you have a better chance of finally getting the car fixed right if there is a problem that can be detected. The manufacturer is bound by the arbitrator's decision, but you still have the right to sue the manufacturer if you are dissatisfied with the arbitrator's decision.

INVESTIGATE SECRET AUTOMOBILE WARRANTIES

Many automobile manufacturers have "secret warranties" in addition to the written warranty you receive. Often, the secret warranty applies when a manufacturer is aware that a particular vehicle is prone to a problem shortly after the standard warranty runs out and doesn't want the bad publicity that lawsuits will generate. Normally, however, the manufacturer will make the repair without charge only for consumers who persistently complain. The Center for Auto Safety (listed below) has information on secret warranties. Most dealers and manufacturers will deny that secret warranties exist—don't believe them.

Beginning January 1, 1994, a manufacturer must inform car owners and leasers about any secret warranties it has. Dealers, too, must inform customers whether their repairs are covered by a free-repair program. Dealers must also post notices telling consumers how to obtain information on free-repair programs. Civil Code § 1795.90 and following.

More Information/Where to Complain

The California Department of Consumer Affairs has a free booklet called *Lemon-Aid for New Car Buyers.* For a copy, contact the Department of Consumer Affairs, Publications, 400 R Street, Sacramento, CA 95814. For single copies, you can call the BAR at (916) 445-1254, or the New Motor Vehicle Board at (916) 445-1888. For multiple copies, call the BAR at (916) 323-7239.

Lemon Book, written by Ralph Nader and Clarence Ditlow (Moyer Bell Limited), has useful information on buying new and used cars, how to avoid buying a lemon and legal remedies for lemon owners.

The National Highway Traffic Safety Administration has an auto safety "hotline" you can call to find out if your vehicle has a federally mandated recall or is under investigation for safety problems. Also, you can report defects and request other safety information. The Administration can be reached at (800) 424-9393 between 5:00 a.m. and 1:00 p.m., pacific standard time. For more detailed information about defects and problems that the "hotline" can't answer, call the Technical Reference Division at (202) 366-2768. There may be a charge ($20 to $35 range) for this service depending on the scope of the information you need.

The Center for Auto Safety (Ralph Nader's group) can provide you with the following information:

- available complaint information about your year, make and model of car
- information about secret warranties, or
- lists of attorneys in your area who specialize in lemon law cases.

For any of this information, send a business-size, self-addressed, stamped envelope with 52¢ postage to the Center for Auto Safety, 2001 S Street, NW, Suite 410, Washington, DC 20009. If you have questions, you can call the Center at (202) 328-7700.

The California Department of Motor Vehicles licenses and regulates new and used car dealers and salespersons. It will investigate problems with a dealer, such as misrepresentation (selling a used car as new, last year's model as this year's) failure to honor a warranty, failure to transfer documents (title, registration, license plates), failure to return a down payment, trade-in or deposit on a sale that fell through, odometer tampering or overcharging for license fees.

You can obtain and file a complaint form at any DMV field office. (Check the phone book white pages Government listings.)

The California New Motor Vehicle Board regulates dealers, manufacturers and distributors of new cars, trucks and motorcycles. If you think you have a lemon law case, file a complaint with the Board. The Board will give you helpful advice to make sure you follow proper procedures and will make inquiries on your behalf with dealers and manufacturers. It cannot, however, enforce the lemon law. In addition, the Board has jurisdiction over warranty disputes, manufacturer's defects, questionable sales practices and advertising. The Board can be reached at 1507 21st Street, Suite 330, Sacramento, CA 95814, (916) 445-1888.

RESPONSIBILITIES OF AUTOMOBILE OWNERSHIP

Registration and Smog Tests

Every year, car owners must renew their auto registration and pay a fee. Generally, a bill comes in the mail; even if you do not receive a bill, you are required to renew by the registration date to avoid paying late fees. After paying the fee, the current registration is returned to you along with a sticker indicating the month your registration expires.

Any unpaid parking tickets will show up on your vehicle registration. You cannot register your vehicle without paying off the outstanding tickets. If you believe the ticket is not yours, you can pay the registration fee (without paying the ticket). DMV can tell you who reported the unpaid ticket. Write to that court or agency (which may be a private company under contract with the city to collect parking fines) explaining why the unpaid ticket isn't yours. Include a copy of your auto registration and the color, model and other descriptions of your car. You probably will not get a written response—you'll have to keep checking with DMV to see if your record has been cleared.

Registering a Used Car

A car's original registration date remains the same for the life of the car. If your new car was originally registered in March, it will always have a March registration date as indicated by a sticker on the back license plate. When you buy a used car, if the vehicle's registration is current, you only pay a small transfer fee as the new owner.

Registering an Out-of-State Car

Vehicles based or used primarily in California must be registered within 20 days of being brought into the state. (There are exceptions for military personnel and their dependents.) Vehicle Code § 4000.4. If you fail to do this, you may be cited and fined, or you may get a fix-it ticket that allows you to get the car registered in a certain time period for a $10 fee.

BUYING AN UNREGISTERED CAR CAN BE COSTLY

Always look at the registration month and year on the back license plate to avoid any surprises later. If you buy a used car with an expired registration, you will have to pay the past year's registration fee to make it current. (You can try to defray the cost by negotiating with the seller to subtract the amount from the price.) You could end up paying for the coming year's registration shortly after paying for the prior year's registration.

Smog Tests

Your car must pass a smog test every other year in order to renew your registration. Comparison shop before getting a smog check; the rates range from $20 to $73 or more. Most vehicles that don't pass the smog check inspections need only minor, inexpensive repairs or adjustments, because of problems such as a carburetor mixture that is too rich, spark plugs or wires that need cleaning or replacing, a clogged filter or a vacuum leak.

Smog check stations may charge varying amounts to bring your car into compliance depending on the model year of your vehicle:

Model Year	Allowed Charge
1966-71	$ 50
1972-74	$ 90
1975-79	$ 125
1980-89	$ 175
1990 and newer	$ 300

If your vehicle cannot be brought into compliance within the cost limit, call the Bureau of Automotive Repair (BAR) at (800) 952-5210. BAR may refer you to a Referee Station to issue you a waiver. If your emissions control equipment (smog equipment) has been removed, modified or disconnected, the cost limits do not apply—you must pay whatever it takes to get your car to comply.

- New cars: If your car is still under warranty, you are entitled to have defects that cause it to fail a smog test corrected for free by the dealer.
- Used cars: The seller is required to give the buyer an original smog certificate, not more than 90 days old. If the vehicle is being transferred to a person's grandparent, parent, spouse, child or grandchild, the old owner does not have to supply a smog certificate. If you renewed your car registration (which required a smog certificate) within 90 days of selling your car, you will have to pay for another smog check in order to provide the buyer with an original smog certificate. DMV will not accept a computer printout of the first smog certificate.
- Diesel vehicles: Diesel vehicles are exempt from smog checks. Owners can fill out the back of their auto renewal registration exempting themselves if the vehicle

registration indicates the vehicle is a diesel. If the registration says "gasoline fueled," the owner must have the car examined by a BAR referee station to get an exemption.

- Out-of-state purchased vehicles: California smog controls are the most stringent in the nation—in fact, the term "49 stater" refers to a vehicle with smog control devices legal in all states but California. Be careful when purchasing an automobile in another state or overseas that you plan to bring into California. Some cars can never be registered in this state.

Where to Complain

If you have a complaint (or suspect fraud) about a mechanic doing smog inspections, contact the Bureau of Automotive Repair (BAR) at (800) 952-5210.

Driver's Licenses

Renewal by Mail

Drivers under age 70 who have no traffic convictions for moving violations and have no more than one non-citable accident during the past two years are eligible to renew their driver's license by mail. Most drivers with good driving records (parking tickets don't count) will be eligible for up to two renewals by mail without taking any written test. If you want a new picture, go to a DMV office and pay $12—you won't have to take a driver's test if you are otherwise exempt. Driver's license renewals by mail are sent to you approximately 60 days before your license expires. You can also apply for mail renewal without waiting to see if the DMV will send you a notice. To do this, request a Renew-by-Mail form from a local DMV office or by calling DMV's main office at (916) 657-7669.

Revoked or Suspended Driver's License

Your driver's license can be suspended or revoked for reckless driving, driving under the influence (DUI) of drugs or alcohol, not having insurance/financial responsibility, filing a fraudulent license application, or having too many moving violations. If your license is revoked or suspended for reasons other than driving under the influence, make an appointment for advice with a driver safety referee at any DMV office. Depending on the reason for the revocation or suspension, you may be able to retain limited driving privileges, such as driving to and from work. It is up to the discretion of the driver safety referee.

If You Are in an Accident

If you are in an auto accident on a public street or highway, or on private property, resulting in injury or death of any person, or property damage of $500 or more to property other than your own, you must file an accident report (form SR-1) with the DMV within ten days. Even if you filed a report with the police or your insurance company, you still must report the accident to the DMV. If you fail to report an accident or to provide insurance information to the DMV, the DMV will suspend your driver's license until you do file the report.

If You Don't Have Insurance

If you are in an accident that must be reported to the DMV, you'll need to provide insurance or financial responsibility information. If you do not have insurance, your driver's license will be suspended for a year. If you get insurance and pay a $250 fine to the DMV, you may be able to get a restricted license which allows you to drive to and from (and in) your work. Falsifying proof of insurance can result in fines of up to $500 and/or 30 days in jail. Vehicle Code § 16028. If you buy insurance to regain your driving privileges, you must keep that insurance for three years.

If you are trying to save money, don't think you can get away with canceling that insurance policy in a few months or next year. If you cancel the policy, the insurance company will notify the DMV and your license will be suspended again.

If You Tint Your Windows

Automobile tinted windows may or may not be legal, depending on who did the tinting. Only the following tinted windows are legal in California:

- automobile windows tinted by the manufacturer in the factory, and
- automobile windows tinted by the dealership and located in the side rear (rear passenger seats) or the rear of the car—and you must have two outside mirrors.

Other tinted windows are not legal because the tinting tends to be too dark. The California Highway Patrol (CHP) may cite you if you're tinted window is illegal. The CHP will give you a fix-it ticket. If you remove the tinting, you won't have to pay the penalty and the ticket will be dismissed.

If You Sell Your Vehicle

When you sell your car, fill out the yellow notice of release of liability that is kept with your pink slip (the title/ownership paper) and mail it within five days to the DMV. (DMV has copies of this form if you need one.) If you don't send the release of liability form to the DMV, you will still be considered the registered owner and may be held responsible for future parking tickets or if the car is in an accident. The release must be filled out completely and accurately or it will not release your liability. Make a photocopy for your records and keep it indefinitely. The information required includes: vehicle license number, auto manufacturer, vehicle identification number, date, selling price, the odometer reading, buyer's name and address, and seller's name, address and signature.

AUTOMOBILE RENTALS

If you have the time before renting a car, compare price differences for the same type of car—compact, economy, mid-size or luxury. Ask the base rate, per-mile charge, free mileage allowance, cost of additional miles, daily, weekend or weekly rates, drop-off charges, and available discounts (such as AAA membership).

Bear in mind that most, if not all, rental contracts state that all charges are subject to a final audit after you turn in the car and pay. If a mistake has been made, an additional charge will appear on your credit card.

California's Automobile Rental Laws

Several consumer protection laws have been adopted in California to protect car renters. They include the following:

- A rental company cannot require that you purchase optional insurance, goods or services, such as Collision Damage Waiver (CDW)—collision protection for drivers.
- A rental company may not charge more than $9 a day for CDW.
- A rental company may not engage in any unfair, deceptive or coercive conduct to induce you to purchase optional features such as CDW.
- A rental company may not debit or block your credit card account for an amount equal to a deposit if you decline to purchase optional services such as CDW.
- A rental company may not seek to recover any portion of a claim arising out of damage to, or loss of, the rented vehicle by processing a credit card charge or debit or block your credit card.
- A rental company may only advertise, quote and charge a rental rate that includes the entire amount, except taxes and a mileage charge, if any.

CDW Protection

If you buy CDW, the rental company cannot hold you responsible for damage, unless (this is a partial list):

- Damage or loss is a result of intentional, willful, wanton or reckless conduct—some rental companies try to use this terminology to refuse to pay off on routine negligence.
- You were driving under the influence of drugs or alcohol.
- You were driving while towing or pushing something.
- You were driving on an unpaved road.
- You were driving in a speed contest, or using the car in connection with a felony.

Who Pays for Rental Car Damage

You are responsible for all collision damage to a rented vehicle even if someone else causes the damage—if the other person does pay, you should be reimbursed—or the cause is unknown. Your liability extends to the cost of repair up to the value of the vehicle, as well as loss of use, and towing, storage and impound fees. Your own auto insurance policy will likely cover this (less your deductible) for a rented vehicle. So check with your insurance agent before purchasing Collision Damage Waiver coverage. In addition, Visa and MasterCard provide the same protection offered by CDW for some renters who use their credit card to pay for the car rental. These companies have cut back their coverage, however, so be sure you know exactly what is or is not covered before assuming your credit card company will pay for damage.

BEWARE OF UNREGISTERED RENTAL CARS

The California Vehicle Code states that the driver (not the owner) is responsible for having current registration tags. When you rent a car, always ask for the name of the manager of the rental office and write it on the rental contract. If the California Highway Patrol stops you for a late or expired registration, the officer will issue the citation to the rental agency manager only if you have his name; otherwise the officer will cite you. Out-of-state policies vary; don't risk the kindness of the officer—have the manager's name.

TRAFFIC TICKETS

Traffic tickets are one of the unavoidable hassles of modern life. If the other person gets one, she probably deserved it (and possibly may drive more responsibly in the future). On the other hand, if you get one, chances are the officer was being unreasonable. So much for human nature. Here is some practical information that should help if you are ticketed.

Moving Violations

Many traffic offenses are infractions, which means that you cannot be sentenced to jail if you are convicted. The maximum fine for a first offense is $290. Most of these offenses are reported to the DMV, and go on your driving record; this may affect your insurance rates. Your license may also be suspended if you get numerous violations.

Speeding

It is always illegal to exceed 55 MPH, unless you are on a freeway where the posted speed limit is 65 MPH. Vehicle Code §§ 22349, 22356. A speeding citation can also be given if you exceed a safe speed. This is called the basic speed law. The basic speed law prohibits only driving faster than is reasonable or prudent, considering conditions such as weather, visibility, traffic and the condition and size of the roadway, or driving at a speed that endangers people or property. Surprisingly, it is not necessarily illegal to exceed the posted limit on a street. The posted limit is presumed to be the fastest speed at which you can drive safely, but if the conditions merit, you may be speeding while driving beneath the posted limit, or driving safely above the limit. Vehicle Code §§ 22350, 22351.

Not Stopping

You can be cited if you fail to come to a complete stop at a stop sign. You must stop at the limit line, crosswalk or the entrance to the intersection. You can also be cited for failure to stop if you enter an intersection while a stop light is red. (But as long as your front bumper enters the intersection while the light is yellow, you have not committed this offense.) Vehicle Code §§ 22450, 21453.

Blocking the Box

You cannot enter an intersection unless there is enough room for you to get across without blocking traffic from either side. This is known as the Anti-Gridlock act. It is most often enforced when traffic is heavy or stopped, and vehicles are stuck in the intersection after the light changes. Vehicle Code § 22526.

Improper Turning

There are several offenses related to turning (Vehicle Code §§ 22100-22106):

- *Staying to the right or left edge of the road:* You must stay as close as practicable to the right or left edge of the street (traveling in your direction) when turning right or left.

- *Prohibited U-turns:* You may not make a U-turn if a sign prohibits it. In a business district, you can make a U-turn only at an intersection or opening in a divided highway. In a residential district, you can make a U-turn at any intersection that has a stop sign or light, or anywhere else as long as no car is approaching within 200 feet.

- *Unsafe turning and lane changes:* You must pull out and back up from a stopped position safely. You must signal turns for 100 feet before turning, and you must signal lane changes similarly if there is anyone behind you in any lane traveling in your direction.

Failure to Yield to Pedestrians

Drivers must yield the right-of-way to pedestrians who are crossing the street in a marked crosswalk or who are crossing at an intersection in an unmarked crosswalk. An unmarked crosswalk is the part of the street that would connect sidewalks on either side of an intersection. Vehicle Code § 21950(a).

Miscellaneous Violations

A number of moving violations can be fairly lumped together under the category of rudeness. These include failure to yield the right of way, failure to yield to pedestrians, driving too slowly, blocking traffic, tailgating, driving improperly in a car-pool lane and improper passing.

Dealing With an Infraction Citation

You have several options for dealing with infraction citations. You can:

- pay the fine
- go to traffic school and pay the fine (if you do this, the offense won't go on your record)
- plead "guilty with an explanation" at an informal hearing or arraignment, and hope that the judge will give you a smaller fine, or
- plead not guilty and fight the ticket.

If you decide to fight the ticket, you will appear before a judge at a trial. You may bring witnesses or evidence if you wish, and you will have the opportunity to cross-examine the officer who cited you. If the officer does not show up, you will be found innocent: the law requires that you be proven guilty, and only the officer's testimony can do that. This may change, however, as some courts allow the officer's notes to be introduced at trial, even if the officer isn't present.

Additional Resources

Fight Your Ticket, by attorney David Brown (Nolo Press), is an excellent guide to fighting moving violations. It doesn't cover parking tickets.

Parking Tickets

Parking tickets are big business for the cities and towns that issue them—San Francisco, for example, took in $44 million on parking citations in fiscal year 1992.

If You Don't Pay

Parking tickets won't affect your driving record, as long as you take care of them by either paying the fine or fighting the ticket. But if you accumulate too many parking tickets or wait too long to pay them, the penalties can be severe. The issuing city or county will notify the DMV, which will refuse to renew your registration until you have paid your fines plus an administrative fee. If you get five or more parking tickets in a five-day period, or if your car has no valid license plates, your car can be immobilized (using a Denver Boot) or towed and stored until you pay the fines. Vehicle Code §§ 22651, 22651.7.

How to Fight a Parking Ticket

As of July 1, 1993, parking tickets are no longer processed by the courts (except for appeals). They are, instead, handled by the city or county which issued the ticket, or a private business which handles tickets for the city or county. To contest a parking ticket, you now have to contact the office listed on the ticket and explain in writing within 21 days why you don't think you should have to pay. If the office won't dismiss the ticket within ten days of receiving your letter, then you can request a hearing by mailing the fine within 15 days. You will then be notified by mail of a hearing date. If you win, the fine is refunded to you.

If a Parking Ticket Is Not Yours

When a parking ticket left on a windshield is not paid, the traffic agency will mail a notice to the registered owner. Traffic agencies have computer access to DMV records; if the meter person transposes numbers on a car license plate when writing the ticket or the agency employee enters the wrong license number into the computer, notice to pay up will be sent to the wrong person.

If you receive such a notice and the ticket isn't for you, write to the processing agency, whose address and phone number is on the ticket. Enclose the following:

- either the original or a photocopy of the ticket—keep the other for yourself
- an explanation of where you were at the time—for example, your car was in the company parking lot while you were at work and your boss can corroborate
- a photocopy of your current automobile registration, and
- any descriptions of your vehicle not on the registration, such as color and model of the car, to show that your car does not match the description on the original ticket.

This should solve the problem, although don't expect the processing agency to send you a notice clearing your record. Unless you follow-up, you may not know if the problem was resolved until you re-register your car.

Seat Belt and Child Restraint Requirements

California requires all passengers to wear a seat belt or other safety restraint.

Seat Belts

Every passenger over the age of four must wear a seat belt, unless a disability prevents him from doing so. If any passenger is not wearing a seat belt when the car is pulled over, the driver may get a ticket. In addition, any passenger over the age of 16 who is not wearing a seat belt may be personally cited. The fine for a first offense is $20.

The owner of a vehicle is personally responsible for maintaining seat belts in working order. If a car is pulled over and the seat belts are not in usable condition, the owner may be cited, even if she is not in the car at the time.

The law used to prohibit officers from stopping cars only for suspected seat belt violations; only if the driver was pulled over for another suspected offense could the officer issue a seat belt citation. Police and highway patrol officers, however, are now allowed to stop drivers for seat belt violations alone. Vehicle Code § 27315.

Car Seats for Children

Every child under the age of four or weighing less than 40 pounds must be in a "child passenger restraint system"—a government-approved child car seat, usually with a harness, that fits into a passenger seat—while riding in a vehicle. The person who gets the ticket is the child's parent or the driver, if no parent is in the car. The fine for a first offense is $100.

A police officer can stop a car if she suspects that a child in the car is not in a proper car seat. Vehicle Code §§ 27360, 27361.

TOWING CARS FROM PRIVATE PROPERTY

A private property owner may have a vehicle towed from his property if signs are clearly posted at every entrance. The signs must:

- be at least 17 x 22 inches in size
- contain lettering not less than one inch in height
- state that public parking is prohibited
- state that vehicles will be towed at owner's expense
- contain the telephone number of the local law enforcement agency, and
- include a statement that a citation may be issued for the violation under Vehicle Code § 22658(a). (Including this statement is optional.)

If you remove a vehicle from your property, beware of the towing and/or storage charge you pass on to the owner of the vehicle. Such a charge is considered excessive if it is greater than a charge that would have been requested by a law enforcement agency. A person who charges an excessive towing or storage charge is liable to the vehicle owner for four times the amount charged. Vehicle Code § 22658 (i) and (j).

TRUCKS/TRUCKERS

You may have some relief from trucks that spew flying rocks off the back of their open-bed big rigs. Under California law, truckers are required to cover their loads with a tarp. In addition, they must install mud flaps and seal cargo areas; however, the law allows truckers to leave their loads uncovered if they do not fill the truck container above six inches from the top.

If Flying Debris Damages Your Vehicle

- Get the Cal. T., C.A. or PUC number on the driver's side of the truck. These are the California Public Utilities Commission (CPUC) license numbers. With one of the numbers, CPUC can give you the company's insurance company and policy number. Call CPUC at (800) 877-8867.
- Note the time and the location on the road.
- File a report in person with the California Highway Patrol; the nearest office can be found in the telephone book white pages, Government section, State of California.
- The trucking company is apt to deny responsibility even if its records show the truck was in the location at the time the incident occurred. If so, either contact your own insurance company if you have "comprehensive coverage" and the damage estimate exceeds your deductible, or take the trucking company to Small Claims Court.

TIP

WINDSHIELD REPAIR

Several glass companies (look in the yellow pages of your telephone book) repair pits and small cracks in windshields for much less money than the cost of replacing the window. This procedure works best when the damage occurs in the corners or outer edges of the windshield. It may not be a good idea if the area to be repaired is in the center of your line of vision—a repair instead of a replacement could distort your ability to see clearly.

REAL ESTATE, HOMES AND NEIGHBORS

HOME SALES

REAL ESTATE

Buying or selling a house is a major undertaking. For many families, it's the largest financial transaction they will ever make. To help make good decisions and reduce anxiety, inform yourself about all aspects of the transaction.

Residential Property Disclosure Rules

California law requires the seller of a home to disclose significant defects when transferring (selling) residential property of one to four units. (Sales pursuant to a probate sale, bankruptcy sale, foreclosure sale, guardianship sale, between co-owners or spouses, or by a government entity are excepted.) This is done by filling out a "Real Estate Transfer Disclosure Statement." Civil Code § 1102. The defects to disclose include:

- neighborhood nuisances, such as noise and traffic
- environmental hazards
- whether or not work done on the house was according to local building codes
- restrictions on the use of the property
- defects such as a leaky roof or poor electrical wiring, and
- whether or not the house lies in a flood hazard or earthquake hazard zone or has any potential earthquake problems.

The seller has no liability for problems that arise after the sale as long as she discloses the known defects beforehand. If she (or her agent) fails to disclose a known defect in a house you buy, however, you have a good chance of recovering damages if you sue. The statute of limitations is only two years, so do not delay if filing a lawsuit becomes necessary.

The Real Estate Transfer Disclosure Statement clearly states that it is not a warranty, and is not a substitute for a buyer having a home inspection or buying a home warranty from an insurance company.

Property You Want to Buy Must Be Appraised

All financial institutions require a property appraisal (by a licensed real estate appraiser) before agreeing to finance a purchase or to refinance an existing loan. Some appraisers are criticized for making appraisals to satisfy the needs of one or another party to a transaction—that is, of not being objective. If you are unhappy with the result of your appraisal, you can often insist on a second one. (See section below on Home Inspections for more information.)

RESIDENTIAL DEFECTS AND DISCLOSURES

Proving that a seller knew about a defect before the sale and failed to disclose it can be tough. Sure, if there are water stains on the ceiling it would seem obvious there is, or was, a leaking roof or plumbing, but other defects are less obvious. If you honestly feel a defect should have been known to the seller and disclosed to you, contact the agent/broker and the seller and ask for the money to correct the problem. If you are turned down and believe you can document that the defect was longstanding and should have been known to the seller, you may want to sue both the agent/broker and seller in Small Claims Court (up to $5,000). If more is involved, consider obtaining legal advice.

Get a Copy of the Appraisal

Lenders require homebuyers to pay for real estate appraisals conducted by the lender. Most major banks in California make those appraisals available to homebuyers on demand. A lender may refuse, however to give you a copy of the appraisal you paid for. If that happens, tell the lender you will sue in Small Claims Court for the cost of, or a copy of, the appraisal. I bet you will get the appraisal. Not many lenders will try to justify this ridiculous nondisclosure policy in front of a judge.

Fixtures Normally Included in a House Sale

A contract to sell real estate must be in writing, signed by both the buyer and the seller, to be valid. The contract should specifically delineate what is and what is not included in the sale. As a general rule, anything that is permanently attached by means of cement, plaster, nails, bolts or screws is considered a fixture and is included in the sale as part of the home. This includes wall-to-wall carpeting, chandeliers, drapery rods, bookcases, built-in appliances and cabinets affixed to the walls. If the appliances, rugs or window coverings are not built-in, they normally are not part of the sale and belong to the seller. Despite this general rule, sellers and buyers often negotiate to remove a fixture which otherwise would be included in the sale or to include portable items which otherwise would belong to the seller.

Buyers—Getting a Deposit Back if You Change Your Mind

When you submit a written offer to purchase a house, it's common for your to spell out exactly what will happen to your deposit if the deal falls through. If the seller accepts your offer and a contract is formed, you will make out your deposit check to a title or escrow company which will deposit it in the company's trust account. Most offers are contingent upon the buyer getting financing and the house getting a clean bill of health when inspected. If a required pest control, general contractor, soils or other report is unsatisfactory, you are entitled to get your deposit back.

If all your contingencies can be satisfied under the terms of your offer and you still back out, however, the seller is legally entitled to keep at least a portion of your deposit. To avoid court fights as to how much the seller has been damaged and, therefore, how much of the deposit he should keep, most contracts have a "liquidated damages" clause setting out in advance how much the seller gets to keep if the buyer breaks the contract. California law generally prohibits sellers from keeping more than 3% of the agreed-upon sale price as liquidated damages.

BUYER'S DEPOSIT—RECOVERY RIGHTS

It is not unusual for a seller to refuse to sign a deposit release allowing the buyer to recover his deposit if a sale does not go through. Neither party can have the deposit without the other party's signature; the money just stays in the trust account. The best protection for a buyer is to make a modest deposit in the first place, preferably 1% of the sales price, which is below the Small Claims Court limit of $5,000 for many houses. If the seller refuses to release the deposit, and the buyer has a valid reason spelled out in the contract entitling him to have the money returned, the buyer should send a demand letter to the seller advising that he will take the seller to Small Claims Court and ask for an order that the money be returned.

Additional Resources

How to Buy a House in California, by Ralph Warner, Ira Serkes and George Devine (Nolo Press), covers every aspect of buying a house in California, including raising money for the down payment, choosing the best mortgage, working with real estate agents and proceeding through escrow.

For Sale by Owner, by George Devine (Nolo Press), provides everything a person needs to handle the sale of his house from putting the house on the market to transferring title.

HOME INSPECTIONS

A thorough home inspection of a house should almost always be done when you buy or sell. A home inspector—who may be a general contractor or a licensed pest control inspector—will examine the major systems of a home, from the foundation to the roof and everything in between. The inspection will cover the plumbing and electrical work, heating and air conditioning systems, walls (inspectors do not move furniture), ceilings, floors, windows and doors. The inspector will give you both an oral and a written report, with average costs ranging from $200 to $400. Home inspectors give you an evaluation of the condition of a home, not a guarantee. Other inspectors conduct structural pest control inspections for about $150.

Home inspectors do not normally:

- check for asbestos, radon or other environmental hazards—they may tell you if the house has asbestos insulation and the seller must disclose any known asbestos; otherwise, you need a specialized inspection by an expert
- check the workings of appliances
- verify if home improvement work on the building was done with necessary permits
- provide structural pest control service (except for inspectors so designated), or
- evaluate soil conditions.

General Contractors and Structural Pest Control Inspectors

For a house to be thoroughly inspected, you will probably need two inspections—one by a licensed general contractor (licensed as a contractor, not as a home inspector) and another by a structural pest control inspector to check for termite and pest damage. If you are a buyer, make your written offer to buy contingent upon receiving satisfactory inspection reports from both.

If you or your general contractor suspects additional problems, consider hiring a specialist to look at the house's wiring, plumbing, roofing or foundation. This is especially wise for an older home in a high price range. Obviously, you will have to determine whether the extra cost is worth the potential benefit.

ACCOMPANY YOUR HOME INSPECTOR

If you hire someone to inspect a house, go with her on her inspection—it should take about two hours. Wear comfortable clothes—you should be going into attics and crawl spaces. Don't be afraid to ask questions along the way. You are probably engaged in one of the most expensive transactions of your life—you should see for yourself the true condition of the house you are selling or considering buying. The more expensive the house, the more you want to be sure you're getting your money's worth. If the inspector fails to thoroughly check any area—perhaps it's hard to reach—pay extra for a more thorough inspection.

For Buyers

A thorough home inspection reveals the real condition of the structural, mechanical, electrical, and other systems of a home. With this information, you can decide whether current or potential problems are worth the repair price and hassle, or if you want to find another home. Often, when inspections reveal expensive problems, a buyer will want to renegotiate the price of the house with the seller. A purchase offer should be contingent upon approval of the inspection results.

For Sellers

By hiring a home inspector before putting your home on the market, you can learn what deferred maintenance needs correcting. By getting your home in tip-top shape, you may be able to get a better price. Even if you do not make the repairs, presenting the buyer with a detailed written report of the inspection along with the required Real Estate Transfer Disclosure Statement should help avoid the problem of renegotiating the contract at the last minute.

Finding a Home Inspector

Get recommendations from your real estate agent, as well as friends, neighbors, co-workers or relatives.

There are many semi-shady practices in the house inspection business. For example, some real estate agents recommend inspectors they know will not be too critical of a home's condition. That's not what you want. You want an extremely thorough home inspector, who can be a deal breaker if a report scares off potential buyers. Also, do not use a home inspector who also does repair work, as that person may reccomend expensive and unnecessary work if he thinks he'll get the job. Finally avoid new inspectors who have little or no training or experience.

One mark of a qualified home inspector is membership in the California Real Estate Inspection Association, a professional organization with extensive experience requirements as well as high standards for membership. This organization does not allow its members to do repair work.

More Information

For a referral of members, call the California Real Estate Inspection Association at (800) 388-8433.

How to Buy a House in California, by attorney Ralph Warner, Ira Serkes and George Devine (Nolo Press), is available in libraries and bookstores.

How to Inspect a House, by George Hoffman (Wesley-Addison), provides a good overview of how to inspect most structural elements of a house for major problems. It is available in libraries and bookstores.

The Termite Report, by Donald V. Pearman (Pear Publishing), provides a guide to discovering and repairing many hidden structural problems caused by termites, beetles and dry rot.

ESCROW

When buying or selling a house or other real estate, the transfer of money and related ownership documents is normally handled by a neutral and knowledgeable third party, normally an escrow or title company. The escrow holder carries out the written instructions given by the principal parties involved.

A typical escrow holder *does* the following:

- acts as a neutral "third party" communications link to all participants
- prepares escrow instructions under the authority of the contract between buyer and seller calling for the removal of various contingencies (such as financing and pest control report) before the deal goes through

- requests a preliminary title search (to find any liens or other encumbrances)
- requests a "beneficiary's statement" from the current lender stating the amount of the existing mortgage that must be paid off
- complies with the new mortgage lender's specifications
- receives purchase funds from the buyer
- prepares or secures the new deed and other documents
- prorates taxes, interest, insurance and rents according to their contract
- records deeds and any other requested documents
- requests issuance of the title insurance policy
- closes escrow when all instructions from buyer and seller have been completed
- disburses funds, including charges for title insurance, recording fees, real estate commissions, loan payoffs and sale proceeds, and
- prepares final statements for all parties outlining the disposition of all funds (useful in tax preparation).

The escrow holder *does not*:
- offer legal advice
- negotiate the transaction, or
- offer investment advice.

Title Searches and Insurance

When buying a house, you and your lender want to make sure the property is clearly yours and that no person or government entity has any rights, liens, claims or encumbrances against it. A title insurance company does an extensive search of relevant public records (available at the County Recorder's office) to determine if anyone has an ownership interest in the property you are buying. Usually, any title problems that are found, such as judgments or tax liens, can be cleared up before you purchase the property.

Once the record has been researched, the title company generally issues two types of title insurance policies:
- Lender's policies to cover the financial lending institution for the life of the loan. All institutional lenders require home buyers to purchase title insurance to protect the lender's investment in the home.
- Owner's policies to protect the buyer. Owner's title insurance is not required, but it's wise to buy it because the lender's policy doesn't cover you.

The major expense is in buying the lender's policy. The homeowner's policy costs a fraction of the lender's policy—for example, if the lender's policy costs $1,000, the homeowner's policy would probably cost about $100. Once a title insurance policy is issued, if a claim is ever filed against your covered property, the title company will pay the legal fees involved in defending your rights, as well as any covered losses arising from a valid claim. In California, there is a five-year statute of limitations to file a lawsuit on real estate title.

Where to Complain

Escrow companies—typically used in Southern California—perform escrow services only, although they usually arrange for a title company to issue title insurance. These are regulated by the California Department of Corporations.

Title companies—typically used in Northern California—issue title insurance and perform escrow functions. They are regulated by the California Department of Insurance. To file a complaint, call, (800) 927-HELP.

MORTGAGES (DEEDS OF TRUST)

Most homebuyers borrow money from a bank or other lender to finance the purchase. Home loans are usually called mortgages, although technically the legal instrument recorded at the County Recorder's Office is a deed of trust, not a mortgage.

Various entities, including banks, credit unions, savings and loans, insurance companies and mortgage companies, make home loans. Most financial institutions that lend money don't keep the majority of the loans they make in their portfolio, but rather sell them to investors on the "secondary mortgage market." Several large institutions, including the Federal National Mortgage Association (FNMA—Fannie Mae) and Federal Home Loan Mortgage Corporation (FHLMC—Freddie Mac), buy a large portion of these mortgages. But they buy only ones that conform to their rules, such as the size of loans made. The result is that most lenders follow these rules and many mortgages are remarkably similar.

To bypass lender rules and restrictions, many homebuyers borrow some or all mortgage money privately, that is, from parents, other relatives and friends. A second mortgage—financing by the seller—is another private source of mortgage money. Government-guaranteed financing is also an option for people purchasing moderately priced houses in many areas of California.

Mortgages come in many varieties. What's best for you depends on many variables—your income, amount of down payment, your credit history, the cost and location of the house you're buying and how long you plan on owning your home. *How to Buy a House in California*, by Ralph Warner, Ira Serkes and George Devine (Nolo Press), covers every aspect of buying a house in California. It particularly focuses on financing strategies that can save you thousands of dollars. Here's a brief overview of mortgages and home financing.

Fixed Rate Mortgage

The interest rate and the amount you pay each month remain the same over the entire mortgage term—typically 15 or 30 years—no matter what interest rates in general do. A fixed rate mortgage offers two main advantages:

- monthly payments don't change, even if interest rates rise, and
- you get the peace of mind of knowing exactly how much your total mortgage will cost.

Variations of a standard fixed rate mortgage are available that offer competitive interest rates and are attractive to people who will move or pay off their mortgages soon. These include:

- short-term fixed rate mortgages
- five-and seven-year fixed rate loans with balloon payments (of the remaining balance) at the end, and
- two-step mortgages with a lower-than-normal fixed rate for the first few years, which later steps up to the prevailing market rate after the initial period (often five years) ends.

SHORT-TERM FIXED RATE MORTGAGES VS. PREPAYING YOUR MORTGAGE

If you don't want to legally obligate yourself to the higher monthly payment of a short-term mortgage, you can still achieve huge interest savings by voluntarily paying more principal each month on a longer-term loan. Even prepaying a small amount each month makes a large difference in your total payment. For example, by paying an extra $50 per month on a 30-year, 8% fixed rate $100,000 mortgage, you'd repay the loan in 24 (not 30) years and save nearly $40,000 in interest. If you don't want to pay extra each month, consider making a yearly lump sum payment—perhaps when you receive your tax refund.

The Banker's Secret, by Marc Eisenson, is an easy-to-use computer program that comes with a manual explaining prepayment rules. It quickly calculates how much money and how many years you cut off a mortgage by pre-paying. A book with the same title is also available. For price and order information, contact Good Advice Press, P.O. Box 78, Elizaville, NY 12523, (800) 255-0899.

Adjustable Rate Mortgage (ARM)

The interest rates on these mortgages fluctuate according to interest rates in the economy. Initial interest rates are always lower than for fixed rate mortgages, which means ARMs let you qualify with a substantially lower income than for a comparable-size fixed rate loan. But if general interest rates go up too, so will ARM rates.

To avoid constant and drastic fluctuations, ARMs typically regulate (cap) how much and how often the interest rate and/or payments can change in a year and over the life of the loan. The interest rates of different ARMs are tied to different financial indexes, including the rates paid on three-month, six-month or one-year United States Treasury Bills (T-bills), the rate at which the London bank lends money (LIBOR) and the six-month CD rate, which is based on a mixture of long- and short-term treasury securities. Some of these indexes fluctuate up or down more quickly than others. In addition to looking at the volatility of an index, buyers need to consider the margin—the number of interest points the lender adds to the index to arrive at the interest rate of a particular ARM.

⚠ Beware of negative amortization, sometimes referred to by lenders as "deferred interest" or "interest advances." In simple terms, this provision takes away most of the advantages of a yearly percentage point cap typically found in ARMs, so that what you owe on your total mortgage will increase even though you made all required payments. While lenders who offer loans with negative amortization normally charge a slightly lower interest rate than do those lenders who market ARM loans without negative amortization, the difference isn't usually large enough to compensate for the added risk.

Several variations of ARMs are available, including the FIRM, which starts out as fixed rate loan tied to the then current interest rate and then changes to an adjustable rate loan after a certain number of years. Convertible ARMS are another option. While the interest rates of a convertible ARM are initially tied to the fluctuations of an interest-sensitive index (plus the lender's margin), a buyer can change to a fixed rate mortgage after a certain period of time—for example, two years—during a specified period (called the conversion window—it usually lasts about two weeks), without having to pay new loan fees.

An adjustable rate mortgage is sure to be cheaper than a fixed rate loan if you live in the house for less than about five to seven years and your ARM has no negative amortization feature, because you get all the benefit of the intitial lower interest rate.

Also, unlike fixed rate loans, most adjustable rate mortgages are assumable, meaning a buyer can take the loan over from a seller.

⚠ Avoid mortgages with prepayment penalities. Whether you have a fixed or an adjustable rate mortgage, you may want to pay it off early, either to save interest on your original mortgage or to refinance if interest rates drop. You want to be able to do this without paying the lender a penalty for the privilege. Generally, this isn't a problem, as loans rarely contain a penalty for early payment (called a prepayment penalty).

Down Payments and Private Mortgage Insurance (PMI)

Down payments are always a percentage of a house's purchase price, not a specific dollar figure. Most buyers put down 10%-25%, unless they qualify for one of the government mortgage guarantee or insurance programs which allow for no, or a very low, down payment.

If you take out a low down payment loan (less than 20%), be prepared to pay a slightly higher rate of interest and more points, and to show that you have an excellent credit history. In addition, you will probably have to purchase private mortgage insurance (PMI), which pays back the lender if you default and the foreclosure sale price is less than the amount you owe the lender (the mortgage and the costs of sale).

For a loan with 10% down, PMI costs about .5% of the loan at close of escrow for the first year's premium, with lower rates in subsequent years. You may drop PMI once your loan is no more than 75% of either the original purchase price or the current fair market value of the house, and you meet the following requirements (Civil Code § 2954.7):

- the house was purchased after January 1, 1991
- you own and live in a one-to-four-unit residential building
- you wait at least two years after taking out the loan
- the loan was not made by the California Housing Finance Agency
- you have not been more than 30-days overdue on any mortgage payment during the previous two years, and

- you make a written request to the lender based on an appraisal paid for by the homeowner.

Many lenders allow homeowners who purchased their home before January 1991 to drop PMI if they meet these same criteria.

Points, Interest Rates and Other Lender Fees

There are a variety of fees—and fee amounts—associated with getting a mortgage. Loan application fees of several hundred dollars cover the lender's cost of processing your loan. In addition, many lenders charge a fee for checking your credit. And if you make a low down payment, you'll likely be required to purchase private mortgage insurance. These items and others, such as the fee to appraise the house you want to purchase, are called closing costs and typically add 2% to 5% to the cost of your mortgage. Some lenders don't charge all these fees; those that do charge varying amounts.

Points comprise the largest part of lender fees. One point equals 1% of the loan principal. For example, two points on a $250,000 loan is $5,000.

Comparing Points to Interest

There is a direct relationship between the number of points lenders charge and the interest rates they quote for the same type (such as a fixed rate) mortgage. The more points you pay, the lower your rate of interest, and vice versa.

One method to compare loans with different points is to use the Annual Percentage Rate (APR) which lenders must disclose to borrowers under federal law. The APR can be misleading, however, because its method of calculating the cost of a loan as a yearly rate assumes that the loan will not be paid off until the loan term ends. While many loans are for 30 years, people generally pay off their loans before the loan term ends because they either move or refinance sooner; the result is that a loan with lots of points may be more expensive than one with fewer points (and a higher interest rate), even though the APR is the same.

So before comparing points to interest, factor in how long you plan to own your house. The longer you live in your house (or pay on the mortgage), the better off you'll be paying more points up front in return for a lower interest rate

Government-Assisted Loans

Four government-assisted mortgage programs are available to help Californians buy homes. These programs differ significantly in the types of homes that qualify, loan conditions and fees, but have a common purpose—to help an average family buy a modest house, with a very low down payment.

Federal Housing Administration (FHA)

The FHA (an agency of the U.S. Department of Housing and Urban Development—HUD) insures loans made to all U.S. citizens and permanent residents who meet financial qualification rules. Under its most popular program, if the buyer defaults and the lender forecloses, the FHA pays 100% of the amount insured. The major attraction of an FHA-insured loan is the low down payment—usually about 5%-7% of the the purchase price and closing costs. To find out more about FHA loans, call one of HUD's offices in California:

- Fresno—(209) 487-5604
- Los Angeles—(213) 251-7095
- Orange—(714) 836-2510
- Sacramento—(916) 551-1351
- San Diego—(619) 557-5305
- San Francisco—(415) 556-5900
- Santa Ana—(714) 957-7335.

FHA Mortgage Insurance Distributive Shares and Refunds

FHA-insured mortgages placed before September 1983 charged the borrower 1/2% a year for mortgage insurance premiums. If the mortgage had been in effect at least seven years before being paid off (through final payment or refinancing), sometimes refunds of excessive mortgage insurance premiums (called "distributive shares") may be due to the person making the final payment.

In addition, many FHA-insured mortgages taken out after September 1983 charged the borrower a one-time Mortgage Insurance Premium (MIP) at the time the mortgage went into effect. If you pay off one of these loans early (often by selling or refinancing), you may be eligible for a partial refund. No refund is owed if the mortgage runs its full 20, 25 or 30 years.

How to Apply for a Distributive Share or a Refund

If you have paid off an FHA-insured loan in full on a loan paid off before November 5, 1990, or taken out after September 1983 and have not received a distributive share or refund, send HUD the following information:

- your name
- your current address
- your work and home phone numbers
- the address of the FHA property paid off
- the date of your first payment
- the date the loan was paid off, and
- your FHA case number (not your loan number)—most California FHA case numbers begin with 64 or 042; the number should be on your loan papers; if you can't find it, ask your mortgage lender or the title company, or check the County Recorder's office.

Sign and date your letter and mail it to Department of Housing and Urban Development, Mortgage Insurance Accounting, Attn: Home Mortgage Branch, P.O. Box 23699, Washington, DC 20410-3699. If you have any questions, call HUD at (800) 697-6967.

Once you have sent the information, HUD takes two to four months to process your request. But some refunds and shares are over $1,000, which certainly makes it worth the effort.

AVOID FHA MORTGAGE REFUND SERVICES

Businesses have sprung up trying to cash in on the fact that many people entitled to FHA mortgage insurance refunds don't know about it. These services charge a fee of 25% to 50% of the refund amount. This is silly—don't pay someone money to do what you can do yourself for free by simply filing Form 2042.

California Housing Financing Agency (CHFA)

The CHFA provides mortgage financing for first-time homebuyers (or people who haven't owned a home in three years) who want to buy a previously occupied, affordable house. Funds are limited and tend to be most commonly available in geographical areas targeted by CHFA. You can contact CHFA at either of its locations:

- 5711 Slauson Avenue, Culver City, CA 90230, (213) 736-2355
- 1121 L Street, 7th Floor, Sacramento, CA 95814, (916) 322-3991.

Veterans Administration (VA)

The basic VA loan offers men and women who are now in the service and qualified veterans fixed rate mortgages with no down payment and interest rates that are usually slightly below the current market rate. The VA doesn't make mortgage loans, but guarantees part of the house loan you get from a private lender. To contact the VA, call (800) 827-1000. This is the national VA number; your call will be automatically forwarded to the closest VA office.

California Department of Veterans Affairs (Cal-Vet)

This program provides mortgage loans with lower-than-market rate interest to qualified California veterans who served during designated "war periods." Cal-Vet loans are made directly by the program, not by private mortgage lenders. You can hear recorded information 24 hours a day by calling (800) 952-5626. If you need additional information, contact Cal-Vet at one of the following offices:

- Bakersfield—(805) 395-2869
- Concord—(510) 602-5070
- Fresno—(209) 445-5466
- Oxnard—(805) 983-7477
- Redding—(916) 224-4955
- Sacramento North—(916) 722-1841
- Sacramento South—(916) 262-2555
- San Bernardino—(909) 383-4282
- San Diego—(619) 627-3966
- Sante Fe Springs—(310) 944-3585.

Escrow/Impound Accounts

An escrow or impound account is a fund required by many lenders to cover the payment of property taxes and hazard insurance on your home. You pay the lender, and the lender pays your tax and insurance bill. To have the necessary funds, the lender adds one-twelfth of the tax and insurance total to your monthly mortgage payment. The federal Real Estate Settlement Procedures Act allows the lender, annually, to add two extra months' payments, prorated monthly, to cover possible tax or insurance increases.

Who Must Have an Escrow Account?

Escrow accounts are required for Veterans Administration (VA) mortgages, FHA-insured mortgages and loans for which private lenders require a borrower to purchase Private Mortgage Insurance (PMI). If you can avoid an escrow account and pay your own tax and insurance obligations, it will be cheaper because you don't have to pay until payments are really due. (An escrow account collects money in advance.) Most lenders, however, require escrow accounts for any homebuyer whose down payment is less than 10% of the purchase price. California law prohibits lenders from forcing borrowers to use an escrow account if their down payment is greater than 10%. Civil Code § 2954.

Verifying the Accuracy of the Account

If you want to verify that your lender is charging the correct amount, call your insurance company and your tax assessor and ascertain the annual payments due. Then check the lender's annual statement of how much has been paid and how much is left in the account. It should add up. If there is an excess amount of money in the account, ask your lender to reduce your payments to the correct amount needed.

Interest Payment Required

The law requires lenders to pay at least 2% simple interest per year for money in escrow accounts for real property containing one to four family residences. Civil Code § 2954.8.

More Information/Where to Complain

For more information, get a copy of "Escrow Questions," Division of Credit Practices, Federal Trade Commission, Washington, DC 20580, (202) 326-2222.

Always try to resolve any dispute directly with your lender, going to the top if necessary. If that does not work, contact the financial institution regulatory agency.

If you think your lender may have violated the Real Estate Settlement Procedures Act, contact the Department of Housing and Urban Development, Washington, DC 20410, (202) 703-1422.

HOME EQUITY CONVERSION AND REVERSE MORTGAGES

Home equity conversion is the general term for a variety of plans designed to help older homeowners make use of the accumulated value (equity) in their homes without requiring them to move, give up title to the property or make payments on a loan. The most common types of home equity conversion plans are reverse mortgages and deferral loans for property tax and home repair.

Home equity conversion plans can raise a senior citizen's standard of living and help an older person maintain independence by providing cash for everyday living expenses, home maintenance and repair, or to finance in-home care.

Reverse Mortgages

Reverse mortgages are loans against the equity in the home that provide cash advances to a homeowner and require no repayment until the end of the loan term or when the home is sold. The borrower can receive the cash in several ways—a lump sum, regular monthly payments, a line of credit or a combination.

To qualify, you must be at least 62 years old and own your home free and clear or have a very small mortgage that can be paid off with an initial lump sum payment from the reverse mortgage.

All reverse mortgages will cost you money—closing costs (title insurance, escrow fees and appraisal fees), loan origination fees, accrued interest and, in most cases, an additional charge to offset the lender's risk of you not repaying.

There are three basic types of reverse mortgages—fixed term, tenure and portable.

Fixed Term Reverse Mortgages

You receive monthly advances for a specified period of time. At the end of the period, the advances stop and you must repay the loan.

Tenure Reverse Mortgages

You receive monthly advances as long as you stay in your home. Once you leave (for example, sell your house), you must repay the loan.

Portable Reverse Mortgages

You receive an advance in order to purchase an annuity that will pay you a fixed amount as long as you are alive, no matter where you live.

Deferral Payment Loans

Deferral payment loans are need-based loans used for a special purpose—to make property tax payments or to pay for home repairs. The cost of these loans is very low and repayment is deferred as long as you live in your home. Deferral payment loans are generally available through state or local government agencies.

There are two types of deferral payment loans—property tax and home repairs.

Property Tax Deferral Loans

The State of California will provide vouchers to approved applicants to pay their property taxes. You must apply and qualify each year.

Home Repair Deferral Loans

These are loans for home repairs at no or very low interest.

Other Options to Tap the Equity in a Home

Several other programs exist for older people who want to use the equity in their homes. These include:

Sale-Leaseback

This is a sale where you rent back your home for life from the buyer. The rental payments are deducted from the mortgage payment, giving you a monthly check for the difference.

Life Estate Sale

You sell your home at a discounted price which reflects your right to live in the house for the rest of your life. The price is based on the home's value and your age and life expectancy. Usually, the entire amount of money is given at the closing of the transaction.

Hospital Foundation Loans

These programs (tied in with charitable gifts) are fixed term reverse mortgages, but usually have a maximum time limit of ten years. You will have to check with various hospitals to see if they have such a program.

Deed/Annuity or Remainderman Interest Sale

Some universities, religious organizations and hospitals have programs under which you transfer title to the institution in exchange for income and the right to stay in the home for your lifetime. Contact the various institutions to see if they have such a plan.

Additional Resources

Several nonprofit senior service groups provide counseling on home equity conversions and reverse mortgages. Check with your local senior center for a referral. Also, you can obtain the following publications:

Reverse Mortgages, Federal Trade Commission, Office of Consumer Education, Washington, DC 20580—free.

Homemade Money, American Association of Retired Persons (AARP), Home Equity Information Center, Consumer Affairs Division, 601 E Street NW, Washington, DC 20049—free.

Money From Home: A Consumer's Guide to Home Equity Conversion Mortgages, Fannie Mae, Consumer Education Group, 3900 Wisconsin Avenue NW, Washington, DC 20016-2899—free.

Retirement Income on the House: Cashing in on Your Home With a Reverse Mortgage, by Ken Scholen, National Center for Home Equity Conversion, 7373 147th Street West, Suite 115, Apple Valley, MN 55124—$24.95.

Reverse Mortgages—Cashing in on Your Home, put out by the Human Investment Project, Inc., 364 S. Railroad Avenue, San Mateo, CA 94401, (415) 348-6660—$20 video.

HOMEOWNER'S INSURANCE

If you are financing your home, your lender will require that you carry hazard insurance to pay the lender in the event your house is destroyed by fire, wind, hail, vandalism or another similar act. Even if your home is fully paid for, don't balk at the insurance. You're going to want what's required and probably more. Virtually all homeowners buy comprehensive homeowner's insurance, not just the minimum required by the lender.

Homeowner's insurance covers two areas: personal liability and property damage:

- *Personal Liability Coverage* provides protection if you, a family member or your pet injures someone or damages someone else's property no matter where this occurs. (Injuries caused by motor vehicles are excluded.) For example, if you accidentally hit someone on the head with a golf ball, your homeowner's coverage will protect you. If you are sued, the insurance company will defend you and pay any judgment. Liability insurance also covers medical expenses for guests (non-family) injured on your premises.

- *Property Damage Coverage* includes the dwelling, other separate structures on your premises (such as a garage, storage facility or fence), personal property (including furniture, clothes and personal belongings) and loss of use/additional living expenses. For instance, if you have to move out of your home temporarily because of a fire, the policy will pay for the expense of reasonable accommodations, up to the policy limit, over and above your normal living expenses. Insurance won't cover loss of use if you have to move out because of something your policy doesn't cover.

Personal property is usually insured for 50% of the dwelling limit, which is usually more than adequate; however, if you have particularly valuable property, you can purchase increased limits for an additional charge. Some types of property aren't routinely covered—you must pay extra and list separately under most policies.

Public Adjusters

Public adjusters are independent business people who work for the general public, not an insurance company. Public adjusters are generally professional specialists who understand the complexities and intricacies of insurance policies. They help you by filing your claim with your insurance company, and may be able to get a better settlement than you might get on your own. Public adjusters make money by taking a percentage of the insurance company's settlement with you. When you suffer a property loss due to fire and other allied casualties, filing your own claim and handling all the details may make the best sense. If you feel overwhelmed or just don't have the time to cope with all the details, however, retaining a public adjuster to help can make sense. This can be especially true if you have never read your insurance policy and don't know what coverage you have until you file a claim.

Finding a Public Adjuster

If you have a fire in your home, you will likely be contacted by several public adjusters. Never sign anything in a hurry or under pressure. How do you make a good choice? Members of trade associations with high standards are often a good place to start. Public adjusters who are members of the National Association of Public Insurance Adjusters are supposedly held to a strict code of ethics. Also, because public adjusters are often retained by banks and lawyers who handle insurance cases, these may be good sources for a referral. Always ask any public adjuster for references and check them. If the adjuster can't refer you to several local people who have happily used her services, stay away. Public adjusters are listed under Adjusters in your telephone book yellow pages.

What Does Your Insurance Cover?

Here are several items that may or may not be covered by your homeowner's policy.

Jewelry, Furs and Other Valuables

Most homeowner policies provide $1,000 for loss by theft; some companies provide more coverage. To properly protect your valuable property, such as jewelry, furs, expensive art, computer equipment, silverware, cameras, and stamp and coin collections, you should purchase additional insurance coverage—often called a Scheduled Personal Articles Floater. This insurance is usually quite reasonably priced. You will have to give your insurance company an itemized list schedule of what you want covered. It may require a professional appraisal or a bill of sale to verify the value of these items.

RECORDKEEPING FOR INSURANCE

Smart homeowners will make and keep in a safe-deposit box, or other secure place away from home, an inventory, including photographs and/or video tapes, of all items of importance or value. Keeping good records of what you own, and how much valuable items are worth, will make life much easier if you ever have to file a claim with your insurance company. *Nolo's Personal RecordKeeper* software includes a complete home inventory section to make this job easier.

For detailed information on how to do a home inventory, mark valuable property items and improve home security, see *Safe Homes, Safe Neighborhoods: Stopping Crime Where You Live*, by Stephanie Mann with M.C. Blakeman (Nolo Press).

If your property is particularly valuable, it's a good idea to have it appraised every few years and, of course, raise your insurance coverage accordingly.

Replacement Costs

In theory, most homeowner's policies offered today cover replacement cost of the contents and dwelling up to the policy limit. Insurance companies, however, often dispute the amount the insured claims as the reasonable replacement cost. They sometimes also dispute whether the property ever existed, or if it did, whether you owned it. (This is where documentation comes in.) You can also buy replacement cost guaranty coverage that supposedly guarantees rebuilding your home even if the cost exceeds the policy limit. If you want replacement cost guaranty coverage for both contents and dwelling, be sure to specify that to your agent.

Some insurance companies still sell standard, non-replacement cost homeowner's insurance. Although it's cheaper than replacement cost insurance, this coverage only pays the actual cash value at the time of the loss or damage. Basically, this amounts to what you could get for your belongings if you sold them. It is more sensible to buy replacement cost coverage.

If you have replacement cost coverage for personal property, the insurance company may only reimburse you for the actual cash value—depreciated value—if you do not replace the item. If you do replace the item, the insurance company will pay the additional amount of money owed. Some companies will buy the replacement items for you because they can often buy merchandise wholesale.

If your insurance company won't pay you an amount you consider fair, your first step is to document every loss and fight like mad. You have the right to an appraisal or you can hire a public adjuster. If this fails, you can demand an appraisal. You and the insurance company each select a competent, independent appraiser, who may charge 5%-10% of the total appraisal amount. The two appraisers select an umpire. If the two appraisers cannot reach an agreement, they submit their differences to the umpire. The end result is a written agreement signed by at least two of the three, which sets the amount of the loss. Each party pays his own appraiser's fee, but the umpire's fee is split between you and the insurance company.

Bringing Your House Up to Code

Check your policy carefully, especially if you have an older home where rebuilding will likely entail complying with new building codes. Even if you suffer fairly minor damage, you may have to rebuild to new code provisions. Some policies specifically exclude paying for costs to meet any building codes, ordinances or laws requiring repairs or reconstruction. Other policies will pay up to 10% (15% in a few cases) of the limit of liability for the increased cost incurred to repair or rebuild the structure and bringing it up to code. For example, if you have $150,000 coverage, your insurance company would pay up to $15,000 of the cost of bringing the house up to code.

The state Supreme Court has ruled that an insurance company does not have to pay extra costs because of new building codes unless it's specified in the policy. The case involved a garage with a wood floor which burned in a fire. The new building code required a cement floor and a new foundation, at an additional cost of approximately $29,000. The insurance company refused to pay.

Earthquakes

Earthquake insurance is not included in a standard homeowner's policy, but for an additional fee you may be able to add the coverage to your policy or purchase a separate earthquake policy. Earthquake coverage may not be available for some houses, however, such as ones right on active faults or built on artificial fill. When you take out a homeowner's policy, the insurance company is required to offer you earthquake coverage (at an additional cost). The company is also obligated to offer earthquake coverage every other year. Many earthquake insurance policies have a

10%-15% deductible. A 10% deductible applies to 10% of the insurance coverage you purchased, not 10% of the damage. For example, if you bought earthquake insurance coverage of $300,000, you would have to pay for the first $30,000 of damage before the insurance company would have to pay anything.

Floods
If your home is located in a federally designated "flood zone," your lender will require you to purchase flood insurance. Even if your house is paid off, you may want to continue this insurance.

Flood insurance is written and administered by the National Flood Insurance Program (NFIP). It can be reached at (800) 638-6620, Monday through Friday, 5:00 a.m. to 5:00 p.m., pacific standard time. You can listen to a variety of recorded messages anytime.

FLOOD ZONES CHANGE

If you believe flood coverage required by a lender is unnecessary—for instance, you live on a hill—check with your city planning and zoning office, annually, to see if your home is still officially located in a flood zone. Flood zone maps change frequently, and you may find you are no longer so classified. Many homeowners have paid needlessly for flood insurance after their homes were removed from a flood zone map. It is unlikely you will ever get money refunded after the fact—but it can pay to check every year or two.

Household Employees
Standard homeowner's policies provide household employees workers' compensation insurance coverage if they are injured on the job, and many companies do not charge extra for this coverage. Give your insurance company the names of any household employees. Your employee must have worked at least 90 days, at least 52 hours, and earned at least $100 in the period just prior to the accident to be eligible for workers' compensation coverage. California law requires that this coverage be included on comprehensive personal liability policies (Section 11 on your homeowner's policy) and cannot be deleted. The company may charge an extra amount for household employees who work more than ten hours per week.

Plumbing Problems
Problems caused by an accidental or sudden discharge of your plumbing system or an explosion (a named peril in your policy) are normally covered. Problems such

as rotten wood or loose floorboards that result from continuous leaking or other plumbing problems are generally excluded from coverage. And remember that the plumbing damage itself (the replacement of broken pipes or a cracked water heater) will likely not be covered—just the resulting damage.

Lost Luggage
If the airline doesn't adequately compensate you for the loss, your homeowner's policy may cover the difference.

If You Live in a High-Crime Area

If you install required safety devices, you may be eligible for subsidized insurance with the Federal Crime Insurance Program (FCIP). This will cover you for robbery or burglary losses. You might also get a discount if you have a security system. For more details, ask your insurance agent or call the FCIP at (800) 638-8780.

More Information/Where to Complain

The California Department of Insurance maintains a toll-free hotline, (800) 927-HELP. In addition, it publishes a free pamphlet called a "Buyer's Guide to Homeowner's Insurance."

To protect consumers against an insurance company that's going belly-up, a surcharge is added to all homeowner's and property insurance policies. The money collected from this surcharge is put in a guaranty fund to cover the cost of claims for any insured whose company becomes insolvent/bankrupt.

HOME WARRANTIES

Existing Home Sale

If you are buying or selling an older home, one of the most effective sales tools is for the seller to provide a home warranty for the buyer. The average cost is approximately $300. These policies typically provide repair and service for all built-in appliances and plumbing, heating and electrical systems. Some plans offer optional additional coverage for air conditioning and swimming pools. Under standard home warranties, if a covered system fails during the coverage period (usually one year), you simply call the warranty company, which sends out a repairperson. Home warranty policies spell out, very clearly, what is and what is not covered and set a dollar limit for certain types of repairs. The best home warranties cover pre-existing conditions that were not known to the seller or discovered in an inspection.

New Home Sale

If you are buying a newly constructed home, the developer generally guarantees workmanship and materials for one year. This guarantee is only as good as the developer making the promise and is worthless if the developer dissolves the corporation and starts another one—when problems arise, there's no one to accept a claim on the guarantee, and you have no one to sue because you can't sue a dissolved corporation.

In addition to developer guarantees, private insurance companies sell new home warranties typically covering workmanship and materials for one year, plumbing, electrical and heating systems for two years and major structural defects for ten years. Some scrupulous developers purchase these extra policies which are an additional important protection to developer guarantees. Of course, all the new appliances also come with the manufacturer's written warranties.

HOMEOWNER'S ASSOCIATIONS

Homeowner's Associations are nonprofit (mutual benefit) corporations. Homeowner's Associations have three components in common:

- Articles of Incorporation, which the association must file with the California Secretary of State
- Declaration of Conditions, Covenants and Restrictions (CC&Rs), which spell out the rules of ownership, and
- Bylaws, which spell out the Board of Directors and membership rules including how much fees can be raised.

In general, the CC&Rs describe the following:

- property (and property rights)
- Homeowner's Association membership and voting rights
- duties and powers of the Association
- assessments
- easements
- use restrictions
- architectural control
- mortgagee rights and protection, and
- damage, destruction and condemnation of common area improvements.

The Bylaws do the following:

- define membership and ownership
- define responsibilities of members
- define meeting requirements
- define voting rights
- define what constitutes a majority, and
- cover the power and duties of the board of directors, including nominations, elections and terms.

You should become familiar with the CC&Rs and the Bylaws before and after purchasing property subject to a Homeowner's Association.

Dissatisfaction With a Homeowner's Association

If you are dissatisfied with the operation of your Homeowner's Association, try the following:

- Obtain up-to-date copies of the CC&Rs and the Bylaws, membership list, minutes and latest financial statements.
- Check the latest California Corporations Code.
- Determine if the corporation is operating in accordance with the Bylaws and California Corporations Code.
- If the board of directors or officers are not following procedures for furnishing records or calling or holding a meeting, or are violating the Bylaws or California Corporations Code, you can take whatever action is necessary. For instance, you can call a special meeting (following your Homeowner's Association procedures) and elect new directors and officers.
- If any situation gets out of hand, you probably need legal advice.

BEWARE THAT FEES CAN GO SKY HIGH

Here's one reason why it's a good idea to read the CC&Rs and the Bylaws before you buy. Homeowner's Associations can assess mandatory fees for common area maintenance and improvements, which can be expensive if your development has recreational facilities, like a swimming pool or tennis courts. Some associations allow their boards to raise regular assessments up to 20% a year; some also allow for establishing special assessments without a membership vote. In addition, if your association decides to sue a developer or city, you will have to share in the cost of the lawsuit.

More Information/Where to Complain

CC&Rs and Bylaws must conform to §§ 5001 through 10014 of the California Corporations Code. You can find the Corporations Code in any law library and in the business or government section of many public libraries.

The Homeowner's Association Manual, by Peter M. Dunbar (Suncoast Professional Publishing), is a practical guide for operating Homeowner's Associations, including membership meetings, board of directors meetings, committees and budgets.

Many Homeowner's Associations belong to one or several condominium organizations (much the same as trade associations). These groups publish useful materials and hold seminars on how to operate in an efficient, cost effective way. In some circumstances they provide helpful information if you are having trouble getting a problem resolved with your association.

If your problem is with the board of directors of the Association, the California State Association of Parliamentarians may be able to help explain the rules that the directors should follow. (Roberts Rules of Order are the most commonly used rules.) The California State Association of Parliamentarians can be reached through a Parliamentarian member, at (415) 566-7826.

MOBILE HOMES

Many Californians happily reside in mobile homes—perhaps the most cost-effective type of housing—and live in mobile home parks. Laws which regulate people's rights in mobile home parks differ from regular landlord-tenant laws and property owners' laws. The California Department of Housing and Community Development implements the state's housing policies, including the enforcement of mobile home construction and mobile home parks' regulations.

More Information/Where to Complain

Housing discrimination matters are handled by the Department of Fair Employment and Housing, at (916) 445-9918, Monday through Friday, between 8:00 a.m. and 5:00 p.m. All other landlord/tenant concerns may be answered by the Department of Consumer Affairs, at (800) 344-9940 (a number that is very hard to get through to).

The Golden State Mobile Home Owners League (GSMOL), a nonprofit membership organization, will try to answer questions about your rights and mobile home park rules. In addition, each year GSMOL puts out a booklet of the Mobile Home Residency Laws, which is free for members and $1.50 for non-members. Contact GSMOL at P.O. Box 876, Garden Grove, CA 92642, or call (800) 888-1727 between 9:00 a.m. and 4:00 p.m. (except noon to 1:00 p.m.).

The California Department of Housing and Community Development provides the following services:

- Mobile Home Ombudsmen (complaint center) for problems against mobile home park owners for Health and Safety Code violations; against dealers, salespeople and manufacturers for problems with the sale or construction of a mobile home; and against sellers of warranties for failing to make good on a new mobile home warranty—(800) 952-5275.
- Titles and Registration for problems with registered ownership of a mobile home—(800) 952-8356.
- Codes and Standards for problems with plumbing and electrical systems and other standards mobile homeowners and park owners must meet—(916) 445-9471.

HOMESTEAD PROTECTION

If a creditor sues you for a debt, wins and tries to force the sale of your home (including houses, boats and movable motor homes) to pay the court judgment against you, California's homestead law protects you. It also protects you if you need to file for bankruptcy to get rid of your debts. If either case, you can avoid the forced sale of your home unless the sale would produce enough money to:

- pay all existing liens (a judgment lien, a mechanic's lien or a tax lien)
- pay mortgages and costs of sale, and
- let you keep your equity in the house, up to the amount protected by the homestead.

If you are:	Your homestead protection is:
Single	$ 50,000
A member of a family unit	$ 75,000
Over 65 or disabled (or your spouse is)	$ 100,000
Over 55 and your income is $15,000 or less	$ 100,000 (or $20,000 if married)

The homestead law doesn't protect you if the creditor is trying to foreclose on the mortgage (deed of trust) itself, or collect a judgment for back child support, spousal support or taxes.

 Always consult a lawyer if a judgment creditor tries to force a sale of your house. You need to file court papers to protect your homestead rights.

Declaration of Homestead

You can get even more homestead protection if you fill out a simple form called a Declaration of Homestead and file it with the County Recorder. If you sell your house voluntarily, or if a creditor who has a court judgment on the property tries to force a sale of the house, recording a homestead declaration protects you in two ways:

- You are entitled to keep the homestead amount from the proceeds of the sale for six months. Creditors cannot take it during that period.

- You can permanently keep creditors from taking this protected amount by investing it in another home, and recording a Declaration of Homestead on the new residence, within six months. Code of Civil Procedure §§ 704.730 and 704.960.

A declared homestead protects only dwellings that are considered real estate—houses, condominiums and mobile homes permanently attached to land.

You may want to record a Declaration of Homestead if it seems likely that a creditor will sue you for a large sum of money. The declared homestead strongly discourages creditors from trying to force a sale of your home to pay off a court judgment, and it can also protect your equity if you want to sell your house and buy another.

If you own a business that operates as a sole proprietorship or partnership, you should definitely record a homestead declaration. If your business is successfully sued, creditors can go after your property, not just business assets, to pay off the judgment.

HOMESTEAD YOUR OWN HOUSE

Owning a home is a matter of public record, which means various opportunity seekers may get your name to try to sell you something. One such gimmick is an offer to provide a homestead on your house for $25. (California law limits these homestead services to charge no more than $25 including notary and filing fees.) It's not worth it—you'll have to fill out the form yourself anyway. If you want to file for homestead protection, you can buy the needed form for $1 or less from an office supply store; by paying a small fee you can file the filled-out form with your County Recorder.

Additional Resources

Homestead Your House, by Ralph Warner, Ed Sherman and Toni Ihara (Nolo Press), contains tear-out homestead forms and instructions, as well as a detailed discussion of how the homestead law works. It is available in public libraries and bookstores.

LANDLORDS AND TENANTS

LANDLORD/TENANT RIGHTS AND RESPONSIBILITIES

Landlords and tenants are both best served when they each understand their legal rights and obligations. All agreements, whether a lease or a month-to-month tenancy, should be in writing. The tenant should read the agreement before renting or leasing an apartment or house, so there is no misunderstanding about the terms. Any changes to the basic agreement (either before the move-in or during the rental period) should be made in writing and initialed by the landlord and tenant.

Tenants have the following obligations in a landlord-tenant relationship:

- Pay the rent on time. There is no grace period provided in the law but some landlords allow three to five days.
- Maintain the premises.
- Abide by the terms of the lease or rental agreement.
- Promptly notify the landlord/manager of any needed repairs.

Condition of Rented Property

Several state and local laws set housing standards for the physical condition of rental property, both when the tenant moves in and during the tenancy.

All rental agreements have an implied warranty of habitability, which means that the landlord has an obligation to maintain the property in a reasonably livable condition. Civil Code § 1941.1. Specifically, the rental unit must have:

- waterproof and weatherproof walls, windows, doors and roof
- plumbing that provides hot and cold running water—must be connected to an appropriate sewage disposal system
- safe heating and electrical systems (lights and wiring must work), and safe gas facilities
- safe stairways, railings and floors
- smoke detector for dwellings in multiple-unit buildings rented after January 1987
- clean premises (when rented) free from garbage, rodents and pests, and
- adequate number of garbage cans or bins with tops.

In addition, the landlord must provide locks for all doors and windows, as well as emergency exits to a hallway or the street.

Landlords do not have to repaint premises or replace carpets and drapes before a tenant moves in, or just because a tenant has lived in a unit for a number of years.

When Premises Are Uninhabitable

A tenant is financially responsible for damage he caused. If a tenant's child flushes a toy down the toilet, the tenant is responsible for the plumber's bill.

A landlord has an obligation to repair any problem that falls under her responsibilities, unless the damage was caused by the tenant. To get repairs made, a tenant should do the following:

1. Promptly notify the landlord about any needed repairs orally, and follow-up in writing. Keep a copy of the letter as proof of the request in case there is a problem later.

2. Wait a reasonable amount of time. Thirty days is considered reasonable for non-emergency repairs to be made, such as a crack in a kitchen counter; however, if the toilet does not flush or the heater breaks down in winter, the repairs must be attended to promptly.

3. If the repairs are not done in a reasonable amount of time, the tenant may be legally eligible to have the repairs made using the "repair and deduct" remedy (Civil Code § 1942). This remedy may be used only for serious problems (no hot water) that were not caused by the tenant and that make the unit "untenable." First, the tenant must give the landlord or manager reasonable notice. If the repairs aren't made, the tenant can get them done and send a copy of the bill to the landlord and deduct that amount from his rent. The tenant cannot deduct more than one month's rent, and cannot do this more than two times in any 12-month period.

4. A tenant can withhold rent if the landlord won't fix a major problem that makes a rental unit uninhabitable after the tenant has notified the landlord of the problem. Using this remedy can be tricky because the tenant wants to avoid the implication that she simply doesn't want to pay rent. It's best for a tenant to put rent money in a "special bank or escrow account" to prove that she will pay the rent if the repairs are made. (Los Angeles and Sacramento have city-run escrow accounts to deal with this situation.) The tenant may want to contact the city building inspector if there are code violations. This local agency can order the landlord to make repairs. Telling the landlord that he will be reported to the building inspector may be enough to solve the problem.

Landlord's Liability for Injuries

A landlord may be liable to the tenant—or others—for injuries caused by dangerous or defective conditions. A landlord may be liable for tenant injuries and property damage resulting from the criminal acts of others, but only if the injury was caused by the landlord's unreasonable act—such as failing to fix a defective lock. A landlord can also be liable for damage or injury caused by tenants.

Tenants' Right to Privacy

A rental unit is a tenant's home and he has a basic right of privacy. The landlord has the right to enter a tenant's premises only:

- in an emergency
- to make needed repairs or to determine if repairs or alterations are needed
- to show the unit to prospective buyers, tenants or repair workers
- if the premises have been abandoned, or
- as a result of a court order.

Unless it is an emergency, your landlord must give you reasonable notice of entry (24 hours is presumed to be reasonable) and enter only during normal business hours. Civil Code § 1954.

Rent Increases

If you have a lease, your rent cannot be raised (unless specified in the lease) until the lease term is up. If you rent on a month-to-month tenancy, and the unit is not covered by rent control, rent can be raised any amount with 30 days' written notice. In most communities with rent control, there are limits to the percentage of increase allowed on an annual basis. (The same 30-day written notice restriction applies.)

Holding Deposits

You should not give a landlord a deposit to hold an apartment unless you really want that unit. By accepting your holding deposit, the landlord will be taking that property off the market. If you change your mind, and the landlord has lost a chance to rent the apartment to someone else, the landlord probably will expect to keep the deposit. In any case make sure there is a clear written understanding of what happens to that deposit: If you take the unit, will it be applied to the first month's rent? If you change your mind, will you get some or all of the money back?

SECURITY DEPOSITS

Defined

A security deposit means any payment or fee collected (over and above the first month's rent) by the landlord to pay for rent owed, damage repairs caused by the tenant, or for cleaning the apartment when vacated. For an unfurnished apartment, a landlord can ask for the equivalent of two months' rent as a security deposit (two-and-one-half months if you have a water bed). For a furnished unit, the landlord can ask for the equivalent of three months' rent as a security deposit (three-and-one-half months if you have a water bed).

Security deposits are completely refundable when you leave if the unit is clean, undamaged and the rent is paid. There is no such thing as a nonrefundable security deposit. A lease or rental agreement that states part of the deposit will automatically be deducted for cleaning will not hold up in court. Even if the landlord calls the deposit a fee for security, cleaning, damage or keys, the landlord must still use the same refund procedure for returning the security deposit.

Interest on Security Deposits

There is no California-wide law that requires a landlord to pay interest on a security deposit, but it's perfectly legal for a landlord to do so and the tenant can ask for it. Some cities have passed local ordinances requiring interest be paid annually, including Berkeley, San Francisco, Santa Cruz and Santa Monica. Check to see what requirements exist locally.

Security Deposits and Rent Increases

If your rent is raised, so can your security deposit, with 30 days' written notice.

Security Deposits and Sold Property

If the property is sold, the former landlord must return the deposit money to you, or transfer it to the new owner. If the former landlord does not transfer the money to the buyer, the new owner is still legally responsible for returning the deposit to you. Civil Code § 1950.5 (h).

Return of Your Security Deposit

Effective January 1, 1994, California law requires a landlord to return a security deposit within three weeks of your vacating the premises. If the landlord deducts any money, he must send an itemized statement indicating how the money was used, also within the three-week period. Civil Code § 1950.5(f). The law includes a penalty provision against landlords who do not comply. A judge can award you $600 in punitive damages for bad faith retention of a security deposit, in addition to your actual damages. Civil Code § 1950.5 (k).

"Clean" and "Undamaged" Defined

The largest issue of landlord/tenant complaints received by the California Department of Consumer Affairs is over the return of security deposits. The major disputes include: What is clean? What is normal wear and tear? What constitutes damage?

Clean

The unit should look the way it did when you moved in for you to be able to claim it was clean, except for normal wear and tear. Was the stove clean? Was the refrigerator clean? Were the windows washed and the cabinets clean? Were the bathroom fixtures clean with no scum build-up on the shower walls? If the answer is yes to these questions, then you should leave it just like that. If you don't, the landlord probably will deduct cleaning charges from the deposit.

Normal Wear and Tear

Over time, any rental unit will need repainting and other refurbishments, such as new carpets and drapes. A landlord cannot automatically charge you for normal repainting, or for normal carpet and drapery cleaning, especially if you lived in the unit for an extended period (two years or more) and used the premises in a reasonable manner. If you have spilled coffee on the carpeting, or the pet stained the carpets or drapes, however, the landlord is justified in charging for necessary cleaning.

Damage

If you make holes in the wall hanging pictures, damage paint moving furniture, break cabinet doors or put cigarette burns in the carpeting, that's obviously damage. In less serious situations, it can sometimes be hard to distinguish damage from ordinary wear and tear. It often makes sense for a landlord and tenant to try to talk out a compromise acceptable to both. You are not responsible for damage done by a previous tenant or the landlord.

Deposits for Last Month's Rent

If a landlord states that a security deposit or a portion of it is for "last month's rent," then that is all it can be used for. The landlord cannot use last month's rent to cover cleaning or damage repair costs. If the landlord does not call the deposit "last month's rent" (most don't), it's a security deposit.

If the Landlord Does Not Return a Deposit

If you have not received the security deposit or itemized statement in the three-week period, you should send a letter to the landlord advising her that if the money is not returned promptly, you will take her to Small Claims Court and ask for $600 in punitive damages for bad faith retention of the security deposit. That letter may be enough to solve the problem. If not, head for court. In a dispute over retention of a security deposit, the landlord has the burden of proving the reasonableness of the amounts claimed.

Sample Demand Letter

John Landlord
4321 Central Street
Hightown, CA 91000

Dear Mr. Landlord:

I moved out of apartment 23 at 210 San Francisco Street on October 31st (more than a month ago), and I still have not received the refund of my $800 security deposit. I thoroughly cleaned the apartment before moving out, including cleaning the stove and refrigerator and scrubbing the shower walls. A good friend, who helped me move out, can attest to the fact that the apartment was spotless. According to the Civil Code § 1950.5(f), I am entitled to the return of my security deposit (and/or an itemized statement of deposit money spent) within three weeks. Please refund my money within one week or I will sue you in Small Claims Court, not only for the $800, but I will ask the judge for $600 in punitive damages for your "bad faith retention of my security deposit." Civil Code § 1950.5(k).

May I hear from you soon?
Sincerely,

Barbara Kaufman
1234 Main Street
Anyplace, CA 94111

TERMINATING A TENANCY

Terminating a Month-to-Month Tenancy

If the tenancy is one from month-to-month, either the tenant or the landlord can give the other a written notice to move with 30 days' notice on any day of the month. For example, if a tenant normally pays rent on the first of each month, and gives notice to move on May 17th, the tenant will be obligated to pay rent through June 16th. If the tenant moves out earlier and the landlord is able to re-rent the premises earlier than the 16th, the tenant is entitled to a prorated refund. The landlord cannot collect rent from a prior tenant and a replacement tenant for the same period of time. To figure the amount of a prorated refund, divide the monthly rent by 30 (even if the month does not have 30 days) to determine the daily rental. Multiply the daily rental by the number of days the premises was re-rented after moving out, and that is the amount of refund that is owed.

In cities with rent control ordinances that require "just cause for eviction," a landlord can terminate a rent control tenancy only for a stated cause covered by the ordinance.

In non-rent control areas, a landlord must serve the written notice on the tenant in person. If that isn't possible, the notice may be handed to someone else on the premises and a second copy of the notice mailed. If someone can't be found on the premises, then the notice can be posted in a conspicuous place on the premises and a second copy of the notice mailed. The tenant giving notice should give a copy to any manager who collects rent, unless the name and address of the owner is posted on the building or stated in the written agreement. Either the landlord or the tenant may also send a notice by certified mail. Typically, what actually happens is a landlord just mails a written notice and the tenant goes along with it, but this does not technically comply with the law unless it is actually received in time.

Breaking a Lease

If a tenant leaves early, and therefore breaks a lease, he should give the landlord as much notice as possible. Technically, the tenant has obligated himself to the full terms of the lease and the landlord can try to hold him responsible for paying the full amount. The landlord also has a legal obligation to try to lease or rent the premises to another tenant as quickly as possible to lessen the amount of money the tenant owes. This is called "mitigation of damages." If the landlord can rent the unit as soon as the tenant moves out, the landlord must set off rent from the new tenant against anything the first tenant owes. Thus, as long as other good tenants, who will pay as much as the first, are available, the first tenant should have to pay little or nothing. To be sure this happens, the tenant who breaks the lease may want to help find a replacement tenant or make the unit accessible at all times for showing to prospective tenants. The landlord can charge the lease-breaking tenant the cost of advertising to get a replacement tenant as well as any money she loses during the transition if she can't find a new tenant to pay as much rent.

When a Lease Is Up

At the end of a fixed-term lease, the tenant and the landlord (as a matter of good business) should remind each other, in writing, that the lease will be expiring and what each other's future plans are. If the tenant keeps occupying the unit after a lease expires (and does not sign a new lease), the tenancy reverts to a month-to-month agreement at the same terms as the lease.

If the Property Is Sold

If the property is sold voluntarily by the landlord, the new owners must assume the same terms and conditions of the existing lease. Some new owners offer to "buy out" existing leases. If the property is involuntarily sold—a foreclosure or judgment sale—then your lease is no longer valid, but you must be given a 30-day written notice to move.

Evictions

Broadly speaking, a landlord who wants to evict a tenant has three options depending on the circumstances: a three-day, a 30-day or a 180-day notice. Because evictions are very technical—there are numerous legal requirements and possible defenses at every step—this is only a brief overview. For more information, see *Tenants' Rights*, by Myron Moskovitz and Ralph Warner, or *The Landlord's Law Book, Vol. 2: Evictions*, by David Brown. Both are published by Nolo Press and are available in libraries and bookstores.

Three-Day Notices

Three-day notices are used for nonpayment of rent, damaged or destroyed property, illegal use of the premises, disturbing the neighbors, or for other violations of the lease/rental agreement. The three-day notice must state the reason for the eviction. Depending on the circumstances, the notice may give the tenant the opportunity to fix the problem, as would be the case in the non-payment of rent.

After the three days are up, if the tenant fixes the problem, that's the end of the matter. If the tenant refuses to correct the situation, the landlord must file and win an "unlawful detainer" lawsuit in order to have the tenant evicted. When a summons, issued by the court, is received, the tenant has five days in which to respond in writing to the court as to why the eviction should not take place. If the tenant does not respond to the summons, a landlord can request a default judgment without a trial or without a judge's hearing the tenant's side of the story.

Common defenses used by tenants in written response to a summons include:

- the wrong amount of rent was listed on the three-day notice
- the notice was defective (that is, it didn't give the tenant the choice to correct the problem or leave)
- the landlord gave false information (rent was paid or the claimed illegal activity didn't occur)
- building code violations make the premises uninhabitable, or
- the eviction notice was in retaliation for a tenant's legitimate complaints.

If the case goes to trial, the tenant should bring evidence and witnesses to substantiate his side of the story. If the tenant wins, he does not have to move, and the tenancy continues, but he may still have to bring his rent current at some later time. And the judge may also order the landlord to pay the tenant's legal fees. If the landlord wins, the tenant must move. The judge may order the tenant to pay the landlord's legal fees. Either can appeal the decision, but such appeals are very technical and difficult.

If the tenant loses and does not move, the landlord may get a "writ of possession" ordering the tenant to vacate the premises within five days. If the tenant still refuses to move, the sheriff can physically remove him.

30-Day Notices

With a month-to-month agreement, the landlord may give a 30-day notice in writing to end the tenancy without a reason. (In some cities with rent control, including Los Angeles, San Francisco, Berkeley and Santa Monica, a landlord can only terminate a tenancy for "just cause.") Generally, a lease cannot be terminated with a 30-day notice. Exceptions would include the same conditions as for a three-day notice, or if a property is involuntarily sold by a foreclosure or judgment sale. If a tenant refuses to move, then the landlord must file and win an "unlawful detainer" lawsuit in order to have the tenant evicted after serving a 30-day notice.

"Just Cause" for an Eviction

In cities with fairly strict rent control, a landlord must have a valid reason ("just cause") for evicting a tenant. These reasons include the same ones used for a three-day notice to vacate, such as failure to pay rent or the violation of a clause in the written agreement. In addition, "just cause" may be used if the landlord wants to use the property as a residence for himself or a close relative, if the tenant will not allow the landlord access to the property or if the landlord intends to do major renovation work on the unit.

Condominium Conversions

When an apartment is being converted to a condominium, 180-day notice is required. You are entitled to a 90-day first option to buy the unit you are inhabiting, after final approval has been granted for the conversion. Some cities offer even greater protection for tenants. Check with the clerk of your city for more details.

Illegal Evictions

It is illegal for a landlord to evict a tenant by force or threat. Code of Civil Procedure §§ 1159-1160. It is also illegal for a landlord to:

- lock the tenant out or change locks
- remove doors or windows
- remove the tenant's furniture or property, or
- shut off any utilities or cause them to be shut off. Civil Code § 789.3.

Any provision in a lease or rental agreement that purports to allow any of these actions is void. In the case of an unlawful lockout, property removal or utility shutoff, the landlord can be penalized up to $100 per day, with a $250 minimum, and must also reimburse the tenant for actual loss.

Landlords cannot legally terminate a tenancy because of race, religion or other arbitrary reasons, or as a means of retaliating against a tenant for exercising any right under the law.

More Information

The following three books explain the laws (including local rent control rules) that California landlords and tenants need to know:

- *Tenants' Rights,* by attorneys Myron Moskovitz and Ralph Warner
- *The Landlord's Law Book, Vol. 1: Rights and Responsibilities,* by attorneys David Brown and Ralph Warner, and
- *The Landlord's Law Book, Vol. 2: Evictions,* by attorney David Brown.

They are all published by Nolo Press and are available in public libraries and bookstores.

Landlord-Tenant, Answers to Tenant Questions, is a free booklet put out by the California Department of Consumer Affairs. Send a stamped, self-addressed, business-size envelope to: Landlord-Tenant, P.O. Box 310, Sacramento, CA 95802.

Many communities have landlord/tenant organizations designed to mediate disputes. To find out if one exists in your community, call a radio, TV or newspaper "Action Line," the Better Business Bureau, City Hall or the board of supervisors or city council.

Tenants only: In some cities, tenants' rights organizations are available to advise tenants. City or county government officials probably know how to find them.

Landlords only: All larger counties have landlord trade groups, often called "apartment associations." They have regular meetings and often provide some staff help for members.

RENTERS' INSURANCE

Renters' insurance provides coverage for the following:

- personal property—protection against fire, theft and other specified hazards, which covers clothing, furniture and most other personal belongings
- loss of use/additional living expenses—money you can use to secure a temporary place to live
- personal liability and medical payments to others injured on the premises, and
- damage to the landlord's property caused by your negligence.

Does a Landlord's Insurance Policy Cover Renters?

Many renters mistakenly believe that a landlord's insurance protects them. Wrong! The landlord's insurance only covers the dwelling (building). It does not cover damage or loss to your personal belongings or your personal liability if someone has an accident in your apartment.

If you have a cooking fire that damages the building, renters' insurance will cover the loss, up to the policy limit. If you do not have insurance, the landlord's insurance company will pay for the damage and then the insurance company will go after you for reimbursement.

DISCRIMINATION IN BUYING OR RENTING

The California Department of Fair Employment and Housing may pursue a complaint regarding discrimination in housing if it is based on race, religion, national origin or ancestry, sex, marital status, physical handicap or retaliation.

More Information/Where to Complain

Contact the California Department of Fair Employment and Housing headquarters at 2014 T Street, Suite 210, Sacramento, CA 95814, (916) 445-9918. It also has district offices all over the state and can be found in the phone book white pages in the Government section.

Most larger cities have housing discrimination hotlines these days—generally listed under the phone book heading Tenants' Associations, or something similar.

NEIGHBORS

EASEMENTS

An easement is a legal right to use someone else's land for a particular purpose. The property owner must allow the easement holder to use the property according to the terms of the easement. And when the property is sold, the new owner must continue to honor the easement.

Written Easements

Easements are usually in writing and recorded (put on file), like property deeds, at the County Recorder's office. They may also be referred to in property deeds or title insurance reports.

Utility easements are the most common kind. For example, the electric company may have the right to string wires across your property. To find out where utility easements are located on your property, call the company or check the maps at the county planning department or city hall. A survey of the property will also show utility easements.

Property may also be subject to private written easements—easements that allow a neighbor to use a driveway or ensure that a neighbor has sewer or solar access, for example. If your property is subject to private easements, get copies of the easement documents from your neighbor or the County Recorder. If you don't know where the easements are and what uses they allow, you could unknowingly interfere with the easement rights and be liable for the damage.

Easements by Necessity

Even if it isn't written down, a legal easement can exist if it's absolutely necessary to cross someone's land for a legitimate purpose. For example, if the only access to a piece of land is by crossing a neighbor's property, the law recognizes an easement allowing access over the neighbor's land. This is called an easement by necessity.

Easements Acquired by Use of Property

Someone can acquire an easement over another's land by using the land without permission, openly and continuously, for five years. Code of Civil Procedure § 321. An easement acquired this way is called a prescriptive easement.

A prescriptive easement can be made part of the public record by suing the property owner in a "quiet title" lawsuit. A property owner who does not want a neighbor or other user to get an easement, but does not want to prevent the use, can accomplish this in two ways:

- by recording "a notice of consent to use of the land" with the County Recorder's office (generally done with property that has public use, such as a private alley used by the public), Civil Code § 813, or
- by granting permission to a user—just by writing a letter authorizing the use until revoked (often used with a neighbor).

ADVERSE POSSESSION

Under certain circumstances, someone who occupies land that belongs to another can gain legal ownership of that land. This process is called adverse possession, and it's more common than you might think.

In California, a trespasser becomes entitled to legal ownership of property after occupying it for five years without permission, openly and exclusively, and paying the property taxes during that time. Code of Civil Procedure § 749.

The trespasser must be physically present on the land, and it must be obvious to anyone, including an owner who investigates, that a trespasser is on the land. For example, someone in a field harvesting crops is obvious, as is a person who plants a garden—or pours a concrete driveway—on a strip of the neighbor's back yard.

To avoid losing land by adverse possession, keep an eye on your property. Check local tax records if you suspect that someone is paying real estate taxes on part or all of property you own.

Giving permission to someone to use part of your property thwarts any claim. Write out your permission, and get a signed acknowledgment by the person who's occupying the property. Or, if you want the person off your land, say so—and follow up with a call to the police or a visit to a lawyer if necessary.

FENCES

Generally, fences built on a boundary line that are being used by both owners are the responsibility of both neighbors. Repairs, maintenance, removal and other decisions should be decided jointly, no matter who built the fence.

If a fence is built entirely on one's own property, decisions about it can be determined by the owner, unless there are restrictions in the deed, or the city or county zoning rules contain specific height and/or appearance restrictions. Also, if the house is located in a newer tract, then the Declaration of Conditions, Covenants and Restrictions (CC&Rs) will likely regulate the size and appearance of fences. If a neighbor's fence is in a state of serious disrepair (for instance, if it is dilapidated or is a source of danger), then you may have a case you can take to Small Claims Court if other efforts fail to solve the problem.

More Information/Where to Complain

First, determine if there are any restrictions in the use of fences by checking with your neighborhood association, if you live in an area with CC&Rs, or the departments of planning, zoning or building inspectors, or the city attorney.

If you can't negotiate a satisfactory solution with your neighbor, many communities have free neighborhood mediation services that handle just this type of dispute. Your city government should know if such a service is available.

TREES

Trees, as much as we love them, can cause problems. Here's a brief overview of tree rules:

Boundary Trees

A boundary tree or hedge belongs to both property owners in direct proportion to the amount of tree trunk (or hedge) on each side. The joint owners have joint responsibility for the care and maintenance of the tree. Each has the right to trim what is on her side of the property, taking reasonable care not to harm the tree. Neither owner can force the other owner to cut or destroy the tree and should not attempt to do so without the neighbor's consent.

Hanging Tree Branches

Technically, branches (and any fruit) of a neighbor's tree that hang over onto your property belong to your neighbor. You can cut tree branches back to the property line, however, as long as doing so doesn't damage the tree.

If your neighbor can pick the fruit hanging over onto your side without trespassing on your property, he is entitled to do so. Practically, however, this may be impossible. Common sense would seem to say that in this situation the fruit is yours to do with what you want.

If a neigbor's tree doesn't overhang your yard but shades your yard and prevents plants from thriving, you have no legal right to force your neighbor to trim or remove the tree. (The reverse is also true if it's your tree, of course.) If you enjoy the shade of your neighbor's tree and he cuts it down, there is probably nothing you can do. If, however, you can act before the tree is down, you may find that local ordinances prohibit removing certain valued species of trees. A few California communities also regulate trees that block sunlight and drop debris. Check your city and county ordinances to see if any such ordinance applies to you.

Nuisance Trees

If your neighbor's tree annoys you (for example, its leaves continually fall in your swimming pool), you have the right to trim or cut the part of the tree causing the problem up to the boundary line. This also applies to the roots of the tree that may be cracking your cement driveway or walk. If, however, you damage your neighbor's tree by these actions, you may be liable for the damage.

Dangerous Trees

A property owner who is aware that her tree is dangerous (for example, it's sick and one big windstorm would probably topple it right on a neighbor's house, or it drops debris on a neighbor's roof causing a fire hazard) must either correct the problem or cut down the offending tree. Her failure to do this could make her liable for any damage the tree causes.

DEALING WITH DANGEROUS TREES

Some homeowners refuse to cut a dangerous tree down, figuring that when it crashes the insurance company will pay. If you face this situation, call your city or county planning or zoning department, environmental health department or fire department—some will order a property owner to cut down an obviously dangerous tree. If this fails, document that the tree is dangerous and consider enlisting the help of a community mediation project (your neighbor must be willing to mediate). If mediation doesn't work, you can sue your neighbor (in Small Claims Court), based on the fact that the danger posed by the tree makes it a legal nuisance, because it interferes with your use and enjoyment of your property. You can ask for money to compensate you or ask the judge to order the neighbor to prune or remove the tree.

View-Blocking Trees

Many cities have ordinances protecting property owners' views. Typically, they do not require pre-existing trees to be cut down, but may require them to be cut back to their size at a certain date, often when the ordinance was passed or when the complaining party took ownership. Check with your planning or zoning department or the city attorney's office to determine if a view ordinance exists in your community. Also, neighborhood associations often have rules limiting the size and type of trees. If you live in a community covered by Conditions, Covenants and Restrictions (CC&Rs), check these as well.

Most ordinances require you to pay for (or share) the cost of trimming a neighbor's view-blocking tree if you invoke the terms of the law to insist that the tree be cut back.

MORE INFORMATION

For more information on all neighbor issues, including easements and adverse possession, trees, fences and boundaries, see *Neighbor Law*, by Cora Jordan (Nolo Press). ■

Safety and Hazards

CROSS-REFERENCES

ASBESTOS

You may worry that your home has asbestos and is a dangerous place. Asbestos in the home is most commonly found in:

- acoustic and sprayed-on (textured, "popcorn" appearance) ceilings—common in homes and buildings built or remodeled between 1945 and 1978
- duct and furnace insulation
- vinyl floor tiles
- outside siding tiles, and
- wallboard and taping compound (not very common).

Disclosures by Homeowners

Owners of residential real estate must give buyers a disclosure form, called a Real Estate Transfer Disclosure Statement. Among other disclosures, sellers must inform buyers of environmental hazards present on the property, including asbestos. Civil Code § 1102.

Disclosures by Landlords

Owners of apartment buildings that have ten or more units and were constructed before 1979 must notify tenants and employees who work in the building if the building contains "asbestos-containing construction materials." The written notice must be given to each tenant and employee individually. Failure to notify can result in a fine of up to $1,000, imprisonment up to one year, or both. Health and Safety Code §§ 25915 through 25924.

More Information

The U. S. Consumer Product Safety Commission offers a useful booklet, called *Asbestos in the Home,* that explains how to recognize asbestos, when to do something about it or when to leave it alone. For a free copy write CPSC, Publications, Washington, DC 20207.

The California Contractor's State License Board has published *A Consumer Guide to Asbestos.* Not only does this booklet have excellent information, but it has listings of dozens of resources, such as the Environmental Protection Agency (EPA) technical assistance number and the names and phone numbers of laboratories that analyze samples. A free copy is available by calling (800) 321-2752.

LEAD POISONING

Lead from a variety of sources poisons a substantial number of young children every year. The source causing the most problems is leaded dust on the floors in older homes (pre-1978, but especially pre-1960). Other sources incude soil, water and tableware (especially from Latin American and Asian countries). Young children living in urban and older rural areas need to be tested and screened regularly up to age six. Parents can do a number of things to reduce the risk from exposure.

Ceramic Ware

Retail stores selling tableware containing lead levels exceeding state Proposition 65 standards (often from improper glazing) are required to post a warning sign and identify the tableware with a yellow upside down triangle. If you use ceramic ware (especially imported) for cooking and eating, you may want to order a home test kit. These simple test kits run about $20-$30. Generally, they will detect only relatively high lead-leaching potential.

More Information

The California Public Health Foundation Tableware Education and Enforcement Program has several helpful free brochures it will send you. Call (800) 644-LEAD.

Several companies sell home test kits by mail. They are listed in the brochures available from the California Public Health Foundation Tableware Education and Enforcement Program.

Consumer Action, a nonprofit consumer education and advocacy group, has produced free publications (in seven different languages) through its Lead Poisoning Prevention Project. Send a self-addressed, stamped, business-size envelope with 52¢ postage to Consumer Action, 116 New Montgomery Street, Suite 233, San Francisco, CA 94105, or call (415) 777-9635.

POISONING

The California Regional Poison Control Centers will answer questions on such diverse topics as:

- animal bites
- bug or insect bites/stings
- food poisoning
- foreign substances in the eye
- over-the-counter medicines
- pesticides, and
- poisons that have been swallowed.

Of the calls the Centers receive, 60% come from the public and 40% come from the medical profession.

The Poison Control Centers maintain six hotlines throughout the state:

- Alameda, Contra Costa, Del Norte, Humboldt, Marin, Mendocino, Napa, San Francisco, San Mateo and Sonoma Counties—(800) 523-2222
- Alpine, Amador, Butte, Calaveras, Colusa, El Dorado, Glenn, Lake, Lassen, Modoc, Nevada, Placer, Plumas, Sacramento, San Joaquin, Shasta, Sierra, Siskiyou, Solano, Stanislaus, Sutter, Tehama, Trinity, Tuolumne, Yolo and Yuba Counties—(800) 342-9293 or (916) 734-3692
- Monterey, San Benito, San Luis Obispo, Santa Clara and Santa Cruz Counties—(800) 662-9886 or (408) 299-5112
- Fresno, Kern, Kings, Madera, Mariposa, Merced and Tulare Counties—(209) 445-1222
- Inyo, Los Angeles, Mono, Orange, Riverside, San Bernardino, Santa Barbara and Ventura Counties—(800) 777-6476 or (213) 222-3212
- Imperial and San Diego Counties—(800) 876-4766 or (619) 543-6000.

GARBAGE

All cities and counties have ordinances requiring the safe and sanitary storage and disposal of garbage. If your neighbor doesn't properly maintain his property—for example, he stores garbage, old tires or rusting automobile parts in his back yard—call your city or county health department and ask the "environmental health division" to investigate your complaint. It can cite your neighbor and order a clean-up of the trash.

HAZARDOUS CHEMICAL OR PRODUCT DISPOSAL

After you've finished painting your garage door, how will you dispose of the old paint? Or how about the used motor oil from your recent oil change? For information on disposing of hazardous chemicals or household products such as motor oil, paint, paint thinner, pesticides, or anything labeled toxic, flammable or corrosive, call your county Hazardous Waste program or Environmental Health Department. Ask if your county has special toxic disposal days or a special toxic disposal cite.

More Information

A regional office of the California Department of Toxic Substances Control might be able to help you dispose of household hazardous materials. Call and ask to speak to the Duty Officer at one of the following offices:

- Region 1, Sacramento—(916) 255-3545
- Region 2, Berkeley—(510) 540-2122
- Region 3, Glendale—(818) 551-2800
- Region 4, Long Beach—(310) 590-4868.

The Ecology Center-Environmental Information Service answers questions over the phone regarding hazardous chemical and product disposal. Call (510) 548-2220, Tuesday through Saturday, 11 a.m. to 5 p.m. You can also visit the Ecology Center's Library at 2530 San Pablo Avenue, Berkeley, CA 94702.

Your local recycling center may offer suggestions on disposing of hazardous household materials.

Chemtrec Center is a health and safety referral service that can give you the name, address and phone number of a manufacturer or other source if you have safety questions about a chemical product. Call (800) 262-8200, Monday through Friday, 6:00 a.m. to 3:00 p.m.

MOLD AND MILDEW

People with severe allergies often have problems with—sometimes life-threatening reactions to—molds and mildews. If you have a problem with mold or mildew build-up, especially in your closets, help is on the way. Calcium chloride crystals, found in hardware stores, do a very good job of absorbing excess moisture.

STRUCTURAL PEST CONTROL

Pest control services must be licensed in California under the Structural Pest Control Board (SPCB). Pest control companies must provide owners and occupants with written information about the pesticides being used, including the active ingredients, the pest to be controlled and a standard warning about the toxic chemicals in the pesticide.

Finding a Pest Control Company

For starters, check with neighbors, friends, relatives and co-workers for recommendations. Generally, trade associations that establish specific rules of education and performance for its members are a good bet—and this is true for pest control companies. Members of the Pest Control Operators of California (PCOC) must abide by a code of ethics and agree to binding arbitration if there is a dispute. Be sure to ask pest control companies if they guarantee their work and for how long.

Before contracting with any pest control service, contact SPCB to verify the company has a current and valid license and to check the company's complaint record. While you are at it, contact your local Better Business Bureau to see if it has any complaints on file about the pest control company.

If a Pest Control Company Goes Out of Business

SPCB requires a licensee to either put up $4,000 in cash or a bond of equal value. If the company goes out of business, that money or bond will remain in force for five years and 30 days. If you discover a problem more than two-years old (the time limit in which SPCB can take action against a pest control operator), ask the SPCB for the name of the bonding company; you may get compensation there.

Do Home Sales Require a Pest Control Report?

California does not require a structural pest control report prior to the sale of a home. Most financial institutions, however, require one before making a loan. Lenders want to make sure they are lending money to pay for a structurally sound house. Even if a lender doesn't require it, buyers should have a structural pest control inspection for their own protection. First check whether or not a seller has commissioned a pest control report. By law, all pest control reports commissioned within the last two years are kept on file at the SPCB.

What Should Be Covered in a Pest Control Report?

If a homeowner requests a "separated report," a pest control company, in its written report, must clearly separate what work needs to be done now from what is likely to be needed in the future. It's wise to make this request; otherwise you could pay a large sum for repairs that aren't really needed now.

A separated report differentiates between:

- corrective measures for existing damage, such as dry rot and fungus, and
- areas deemed likely (or conducive) to have future problems, such as excessively high grade level (dirt) next to the foundation.

Ask the pest control company to also report areas where further inspection may be needed. Although pest control companies are not legally required to provide this information, there are several reasons to ask for it:

- the area may have been inaccessible—such as a very low crawl space
- the pest control worker simply couldn't get into a locked basement, or
- the pest control company charges extra—for example, to drill holes in areas under gutters to check for rot.

More Information/Where to Complain

SPCB licenses and regulates companies in the pest control business. It will not get involved in fee or billing disputes. Nor will it handle a complaint filed more than two years after a problem occurred. Additionally, SPCB provides free brochures on household pest control, inspection and fumigation. Write or call:

- 1422 Howe Avenue, Suite 3, Sacramento CA 95825—(916) 263-2540
- Los Angeles area—(213) 897-7838
- San Francisco area—(415) 557-9114.

Calls to the Los Angeles and San Francisco numbers are automatically forwarded to Sacramento without additional charge.

CRIME VICTIMS

As a California resident, you may be eligible for monetary compensation if you are an injured victim of certain crimes, even if the crime was committed outside of California. Compensation up to $46,000 may be granted for:

- rehabilitation costs
- lost wages, and
- medical bills and funeral expenses not reimbursed by insurance.

Personal property loss—for example, during a home burglary—is not recoverable. There is no guarantee that you will actually get compensation, but if you are a victim it makes sense to promptly submit a claim to see if you qualify. California's program to compensate victims of a crime is administered by the State Board of Control in Sacramento. Penal Code §§ 13835-13961.

Crimes for which victims can be compensated include:

- vehicular crime, such as hit and run, driving under the influence of drugs or alcohol, using a vehicle as a weapon or causing injuries while fleeing the scene of a felony

- personal crime, such as physical or mental harm from being beaten, attempted homicide or sexual abuse—rape or incest (victim may file within three years of turning 18), and
- witnessing a child abduction or attack, or a rape (only certain family members are eligible).

More Information

For more information on the Victims of Crime Program, contact the Board of Control, P.O. Box 3036, Sacramento, CA 95812, (916) 322-4426.

Also, your county Victim-Witness Assistance Program can provide information on eligibility requirements and benefits, and can help you with the complex application procedure. You must provide verifiable supporting documentation to support your claim and file within a year of the crime or explain why the claim was late—perhaps you didn't know about the program. For the phone number in your area, call 800-VICTIMS (842-8467).

SELF-SERVICE GAS SAVVY

To avoid being the victim of a crime at a self-service gas station, lock your doors when using the gas pump. It's easy to become distracted, especially if the station is busy and you must pay first. Unfortunately, this is a great time for a "shoplifter" walking by to reach in and take your purse, wallet, briefcase, packages, tapes or CDs if you've left your car unlocked.

MISSING PERSONS

If you are trying to locate a missing relative or friend, some private organizations or government agencies may help you in your search.

Salvation Army

The Salvation Army has a service that tries to locate blood relatives. If you're in southern California, call the Los Angeles office at (213) 627-0695. If you're in northern California, call the San Francisco office at (415) 861-0755. The person you speak with will probably put you in touch with someone located nearby the missing person's last known address.

Social Security Administration

The Social Security Administration (SSA) may try to help locate a missing person if your request falls under the SSA's "humanitarian reason" requirement. You must write to the SSA and include:

- an explanation of why you are requesting its help in locating the missing person

- your relationship to the missing person
- a letter to the missing person, in an unsealed envelope with the person's name on the outside—SSA will read it to verify that your request falls under the "humanitarian reason" requirement, and
- sufficient identification about the missing person, such as a Social Security number, birthdate or name of the parents.

SSA will send your letter to the missing person's last known employer that the SSA has on record —SSA's records go back about a year. If the person is no longer working and receives Social Security, SSA might send the letter to the home. That is the end of SSA's involvement—you will know if the person received your letter only if he or she responds. If the SSA can't find an address, the agency simply destroys your letter.

Send your letter (remember—don't seal the envelope into which you put the letter) to the Social Security Administration, OCRO—Division of Certification and Coverage, 300 North Greene Street, Baltimore, MD 21201.

Internal Revenue Service

The Internal Revenue Service (IRS) may try to help locate a missing person if your request falls under the IRS's "urgent and compelling reason" requirement. You must write to the IRS and include:

- an explanation of why you are requesting its help in locating the missing person
- your relationship to the missing person
- a letter to the missing person, in an unsealed envelope—the IRS will read it to verify that your request falls under the "urgent and compelling reason" requirement, and
- the missing person's Social Security number.

The IRS sends your letter to the last known home address the IRS has for the missing person. Send your letter (remember—don't seal the envelope into which you put the letter) to one of the following:

- IRS Disclosure Officer, P.O. Box 24014, Service Center, Stop 891, Fresno, CA 93779
- IRS Disclosure Officer, P.O. Box 30208, Laguna Niguel, CA 92607-0208
- IRS Disclosure Officer, 300 North Los Angeles St., Room 5202, Los Angeles, CA 90012
- IRS Disclosure Officer, 1301 Clay Street, Suite 800S, Oakland, CA 94612
- IRS Disclosure Officer, P.O. Box 2900, Stop SA 5201, Sacramento, CA 95812
- IRS Disclosure Officer, 55 South Market St., Stop HQ 4003, San Jose, CA 95113.

Additional Resources

You Can Find Anyone, by Eugene Ferraro (Marathon Press, 407 W. Santa Clara Avenue, Santa Ana, CA 92706). This guidebook (found in some libraries) has some sneaky and a few possibly illegal suggestions to locate people. It may be particularly helpful in trying to collect a debt.

A Nasty Bit of Business, by Fay Faron (Crighton-Morgan Publishing Group), also has some good ideas on finding folks.

HOME SECURITY/ALARM COMPANIES

Burglar Alarms

Burglar alarms come in a wide array of choices and prices. They range from a simple closed-circuit system that trips a siren or buzzer, to more elaborate motion systems that are often hooked up to a police station or other security service.

The California Bureau of Collection and Investigative Services (BCIS) licenses burglar alarm companies and their employees. Contact it if you have a complaint about equipment service warranties, incomplete installations, inadequate operating instructions, or known defects not repaired. As with most state agencies, it will not get involved in fee disputes.

Locksmiths

BCIS also issues permits to locksmiths. Locksmiths install, repair, open, modify and make keys for locks. (A "key duplicator" is a person who makes keys for retail customers, but is not a locksmith.) To get a permit, a locksmith must be fingerprinted and have no criminal record. Locksmiths are required to carry a valid permit while working. Business and Professions Code § 6980 and following.

More Information/Where to Complain

The National Burglar and Fire Alarm Association has free pamphlets giving tips on purchasing a burglar alarm system and working with a home security company. Contact the Association at 7101 Wisconsin Avenue, Bethesda, MD 20814-4805, (301) 907-3202.

Safe Homes, Safe Neighborhoods: Stopping Crime Where You Live, by Stephanie Mann with M.C. Blakeman (Nolo Press), provides detailed information on how to improve home security and reduce neighborhood crime. It's available in libraries and bookstores.

The Bureau of Collection and Investigative Services may be contacted at 400 R Street, Suite 2001, Sacramento, CA 95814, (916) 445-7366. ■

Service Providers

TOPICS

The Mover's Liability for Loss or Damage
If the Mover Doesn't Deliver When Promised
Where to Complain
OSTEOPATHS
Where to Complain
PHARMACISTS
Generic Substitutes
Where to Complain
REAL ESTATE BROKERS AND AGENTS
More Information/Where to Complain
TAX PREPARERS
Where to Complain

CROSS-REFERENCES
Business and Corporations—Stocks, Stockbrokers and Securities Firms
Consumer Rights—Sales—Right of Cancellation (Cooling-Off Period)
Travel—Travel Promoters and Travel Agents

ACCOUNTANTS

Accountants audit, examine, investigate, review and verify financial records and transactions. The California Board of Accountancy licenses and regulates certified public accountants (CPAs) and public accountants. Anyone can do bookkeeping, and many types of people prepare tax returns, but people using the titles "CPA" or "public accountant" must be licensed by the Board.

Mistakes by Accountants

If your accountant makes an error in preparing your tax return, and the IRS or California Franchise Tax Board subsequently bills you for the balance due plus penalties and interest, first try to settle with your accountant. (If your accountant's error is due to incorrect information you provided, don't blame your accountant for any interest and penalties you incur.) If that doesn't work, you can file a complaint with the Board of Accountancy. Although CPAs on the Board staff will contact your accountant and suggest restitution, the Board lacks the authority to enforce payment for negligence. Sometimes, just suggesting that you plan to file a complaint with the Board of Accountancy may be enough to get your accountant to settle with you. Your accountant may agree to pay only for penalties, however, on the theory that you have had the use of your money and could have been earning interest on it.

How to Find an Accountant

The best referral is from a long-term satisfied customer. Ask friends, neighbors, relatives or co-workers for recommendations for the type of accountant services you need. Small business owners are also good sources. Costs can vary widely, so be sure to compare fees.

More Information/Where to Complain

To file a complaint against an accountant, send a written description of the problem or dispute to the California Board of Accountancy, 2135 Butano Drive, Suite 112, Sacramento, CA 95825. The Board can take disciplinary action against an accountant for reasons including dishonesty, fraud or gross negligence.

To verify that a prospective accountant is properly licensed and in good standing, call the Board at (916) 574-2155.

ACUPUNCTURISTS

Acupuncturists are licensed and regulated by the Medical Board of California. (See Doctors section, below.) For many years, acupuncture was considered an alternative or supplemental health practice and not covered by most medical insurance policies. Although insurance companies are not obligated to cover acupuncture, many now classify acupuncture as a primary form of healthcare and pay for the care.

ATTORNEYS

To be a lawyer in California, one must pass an examination sponsored by the California Bar Association. Unfortunately, the Bar examination does not test competence in legal skills, so in looking for a lawyer to help with a particular problem, it's up to you to investigate further.

Lawyer Referral

Lawyers, like everyone else these days, specialize. So your job is not only to find a good lawyer, but one who has expertise in the area of your concern. A good place to get a recommendation is from friends, neighbors, relatives or co-workers who have had a favorable experience with a lawyer. Keep in mind that when asking for a referral, you want to consult a savvy person whose good sense you respect. Small business owners can be good sources of attorney referrals as they often work with lawyers. Their lawyer may not specialize in the area you need help in, but can suggest someone who does. If personal networks don't help, you may want to call your county bar association and ask for their lawyer referral service.

Specify that you want a lawyer who specializes in the area you need, such as personal injury or divorce—not just the next name on the rotating list. If you use a bar association referral, a half-hour consultation should be inexpensive. (Ask the price when calling for an appointment.) If a lawyer recommends an action that may be expensive or time-consuming, get a second opinion.

Certified Legal Specialists

The State Bar of California has a program for "certifying legal specialists" in the following seven areas:

- criminal
- family
- immigration and nationality
- probate
- estate planning and trust
- taxation, and
- workers' compensation.

To become certified, attorneys must pass a written exam in the specialty, have substantial experience in the specialty, complete approved legal education programs, and have their ability and experience evaluated by other attorneys and judges. For more information or a list of certified specialists, write or call the Office of the Board of Legal Specialization, State Bar of California, 100 Van Ness Avenue, 28th Floor, San Francisco, CA 94102, (415) 241-2100.

Answers to Legal Questions

Lawyers at Tele-Lawyer, Inc., answer legal questions and give advice for $3 a minute. The lawyers specialize, so you will get one who can answer your particular questions. If the lawyer can't answer your question during the call, he/she will research it and call you back. You are not charged for research time, but rather only for time on the telephone; the average call lasts 14 minutes. These lawyers have instant access to a computerized database of legal information. The lawyers will review documents and will send you legal forms, if they are needed, free of charge.

Tele-Lawyer only offers advice; it doesn't make referrals to lawyers and its lawyers do not accept cases. For credit card calls, call (800) 835-3529 or (800) 283-5529. For a charge to your phone bill, call (900) 370-7000, (900) 288-6763, (900) 776-7000, or (900) 446-4529. You can write or call Tele-Lawyer for a free brochure at Tele-Lawyer, Inc., P.O. Box 110, Huntington Beach, CA 92648, (714) 536-2325.

More Information/Where to Complain

A free pamphlet, *What Should I Do If I Have a Problem With My Lawyer,* is available by sending a self-addressed, stamped, business-size envelope to: State Bar of California, 555 Franklin Street, San Francisco, CA 94102.

If you are having a problem with your attorney, let her know it. If she doesn't return your phone calls, write a letter detailing your dissatisfaction. If that doesn't get results, tell the attorney you intend to file a complaint with the county bar association or the State Bar of California. Simply advising your attorney that you intend to file a complaint may be enough to resolve a problem without actually having to do so. Most county bar associations have a volunteer committee (of attorneys) on client relations and professional ethics that can handle a garden-variety dispute within approximately 30 days.

Many people distrust some county bar associations' dispute resolution procedures because they use one "independent person" (who may be a lawyer's wife or secretary) and two local lawyers (who may not be objective). (The inclusion of an independent person on a panel is up to the bar's discretion.) The State Bar, after years of using a similarly flawed system, has dramatically improved its procedures for serious discipline cases, such as client abandonment, stealing or failing to meet court dates. Their new system features the State Bar Court with professional judges and investigators. You can file a complaint with the State Bar by writing or calling State Bar of California, 333 South Beaudry Avenue, 9th Floor, Los Angeles, CA 90017-1466, (800) 843-9053.

Fee Disputes

Most county bar associations have "fee dispute panels" to handle complaints about attorney bills. If your local bar association does not, or you or your lawyer believe a fair hearing is not possible locally, then complain to the State Bar, which will hold a hearing in your county. In most cases, if you take your dispute to arbitration, the lawyer must arbitrate. If the amount is more than the Small Claims Court limit, the attorney must tell you about arbitration.

Reimbursement for Theft by an Attorney

The State Bar of California created the Client Security Fund to compensate clients who lose money due to thefts by an attorney. The fund can reimburse you up to $50,000 to cover money or property lost because an attorney was dishonest, not because the attorney acted incompetently. Reimbursement can take anywhere from three months to three years. For an application form, write or call toll-free to the Client Security Fund at the above State Bar address or phone number.

Additional Resources

The citizen group HALT, which advocates for better attorney-client grievance procedures, might help with your complaint. HALT is a Washington, DC nonprofit membership group with several chapters in California. (HALT offers a wide variety of free pamphlets regarding simple legal issues that people frequently run into.) HALT can be reached at 1319 F Street, NW, Suite 300, Washington, DC 20004, (202) 347-9600. Membership is $15, which provides you with a copy of the 146-page manual, *Using a Lawyer and What to Do If Things Go Wrong* (Random House), and a year's subscription to HALT's newsletter.

BUILDERS/CONTRACTORS

How to Choose a Contractor

Ask neighbors, friends, relatives and co-workers for recommendations. Pay particular attention to the opinions of fastidious people. If they were satisfied by a particular contractor, chances are you will be too. Get references from local builder's supply businesses (electrical, plumbing and lumber). They can often suggest reputable local contractors. Ask a contractor to supply you with references that you can check out for yourself.

Any contractor doing home improvement work worth more than $300 (labor and materials) must be licensed by the California Contractor's State License Board (CSLB). You can verify that the license is current and valid, and check the contractor's complaint record by calling the CSLB. CSLB will reveal any legal action that has been taken against the contractor for inadequate or unfinished work, but not the number and specifics of complaints filed.

Using an unlicensed contractor has some drawbacks. First, unlicensed contractors are breaking the law. They can't get building permits, which may be required for the job you are planning. If you have a problem with an unlicensed contractor, you won't have much recourse. The CSLB cannot pursue an unlicensed contractor, so you could be stuck with a shoddy or unfinished job. If this happens with licensed contractors, the CSLB can go after them.

How to Proceed

1. Get competitive bids from several contractors. Make sure each one bids on exactly the same specifications and proposes similar quality materials.
2. Get everything in writing in a contract—the exact work, price, when work is to begin and how long it will take. Both parties should sign the contract to avoid misunderstandings.
3. Make as low a down payment as possible. Under state law, your down payment may not exceed $1,000 or 10% of the job, whichever is less.
4. Be sure the contractor gets a building permit (if necessary) before work begins.
5. Be sure the contractor is insured against claims covering workers' compensation, property damage and personal liability in case of accidents. Ask to see the policies or ask for the name of the insurance carrier and verify that the contractor is insured.
6. Specify in your contract that you want unconditional lien releases from subcontractors and suppliers (with notarized signatures) before making progress payments.
7. Schedule progress payments based on the contractor's satisfactory performance of a like amount of work. Do not let your payments get ahead of the work.

Three-Day Right of Cancellation

California law requires a contractor to give you a three-day notice of your of cancellation, in writing, when you sign a contract in your home or someplace other than the contractor's place of business.

Mechanic's Liens

California law allows anyone who furnishes labor or materials to your home to place a "mechanic's lien" against your home if you do not pay. Even if you paid the general contractor, if he did not pay the subcontractors or material suppliers, they can place a lien on your home by recording it at the County Recorder's office. In some circumstances, this means you would have to pay a bill twice to remove the lien. To prevent this from happening, specify in your contract that you want unconditional lien releases (notarized) from all the subcontractors and suppliers before you pay any bills. Or, if the job has only a contractor and one subcontractor or one material supplier, you can make a check payable to both parties.

In order for a mechanic's lien to be enforced, the contractor must file a lawsuit to foreclose on your home within 90 days of the date the lien was recorded—this can be extended in some cases. If you owe a lot of money, a contractor will probably file a lawsuit. If you owe only a small amount, the contractor uses the lien as a threat to get you to pay voluntarily. If the contractor does not file a lawsuit, the lien becomes void. Even though the lien stays on the County Recorder's records, it will not prevent you from selling or refinancing your home.

More Information/Where to Complain

Getting a Good House: Tips and Tricks for Evaluating New Construction, by carpenter Bob Syvanen (Globe Pequot Press), is an easy-to-use reference with full-page line drawings and minimal text.

Simple Contracts for Personal Use, by attorney Stephen Elias and Marcia Stewart (Nolo Press), includes sample contracts for home repair and remodeling.

The Department of Consumer Affairs has published a very useful booklet called *What You Should Know Before You Hire a Contractor.* A free copy is available from the Contractor's State License Board by calling (800) 321-2752.

If you can't resolve a dispute you are having—such as the contractor won't finish the work or you can't get the contractor to come back for needed repairs—contact the CSLB at the address or phone number above. You can also contact your local Contractor's State License Board office (check your phone book white pages under State Government Offices).

Just threatening to file a complaint may be enough to get the contractor back on the job. Or you can sue in Small Claims Court up to $5,000, which may well be a faster way to resolve a problem. If you win a judgment in Small Claims Court and the contractor doesn't pay, you can submit the judgment to the Registrar of the Contractor's State License Board, P.O. Box 26000, Sacramento, CA 9582, and it will be placed on the licensee's record. If the contractor (licensee) doesn't pay the judgment or file a judgment bond, the contractor's license will be suspended.

CHIROPRACTORS

The California Board of Chiropractic Examiners licenses and regulates chiropractors. The Board also administers regulations protecting the health, welfare and safety of the public concerning chiropractors.

Where to Complain

The Board handles complaints regarding fraud, misrepresentation, incompetence, negligence or unprofessional conduct. It does not get involved in fee disputes. The Board prefers written complaints sent to 3401 Folsom Boulevard, Suite B, Sacramento, CA 95816, (916) 227-2790.

DENTISTS AND ORTHODONTISTS

Finding a good dentist or orthodontist is basic to providing good care for yourself and your family. Your best bet is to ask friends, neighbors, relatives and co-workers for recommendations. Dentists and orthodontists must be licensed to practice in the state. The California Board of Dental Examiners licenses and regulates dentists, orthodontists and dental hygienists.

Where to Complain

If you have a complaint regarding the quality of work, discuss it with your dentist or orthodontist. If you are still dissatisfied, you can complain to the California Board of Dental Examiners or your county's Dental Society—which has a peer review system. Neither will get involved in a fee dispute. Both groups, however, will examine your dental work to determine if the work performed meets appropriate standards. In addition, the Board will investigate if fraud or misrepresentation is involved.

Your local dental society is listed in the phone book business listings starting with your county's name (for example, the Santa Clara County Dental Society).

The California Board of Dental Examiners accepts written complaints only; write to 1432 Howe Avenue, Room 85-B, Sacramento, CA 95825-3241. You can request a consumer complaint form by calling (916) 263-2335.

**COMPLAINING ABOUT A
DENTIST OR ORTHODONTIST**

I have found that it's better to file a complaint with the Dental Society Peer Review System (if the dentist or orthodontist is a member) than with the Board of Dental Examiners. The Dental Society's process is faster and more responsive. The State Board is understaffed and probably won't pursue the dentist or orthodontist efficiently or as aggressively as you might want. While better, the Dental Society is no paragon of efficiency either. Both agencies' processes are too long and too slow: it's a choice between two less-than-perfect systems.

Fee Disputes

For a fee dispute, if you haven't paid the bill, your best bet is to determine what you believe is fair—check other dentists' or orthodontists' rates—and pay that amount with a letter explaining your reasons. You can write a check for partial payment and indicate that it is for payment in full. Your dentist or orthodontist may accept it. But your dentist or orthodontist may cash your check and then turn the unpaid portion over to a collection agency.

If you've paid the bill and your dentist or orthodontist won't refund the amount you consider excessive, consider going to Small Claims Court. Be ready to document that the dentist or orthodontist charged too much.

DOCTORS

The Medical Board of California (formerly called the Board of Medical Quality Assurance) licenses and regulates physicians and surgeons, as well as other healing arts practitioners including:

- acupuncturists
- audiologists
- hearing aid dispensers
- physical therapists
- physicians' assistants
- podiatrists
- psychologists
- registered dispensing opticians
- respiratory care practitioners, and
- speech pathologists.

Chiropractors and osteopaths are not under its jurisdiction.

More Information/Where to Complain

To verify that a physician or other healing arts practitioner is licensed, call the Medical Board of California at (916) 263-2382.

The Board also handles complaints about negligence, incompetence, misrepresentation, unlicensed activity, and the like. It does not handle fee disputes. The toll-free central complaint hotline is (800) 633-2322. If you're in Sacramento, call (916) 263-2424. The mailing address is Medical Board of California, 1426 Howe Avenue, Suite 54, Sacramento, CA 95825.

Fee Disputes

Do not be embarrassed to ask in advance what the doctor's fees will be. If you have a complaint about a fee, discuss it with the doctor's office, first. If the staff is not cooperative, talk to the doctor. If that does not solve the problem, see if your county medical society has a fee dispute panel. These panels can work particularly well to get a fee reduction if the doctor's fees are much higher than your insurance company's schedule of "reasonable and customary charges."

MOVERS

Before moving, get three estimates for transportation and packing. For recommendations of movers, ask friends, neighbors, relatives or co-workers who have moved previously. If you are moving within California, the mover must provide you with a booklet entitled *Before You Move*.

Interstate Moves (Outside of California)

For interstate moves, you may receive one of two kinds of estimates—binding or nonbinding. Whichever you receive must be in writing. Be sure to read your contract with the mover (called a bill of lading) before you sign it.

Binding Estimate

A binding estimate means that once the move is over and you receive the final bill, it cannot be for more than the estimate. A mover may charge a fee to give a binding estimate. You are responsible for paying the bill in cash or by certified check or money order at the time of delivery unless the mover agrees, before you move, to extend credit or to accept payment by credit card.

Nonbinding Estimate

A nonbinding estimate means that there is no guarantee that the final cost will not be more than the estimate. There is no fee for giving a nonbinding estimate. At the time of delivery, the mover cannot require you to pay more than the amount of the original estimate plus 10% if the mover insists on immediate payment. If the mover is willing to give you 30 days to pay the bill, the mover can charge you more than 10% over the nonbinding estimate.

Intrastate Moves (Within California)

The California Public Utilities Commission (CPUC) urges consumers to verify that a moving company has a valid permit issued by CPUC; look for a five-digit permit number preceded by "Cal.T." For permit verification, call toll-free, (800) 877-8867.

Moving companies are not required to give you an estimate for intrastate moves, but many will. If you get an estimate, it must be in writing and it must be given after visually inspecting your goods. Do not accept an oral estimate. Charges on local moves (fewer than 100 constructive miles, accounting for driving conditions) are usually based on an hourly rate. Long distance moves (more than 100 constructive miles), on the other hand, must be based on weight and mileage. As the weight increases, the cost per pound decreases.

Before your move begins, the mover must inform you of a Not to Exceed Price for your move and cannot charge you more than that price. If you added items to be moved (after the original estimate) or request other services (for example, you forgot to tell the mover about the extra flight of stairs at the new apartment) the mover can provide a Change Order for Services at the time of pick-up or before performing the service. Obviously you have to pay more for additional services.

Inventory Report

When the mover arrives to pick up your possessions, you may request an inventory of all articles being moved. The carrier will note the condition of your furniture and goods (in a code that is explained on the top of the inventory sheet). Make sure you agree with any assessments made by the carrier about the condition of your goods at the time of pick-up. If you disagree, make your own comments on the inventory list; otherwise, you may have difficulty getting compensation if damage occurs. Every item and box should be listed on the inventory sheet. If a box or item is missing, you will have proof it was picked up.

The Mover's Liability for Loss or Damage

For both in- and out-of-state moves, protection in case of damage or destruction is limited to 60 cents per pound—which is very low. For moves within California, you must declare the value of your shipment and choose a level of protection. If you don't do this, your goods will be automatically protected for actual cash value (fair market value) up to $20,000 and you may be charged for this. If this is not adequate (often it is not), you can buy additional insurance coverage from the mover or your insurance carrier. Before doing so, check your homeowners' or renters' insurance policy to see whether your possessions will be covered for damage or loss during the move. Some policies cover moving, others do not.

If the Mover Doesn't Deliver When Promised

For moves weighing more than 5,000 pounds or moved more than 75 miles, you may request the shipment be picked up on a specific date and delivered within an agreed span of two consecutive days. If those terms are not met, the carrier must pay you $100 per day for each day of the delay. You must request this service in writing and any claim you make must also be in writing within 30 days of delivery.

Within California, the mover must notify you at least 24 hours in advance if delivery of your goods is delayed. If you have to spend the night in a hotel because of the carrier's negligence, you can try to get compensation by filing a claim with the carrier.

Where to Complain

When the delivery is completed, check carefully for any lost or damaged goods. Even if you don't notice something damaged or missing at delivery, it doesn't affect your right to make a claim later as long as you can tie the loss to the move. To file

217

a claim, leave any damaged items which were placed in boxes or crates in the original container, especially if the external container shows damage. The carrier may or may not inspect your damaged items. Documentation and damaged packing containers will be helpful if you end up suing the mover.

All damage and loss claims must be in writing. You have nine months from the time of the move in which to file a claim. It is best, however, to file a claim as quickly as possible. The mover must acknowledge your claim within 30 days after receipt, and must pay, offer a compromise settlement, or decline in writing within 60 days.

If you don't get satisfaction from the carrier, try filing a complaint with one of two trade associations:

- Intrastate moves—The California Moving and Storage Association (CMSA) will try to help resolve any problem with one of their members regarding your move. Contact CMSA at 4281 Katella Avenue, Suite 205, Los Alamitos, CA 90720-3562, (800) 672-1415. CMSA needs a copy of the bill of lading, estimated cost of services and a brief synopsis of what took place.
- Interstate moves—American Movers Conference has developed an arbitration program for loss or damage claims involving member companies in interstate moves. Both the mover and the consumer must agree to arbitrate in writing. For more information, contact the American Movers Conference, Dispute Settlement Program, 1611 Duke Street, Alexandria, VA 22314, (703) 683-7410.

If one of the trade associations can't help, you may have to contact a government agency. For interstate moves, contact the Interstate Commerce Commission (ICC):

- 360 East Second Street, Suite 304, Los Angeles, CA 90012, (213) 894-4008
- 211 Main Street, Suite 500, San Francisco, CA 94105, (415) 744-6520.

If you want to sue an interstate mover, you need the Motor Carrier (MC), number which can be obtained from the local ICC. With that, the Secretary of the ICC in Washington, D.C. can give you the name of the person to sue (the "agent for process") in California or any state.

For moves within California, contact the California Public Utilities Commission (CPUC) at 505 Van Ness Avenue, San Francisco, CA 94102-3298, (800) 366-4782 or (415) 703-1402. Or you can contact one of the 18 district offices maintained by the CPUC throughout the state. Check the telephone directory white pages, under State Government. The CPUC doesn't have the authority to make carriers settle claims. Nor can it determine the carrier's liability for any loss or damage. If you and the mover agree, your claim may be submitted to an impartial arbitrator for resolution.

OSTEOPATHS

Osteopathy is a system of medicine which holds that disease is chiefly due to derangement of the bones, such as in the vertebrae. The Osteopathic Medical Board licenses doctors of osteopathic medicine (DOs) and enforces regulations governing the practice of osteopathic physicians and surgeons.

Where to Complain

The Osteopathic Medical Board handles complaints involving fraud, misrepresentation and unprofessional conduct. In addition, it wants to hear about advertisements claiming undocumented cures for specific diseases. The Osteopathic Medical Board accepts written complaints at 444 North 3rd Street, Suite A200, Sacramento, CA 95814, (916) 322-4306.

PHARMACISTS

The California Board of Pharmacy regulates and licenses pharmacists. It also enforces federal and state laws and regulations involving the purchasing, storing and selling of drugs.

Generic Substitutes

If a doctor has not indicated "no substitutions" on a new prescription, a pharmacist can substitute a cheaper generic brand for a name brand without obtaining the doctor's permission as long as the savings are passed on to the consumer. Good pharmaceutical practice, however, dictates discussing the option with the patient. Before a pharmacist renews a prescription with a generic substitute, she discusses the substitution with you and your doctor.

A generic drug has the same ingredients as its well-known name counterpart and is FDA approved, but it is cheaper because the manufacturer does not spend money on advertising. Some insurance companies will only pay for generic medicines.

DISCOUNTED DRUGS FOR SENIORS

Many pharmacies offer 10% discounts to seniors. If such a discount isn't posted, ask about it anyway. Also, you may want to check out savings available by ordering prescriptions by mail. The American Association of Retired Persons has information on mail-order pharmacies in its monthly magazine, *Modern Maturity*.

Where to Complain

If a pharmacist makes an error in filling a prescription—wrong drug, wrong label, wrong strength, wrong directions—contact the Board of Pharmacy:

- 400 R Street, Room 4070, Sacramento, CA, 95814, (916) 445-5014 (main office)
- 107 S. Broadway, Room 8015, Los Angeles, CA 90012, (213) 897-3125 (branch office).

REAL ESTATE BROKERS AND AGENTS

You can legally sell or buy a house in California without a real estate broker or agent as long as you are at least 18 years old and sane. You must be aware of the rules governing real estate transfers, such as who must sign the papers, who can conduct the actual sale transaction, and what to do if and when "encumbrances" arise which slow down the transfer of ownership.

Many buyers and sellers don't have the time or inclination to handle a real estate sale on their own. For that reason, they work with a real estate broker or agent.

Brokers and agents (sellers who work under a broker's supervision) must be licensed by the California Department of Real Estate, after successfully passing an examination and fulfilling other requirements. Before choosing someone to work with, interview several agents. Ask for the names of previous clients. Call a few and ask if they were happy with the agent's services.

A potential buyer can work with a real estate professional under any of the following legal relationships:

- buyer's agent—paid a commission by the seller but legally represents only the buyer
- dual agent—paid a commission by the seller but legally represents the buyer and seller
- seller's agent—paid a commission by the seller and legally represents only the seller, or
- buyer's broker—paid a commission by the buyer and legally represents only the buyer.

Whatever relationship you choose must be recorded on a form entitled "Disclosure Regarding Real Estate Agency Relationships."

More Information/Where to Complain

Nolo Press publishes two California real estate books, both of which contain information on real estate brokers and agents. They are *How to Buy a House in California,* by Ralph Warner, Ira Serkes and George Devine, and *For Sale by Owner,* by George Devine.

If you have a problem with a real estate agent or broker that you cannot resolve directly with the person, you can file a complaint with the California Department of Real Estate. It will get involved if you have been subjected to unfair, misleading or fraudulent treatment in a real estate transaction by a licensee. It will not help you in fee disputes or return of deposits. Nor does the Department give legal advice or order a licensee to cancel a contract. The Department can suspend or revoke a license.

If you have lost money due to fraud, misrepresentation or deceit in a transaction with a licensed real estate broker, you may be able to recover some money from the Real Estate Recovery Fund. The Department of Real Estate can tell you what you have to do to get money from the fund.

You can contact the Department of Real Estate to find out if a broker or agent is licensed, to complain about a broker or agent or to obtain an application to file a claim against the Real Estate Recovery Fund as follows:

- 2201 Broadway, Sacramento, CA 95818, (916) 227-0931 (main office)
- 2550 Mariposa, Room 3070, Fresno, CA 93721, (209) 445-5009
- 107 South Broadway, Room 8107, Los Angeles, CA 90012, (213) 897-3399
- 1350 Front Street, Room 3064, San Diego, CA 92101, (619) 525-4192
- 185 Berry Street, Room 3400, San Francisco, CA 94107, (415) 904-5925
- 28 Civic Center Plaza, Room 639, Santa Ana, CA 92701, (714) 558-4491.

TAX PREPARERS

The California Tax Preparer Program regulates tax preparers and interviewers. It also promulgates rules and regulations.

Where to Complain

If you have a problem with a tax preparer, such as dishonesty, fraud, gross negligence in preparing tax forms or willful violation of the Program's rules and regulations, contact the California Tax Preparer Program, 400 R Street, Suite 3140, Sacramento, CA 95814, (916) 324-4977. The organization does not handle fee disputes.

The California Board of Accountancy licenses and regulates certified public accountants (CPAs) and public accountants; it does not regulate tax preparers. ∎

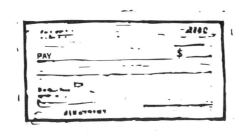

Taxes

TOPICS

CROSS-REFERENCES

Consumer Rights—Products—Mail Order
Consumer Rights—Sales—Auctions
Credit, Loans and Debts—Credit Reporting
Employment—Social Security
Government—Government Agencies—Department of Motor Vehicles
Service Providers—Tax Preparers

FRANCHISE TAX BOARD

The California Franchise Tax Board is responsible for collecting state personal income taxes, state corporation franchise taxes and income taxes, as well as administering the homeowners' and renters' assistance programs (postponement of property taxes and rent rebates).

More Information/Where to Complain

The Franchise Tax Board has a toll-free number—(800) 852-5711.

If you write to protest an FTB's "Notice of Tax to Be Assessed," you must disagree in writing within 60 days of receiving the notice. Send you protest letter to Franchise Tax Board, Protest Unit, P.O. Box 942867, Sacramento, CA 94267-5540.

All other correspondence (filing, billing, complaints or questions) should be sent to the Franchise Tax Board, P.O. Box 942840, Sacramento, CA 94240-0040. You can contact one of the 16 district offices around the state. Check the white pages Government listings, State of California.

INTERNAL REVENUE SERVICE (IRS)

The IRS is the federal agency responsible for collecting income taxes from people who earn income in the United States. Every taxpayer (with a few exceptions) is required to file a tax return and pay the taxes owed.

Every tax return is reviewed for mathematical accuracy and the correct payment amount, and is checked against government and private records filed with the IRS showing your income. If the IRS finds you owe more money than you have paid, it will bill you for the amount it claims you owe. If you don't pay up, the IRS will send you four to nine tax bills, depending on the type of tax owed. If you don't pay the final notice, the IRS normally sets up a delinquent collection account and notifies you that liens may be placed on your property. If you don't pay within 30 days, the IRS will probably start to enforce its liens—usually by garnishing your wages, attaching your bank accounts and possibly forcing the sale of your car or house. The IRS is the only agency that can place a lien, without a court judgment, on assets, such as your bank account, automobile or boat.

Negotiating With the IRS

If you owe less than $10,000, you have an automatic right to be put on an installment plan to pay your taxes before the IRS files a notice of federal tax lien or takes a more aggressive collection stance. The IRS may not necessarily tell you about this right. Be sure to bring it up with the first person you speak to.

IRS Liens and Credit Reports

A notice of federal tax lien is a matter of public record and it will show up on your credit report. The IRS does not report credit information to credit bureaus. Credit bureaus hire businesses to search public records—county recorder's offices, where notices of federal tax liens are filed, are always searched.

If the IRS records a lien in error, ask the IRS to give you a letter explaining the mistake. Send a copy of the letter to the credit bureaus and ask to have the inaccurate information removed from your report.

If You Have a Problem With the IRS

If you receive a notice from the IRS that you disagree with or don't understand, don't ignore it even if you think you are right. That the IRS made a mathematical error is irrelevant at this point. Although the letter suggests you call (it will indicate a specific phone number), writing is preferable. Phone calls are rarely documented—you'll just keep getting bills.

Your written statement should concisely explain why you don't owe the money. Include:

- photocopies of documents which support your position
- your Social Security number or Taxpayer ID number
- the type of tax
- the year in question, and
- your daytime telephone number.

To ensure that your letter gets to the right department, place a photocopy of the IRS notice on top of yours. (Keep the original in a safe place.)

If you don't get satisfaction from your letters or calls and have received at least two notices, call the Problem Resolution Office (PRO); its function is to resolve taxpayer disputes. In California, the PRO has five offices:

- Laguna Niguel—(714) 643-4182
- Los Angeles—(213) 894-6111
- Sacramento—(916) 978-4079
- San Francisco—(415) 556-5046
- San Jose—(408) 291-7132.

More Information

Stand Up to the IRS, by Frederick W. Daily, contains all the information individuals need to contend with an IRS notice or collection effort. It covers negotiating with the IRS, audits, reducing your tax bill, filing for bankruptcy to get rid of your taxes, and much more. Small businesses might want to get ahold of *The Small Business Tax Survival Handbook*, also by Frederick W. Daily. Both books are published by Nolo Press and are available in bookstores and libraries.

"ROLLING OVER" THE PROFIT ON A HOUSE SALE

When you sell a house and purchase another, you can normally defer taxes owed on your profit from the sale. The "rollover residence replacement rule" requires that you defer paying taxes on the profit realized when you buy a replacement principal residence within two years (before or after) of selling the first house, as long as the house purchased costs the same or more than the other house sold for. You can roll over your profit an unlimited number of times, but not more often than once every 24 months unless you must move sooner because of a job change. Internal Revenue Code § 1034.

If You Are 55 or Older

If you are age 55 or older and don't qualify for the "rollover" described above (you're not buying another home or the home you're buying costs less than the one you are selling), you are entitled to claim a once-in-a-lifetime tax exemption on the first $125,000 of profit you realize from the sale of your home. To claim the exemption, only one co-owner spouse needs to be at least 55 on the day of the sale. The seller must have owned and lived in the home any three of the last five years—the years need not be the last three, nor consecutive—before the sale. Internal Revenue Code § 121.

While the once-in-a-lifetime $125,000 exclusion is a real benefit for many people, even if you're eligible you may not want to use it just yet if you do plan to buy another house at a lesser cost than what you sold your house for. The tax savings now may be relatively small and, if you think you'll sell your second house at a great profit some day, you may want to save the exclusion for later use. If you don't plan to buy again, however, use the exclusion now.

If You Are 55 or Older and Planning to Marry

If you are over 55 (and so is your spouse to be) and you each own a home, study the $125,000 exemption rule carefully. If neither of you has used the exemption before and you each own a house, you each may want to sell before getting married so you can both claim the exemption. Once you are married, only one of you will be able to use the exemption.

PROPERTY TAXES

Tax assessors are county officials who establish the value of real property located within their county for tax purposes. Specifically, the tax assessor has the following responsibilities:
- locate all taxable real property in the county and identify the ownership
- establish a value for all real property subject to property tax
- list the value of all real property on the assessment roll
- apply all legal exemptions, and
- assess personal property for businesses.

The tax assessor does not compute property tax bills, collect property taxes (that is done by the Tax Collector's Office), or set property tax rates or rules by which property is appraised.

Basis of Property Taxes

By California law, the assessment year 1975-76 serves as the original base year and the market value base for individual real property assessments. Thereafter, the base year is that year in which the property is purchased, newly constructed or has a change of ownership (with some exceptions). Property taxes are based on 1% to 1.25% (depending on the county) of the market value of the house as of the date of sale.

Increasing Property Taxes

There are several ways in which property taxes may increase.

First, property tax assessments may be increased 2% annually.

Second, property tax assessments may be increased by any bond indebtedness (such as for libraries, street lights or parks) or other special assessments (for example, flood control/sewer service) that local voters approve. Your tax bill will show your tax rate.

Third, if you improve your house by adding or remodeling a room, your tax assessment will reflect the increase in value which results from the improvement. But the assessed value of the unimproved portion of the property will not be increased.

Fourth, transferring ownership of your house will trigger a property tax increase in the following situations:
- If you sell property, the new owner is assessed based on the market value of the property at the time of title transfer.
- If a co-owner sells her portion of the property, the assessment on the portion that was not sold remains at its current rate. The assessment on the portion that was sold will be based on the current fair market value. It makes no difference to whom the sale was.

Transfers in ownership between spouses do not trigger a new assessment. Nor do transfers between a parent and a child.

In the event of new construction or a sale described above, you will receive a supplemental assessment tax bill for the current year. Supplemental assessments tax the difference between the new base year value and the previous value. This is a one-time tax prorated from the purchase date or completion date of new construction. If the change in ownership or completion of construction occurs between June 1 and the last day of February, you will receive only one supplemental assessment. If the change occurs between March 1 and May 31, you will receive two supplemental assessments—one for the remainder of the fiscal year and one for the following fiscal year.

In the case of a sale, the supplemental tax will not be prorated in escrow. This is because the assessor will not have the figures at closing. The bill will come later—sometimes six months to two years later.

How Long the Tax Collector Has to Collect

- For a supplemental tax following a recorded change of ownership or new construction—four years.
- For a supplemental tax following an unrecorded change of ownership—eight years.

If You Disagree With an Assessment

If you disagree with the amount an assessor has raised your taxes as a result of home improvements, you can appeal that decision. If the increase comes as a "supplemental notice," you must file an appeal within 60 days of that notice date. (If you miss that 60-day period, you can try the appeal again next year when the regular assessment comes out, between July 2 and September 15.) If the increased assessment comes as part of your regular assessment on July 1, you have the right to appeal until September 15.

If you think your house has gone down in value, you can appeal to the tax assessor to have your assessment lowered. Come prepared with evidence of what's happened to property values in your neighborhood.

Transferring the Assessed Value of One Home to Another

If you sell a house you bought long ago and buy another at current prices, your property tax liability can go way up. If you are over the age of 55, you can transfer the assessed value of your old home to your new home as long as your new home is:

- purchased or newly constructed as a replacement for your primary residence within two years of the sale of the old property
- of equal or lesser value than the original property, and
- located within the same county or located within another county if the new county will accept the old assessment. About a dozen counties in the state will accept property tax transfers.

This transfer is not automatic—your must file a form with the county assessor's office.

You Never Got a Bill: Can You Be Penalized?

Property taxes, like income taxes, are due annually. It's your responsibility to pay them on time. The California Legislature has authorized automatically imposed penalties if you pay your property taxes late. The law does authorize county tax collectors to cancel or refund penalties under limited conditions. (Few counties will, but you can try filing for a refund.) For example, the law makes allowances for circumstances beyond the taxpayer's control—for example, the Post Office did not postmark your bill or payment properly and you can prove you mailed it on time.

Your Mortgage Company Paid Your Bill Late: Can You Be Penalized?

If you have an escrow or impound account which authorizes your mortgage company to pay your taxes and insurance, it's the company's responsibility to do so. If it fails to pay on time, it is obligated to pay the penalty—not you!

Additional Resources

For $2, you can obtain a copy of the pamphlet, *How to Fight Property Taxes*; contact the National Taxpayers Union Foundation, 325 Pennsylvania Avenue SE, Washington, DC 20003, (202) 543-1303.

Extra Help for Seniors and Disabled

The Property Tax Postponement Program is designed to help home-owning senior citizens and disabled persons whose total gross household income does not exceed $24,000. A qualified homeowner—someone age 62 and over, or blind or disabled—can defer the payment of all or part of her property taxes. The State of California pays the local government the amount owed and places a lien on the homeowner's property. When the property is sold or transferred to a beneficiary at death, the postponed taxes are paid with interest.

For more information, call the State Controller's office at (800) 952-5661 (often busy) or (916) 323-5700.

SALES TAX

The sales tax in California ranges from 7.25% to 8.50%, depending on where you live. The basic state rate is 7.25%; some counties have voted to raise the sales tax to cover the cost of various improvements. For example, the Bay Area Rapid Transit (BART) in the Bay Area and road improvements in the South Bay have added increase in the local sales tax.

The California Board of Equalization administers and collects state and local sales and use tax. The sales and/or use tax applies to all retail sales of tangible personal property unless otherwise exempt. The sales tax is imposed on the retailer for the privilege of selling personal property in this state. The use tax is imposed on someone who purchased personal property not subject to the sales tax from a retailer.

You may be surprised to learn that you must pay a sales tax when purchasing something by mail-order from out-of-state. Because the U.S. Constitution prohibits states from taxing interstate commerce, the tax you pay an out-of-state mail-order company is called a use tax—you use the product in this state.

Below are common situations in which consumers are confused about whether they are required to pay sales/use tax:

Video Rental for Home Use

Yes.

Newspapers and Periodicals

Yes; however, periodicals sold on a subscription basis and delivered by a common carrier are exempt from sales or use tax. Newspapers are considered periodicals and exempt from the tax if the following apply:

- they are issued more than four times a year, but fewer than 60 times a year
- each issue has some relation to prior issues
- each issue is sufficiently similar in style to the previous one so it is clear the papers constitute a series, and

- the papers are sold on a subscription basis and delivered via U.S. mail or a common carrier.

Personal Services

Personal services, such as gardeners, residential or office-cleaning services, attorneys and doctors are not taxable.

Motor Vehicles Bought Out-of-State

If you register a motor vehicle in California, within 90 days of its purchase you must pay a use tax (same amount as the California sales tax) to the DMV. (If you paid tax in another state, you will be given partial credit and will only have to pay any difference if California's tax is higher.) You will not have to pay tax if the seller is a close relative (parent, grandparent, child, spouse or minor brothers and sisters) of the buyer and is not in the automobile business. Nor does a military service member or anyone else who can prove that the automobile was originally purchased for use outside the state. (This would be the case if you had a sudden job transfer.)

Don't think you are getting away with something by simply leaving out-of-state tags on your car. A vehicle based or used primarily in California must be registered in California within 20 days of being brought into the state. If you don't register the car voluntarily you are likely to be cited by a police officer. Vehicle Code § 4000.4.

Auto Rebates

A manufacturer's rebate is taxable. For example, if you pay $13,000 for a car, you have to pay sales tax on the full purchase price, even though the manufacturer refunds you the $1,000 advertised manufacturer's rebate. By contrast, a cash discount from the dealer is not taxable. Thus, if the dealer (not the manufacturer) reduces the selling price of a car from $13,000 to $12,000, you pay sales tax on $12,000.

When Using a "Cents Off" Coupon

Merchants (including restaurants and fast food chains) must charge sales tax on the full purchase price (even if the item is free) if the "cents off" coupon is from the manufacturer of the product, which is usually the case when you clip coupons from magazines and newspapers. The reason for the requirement is that the manufacturer reimburses the merchant for the money it didn't collect from you. When retailers offer their own coupons in local print ads or in mailers to your home, you pay the sales tax only on the actual (discounted) purchase price, because no one reimburses the merchant.

Delivery Charges

It depends. Normally, if anything is purchased for a "delivered price," such as furniture, and is being delivered by the store's own truck, that transportation charge is taxable whether or not the delivery charge is included in the advertised price. In short, when the ownership of the item (title) is passed to the consumer after being delivered and signed for, that transportation charge is taxable. When the delivery is made by United Parcel Service (UPS) or some other common carrier and the delivery is listed as a separate item, however, it's not considered taxable transportation so you do not have to pay tax on the delivery charge.

Food Products

In general, sales tax does not apply to sales of food products for human consumption sold at grocery stores, although there are exceptions:

- carbonated beverages, alcohol, mouthwash, aspirin and other non-prescription over-the-counter medicines (the Board of Equalization classifies these as food items)
- meals or hot prepared food products furnished by restaurants, hotels, soda fountains and the like
- food provided by retailers, such as sandwiches and ice cream, for consumption on the premises at tables, chairs or counters, or from trays, glasses, dishes or other tableware
- "hot prepared food products" which have been prepared for sale in a heated condition (above room temperature), even if the product cools before purchase, such as a grilled sandwich or food on a steam table—a cold tuna sandwich is not considered a hot prepared food product but if it is sold for a combined price with a hot cup of coffee, it will be taxed, and
- food sold in a form suitable for immediate consumption on the seller's premises provided 80% or more of the seller's gross receipts are from the sale of food products and 80% or more of the seller's retail sales of food products are sales subject to tax. Sales tax applies whether the food is consumed there or taken out for consumption elsewhere. Examples include a cup of coffee, pint of milk, slice of pie and individual pastry serving.

Out-of-State Mail-Order Purchases

The Board of Equalization requires an out-of-state company to collect the California sales and use tax if it had a presence in California (such as a store, factory or even just one employee). If a company has no physical presence in California, it is not required to collect the use tax. Now you see why some companies charge sales tax and others don't.

Some companies have built the sales tax into their pricing structure and do pay the tax to the State of California. A U.S. Supreme Court case (*Quill Corporation v. North Dakota*) stopped states from requiring that mail order companies with no physical presence in a state collect the use tax in those states.

Foreign Purchases

The use tax, which has the same rate as the sales tax, applies to all goods brought into the state that are normally subject to sales/use tax, including jewelry, furs, art objects, clothing and souvenirs. There is one exception—the first $400 in purchases, per person, is exempt from the use tax. This law is enforced because the Board of Equalization has access to customs declarations. After the Board reviews your U.S. Customs declaration, the state collectors will send you a tax return form you must fill out, giving the value of your purchases, along with instructions on how to figure and pay the tax.

More Information/Where to Complain

For more information on what is and what is not taxable, or to complain that an improper tax was charged, write or call the nearest California Board of Equalization, Business Taxes Office; locate one of the many offices throughout the state. Check the telephone directory white pages under State Government Offices. ■

TRAVEL

TRAVEL, GENERALLY

Here are two simple but important travel tips:

- Check the expiration date on your credit card to make sure it will be valid the whole time you are away. If it will expire during your trip, contact your bank before you leave and ask to have your replacement card sent early.
- Photocopy or record your traveler's checks' numbers and keep them separate from your traveler's checks—perhaps in the bottom of your suitcase. Leave another copy at home with a family member or friend.

Travel Promoters and Travel Agents

The California Travel Promoters Law requires all travel promoters—defined as a person who sells, provides, furnishes, contracts for, arranges or advertises that she or he can arrange wholesale or retail air or sea transportation—to abide by the following procedures with respect to money received from passengers.

- At least 90% of all money received from customers must be deposited into a federally insured trust account.
- If you pay by credit card or cash, the travel promoter must issue and deliver (put in the mail) your air or sea ticket within 48 hours.
- If you pay by check, the travel promoter must issue and deliver (put in the mail) your air or sea ticket within 48 hours of the earlier of when your payment is credited to the travel promoter's account or when the legal period to hold your check expires.
- If the travel promoter cannot issue your ticket within the 48 hours as required, she must either forward your money to the air or sea carrier who will issue the ticket or deposit your money into her trust account until she can issue the ticket. She cannot offset or reduce the amount you pay by taking a fee for herself.
- If the travel promoter cannot issue your ticket because of an unforeseen condition beyond her control, she must return your money within 30 days.

Business and Professions Code §§ 17540.10, 17450.11.

This law does not cover airline or ocean carriers, or officially appointed agents of those carriers. This means that retail travel agents are not covered under the law, which is really aimed at eliminating travel scams. There is legislation pending in California to be taken up in 1994 that could extend coverage of this law to travel agents, which could prove to be a loss for consumers. Good travel agents hold tickets after purchase in order to attach boarding passes (which cannot be issued earlier than 30 days before your flight). Extending the 48-hour rule to them could mean a loss of services to consumers.

In addition, only a few states (such as California and Florida) have travel promoter laws. If you use a travel promoter in another state you may not have these protections.

A good travel agent can add immeasurably to your travel plans. Ask friends, relatives and co-workers for recommendations. If you use the same travel agent for your business travel and your personal travel, you are likely to get a higher level of service than most people get, such as having your tickets delivered to you and watching for fair reductions.

Travel Clubs

There are legitimate travel clubs that offer discounts on hotels, airlines, ski resorts, golf courses and cruise lines (particularly on a short notice basis). For recommendations, ask friends, neighbors, co-workers or relatives who travel. But be careful—many travel clubs are not so great. Some of the poorer organizations offer a promotion claiming that for a mere $50 a year (automatically charged to your credit card), you'll get great deals on discounted travel. In truth, you might get a $5 rebate check and some travel goods (such as a camera) that are pieces of junk, or be required to pay an arm and a leg for a hotel after getting a cheap flight.

Travel Insurance

If you are spending a lot of money on a trip, you may want to consider buying travel insurance to reimburse you if you have to cancel or shorten your trip. Before you buy, be sure to read the provisions for coverage carefully—these policies often exclude existing illnesses. Thus, if you cut your trip short because you got sick while traveling, be prepared for the travel insurance company to deny coverage if your health problem overseas was a "pre-existing condition."

If you feel the insurance company is giving you the run around, file a complaint with the California Department of Insurance at (800) 927-4357.

Traveling Outside the U.S.

Photocopy your passport (or at least write down the number, date and place of issue). Keep the photocopy in the bottom of your suitcase and leave another at home with a family member or friend. If your passport is lost or stolen, you can get a replacement at a U.S. embassy or consulate if you can offer proof of citizenship or the number, date and place of issue of your original passport.

Consider buying a small amount of foreign currency before you leave home—at least enough to last you for a day or two. This way you will not need to exchange money at your destination (currency offices are often closed at night); instead you will have ready cash for taxis and tips.

Whenever possible, it's best to use your credit card instead of cash because you get the exchange rate given to banks that convert in millions of dollars at a time. This exchange rate is much better than the ones given by exchange dealers. When you exchange U.S. currency for cash, try to use local banks instead of money changers or hotel concierge desks. Banks give better rates than the others.

U.S. State Department

Travelers, experienced or not, should know that the federal government offers several services before, during and after traveling outside of the U.S.

Citizens' Emergency Center

The U.S. State Department's Citizens' Emergency Center provides travelers emergency and assistance services, including:

- warnings to travelers of political problems abroad
- searching for a missing traveler in an emergency at home
- helping transfer money abroad
- assisting Americans abroad who are victims of accidents, disasters or crimes, and
- informing families of the injuries or deaths of Americans abroad.

The Center can be reached at (202) 647-5225.

Problems With Foreign Purchases

The U.S. State Department may be able to help if you have a problem with a foreign purchase—for example, if you never received merchandise ordered and the merchant won't respond to your calls or letters. The State Department will contact the American consulate in the particular country and ask it to check with the merchant on your behalf. Contact the Office of Consular Services, CA/OCS/CCS, Room 4817, U.S. Department of State, 2201 C Street NW, Washington, DC 20520, (202) 647-3666. You also might try to contact the country's own consulate in San Francisco or Los Angeles to see if it can help.

BUYING AND CONVERTING
FOREIGN CURRENCY

Always check the amount of the foreign currency written on a credit card slip before you sign. It is not uncommon to have a "verbally quoted" price of 100 francs appear as 1,000 francs, or 10,000 lira appear as 100,000 lira. Like most scams, this one can be difficult to do anything about later. Also, if a country has recently issued new currency, be aware of scams of people selling the "old" currency at extremely tempting rates.

Do not buy more foreign currency than you plan to use. The exchange rate for buying foreign currency is almost always higher than the rate for selling it. In addition, you often pay a service charge, which means if you convert money twice, you lose twice the amount in service fees.

Before you leave a foreign country, try to spend all your coins or at least convert them into bills. Banks and exchange dealers in other countries seldom accept coins. When they do, they pay much less than their face value.

Where to Complain

Travel Agents

Currently, travel agents are not regulated by any consumer law—remember, however, the California Legislature is considering a bill to extend the Travel Promoters Law to travel agents. Travel agencies that associate with certain professional organizations must often be bonded, and so if the travel agency errs seriously, you may have some recourse.

If an airline was late and you missed your connection, don't blame your travel agent. If the hotel gave you a view of the parking lot and you expected an ocean view, that may not be your travel agent's fault. If, however, you have a valid complaint with an agent that you cannot resolve, contact a radio, TV or newspaper "Action Line" or the Better Business Bureau. If that doesn't work, consider taking the agent to Small Claims Court. If you suspect fraud, contact your local District Attorney's office.

Cruise Lines

No regulatory agency oversees cruise dealers; your travel agent may be able to help. Some cruise lines will compensate dissatisfied travelers who request a partial refund for "problems" on a cruise by offering a discount on a future cruise rather than a cash refund.

Tour Companies

If you have a problem with a tour company and have not been able to get satisfaction, you can try contacting the United States Tour Operators Association (USTOA), 211 East 51st Street, Suite 12B, New York, NY 10022, (212) 944-5727. This is a membership organization that can sometimes help resolve complaints between member tour operators and consumers. When you contact the USTOA, you will first have to find out if the operator is a member. Be aware that most small tour operators are not members, and some of the large tour companies are pulling out; USTOA's "consumer protection" program has been having some problems.

AIRLINES

Airlines offer a wide variety of choices in service and price. If something goes wrong with reservations, tickets, seating, flight schedules or luggage, airlines offer an often confusing array of recourse policies—some fair, others poor.

Low-Fare Tickets

On every flight, tickets are sold at a wide variety of prices. The key to getting the lowest possible fare, generally, is to plan far ahead since most airlines set aside only a few seats on each flight at the lowest rate. In addition, the more flexible you can be in making your travel plans, the more you are likely to save; a cheap discount fare available one day may not be available the next. Airfares can only be locked in when you pay for the tickets. Just making reservations won't guarantee a cheap airfare. Travel agents with access to schedules and prices from a number of airlines can often help you comparison shop.

Nonrefundable Tickets

Most cheap airline tickets are called nonrefundable, which means you can't return them for your money back. Most airlines, however, will change a nonrefundable ticket for a $25-$50 fee. For example, if you buy a ticket to fly San Francisco to New York over Thanksgiving and a family emergency arises meaning that you need to be in Florida during that time, the airline will probably re-ticket you for a fee—assuming that seats are available. If you don't use the ticket, however, the airline will probably not refund your money, except in cases of unexpected emergencies—such as illness or death in the family (with proof—a death certificate or doctor's letter). A few airlines will accept a military or civilian job reassignment; others will accept jury duty or subpoenas.

When Fares Go Down After Purchase

On regular-price tickets, if the fare is reduced you will be able to collect the difference. With nonrefundable tickets, you may or may not be able to get a refund. If the ticket is nonrefundable but the airline permits changes, you probably can get re-ticketed at the lower fare. Your refund will be the difference in the fares less the fee the airline charges for changing a nonrefundable ticket.

Discount Fares for Sudden Death or Illness

Until the early 1990s, most airlines offered relatively generous "bereavement discounts" to people who need to travel suddenly due to the death (or critical illness) of an immediate family member. Because some travelers fabricated hardship stories to get these fares, airlines have cut back the availability of these fares. Those that still offer them, generally require proof of the death or illness. (The airline may contact the hospital or funeral home.) If an airline employee tells you that the discount is not available, ask to speak to a supervisor. If the supervisor says no, call the next airline.

Lost or Stolen Tickets

If your tickets are lost or stolen, an airline will require that you buy replacement tickets—not necessarily at the same fare. If the missing tickets are not used, most airlines will refund the higher-priced ticket in six weeks to six months. Most airlines charge a fee of about $50 for refunding the higher-priced ticket.

Always photocopy your tickets, or record the numbers somewhere—it will definitely speed up the refund process.

TRAVEL SAFEGUARDS

Here are six rules to protect yourself while traveling:

- Always write your name inside your luggage and include an itinerary in case your baggage tags get pulled off. This way, the airline can find you and deliver your unmarked luggage.

- Put your office, not home, address on baggage tags. Thieves have been known to look at baggage tags to discover empty houses.

- Carry car or house keys that you may need on arrival—don't pack them.

- Never pack cash, jewelry, prescriptions or other medicines, cameras, or other valuable items; carry them on your person or in carry-on luggage.

- Carefully save your baggage claim checks—they are proof that you checked luggage. If your luggage is lost, the airline will require you to turn in the claim checks.

- Always remove old baggage tags on arrival so future baggage handlers won't get confused.

Bumping on Oversold Flights

When you show up at the airport and find that your flight has been oversold, you will probably react in one of two ways—thrilled at the opportunity to get a voucher for a free later flight by taking a later flight today, or horrified that you might miss your flight.

Voluntary Bumping

If your flight is oversold , the airline must ask for volunteers who are willing to give up their seats in exchange for compensation. If you are not in a big hurry, you can get cash or, better yet, a free round-trip airline ticket good anywhere in the U.S.

These compensation tickets generally have some restrictions—such as permitting you to confirm reservations only a few days before you want to travel; but for free, they are still a good deal.

Involuntary Bumping

If the airline does not get enough volunteers, it will bump people on its own. If you are bumped involuntarily from a regularly scheduled domestic flight (charter flights and commuter flights with 60 or fewer passengers don't count), the U.S. Department of Transportation requires the airline to compensate you, unless the airline gets you to your destination within an hour of your originally scheduled arrival time.

The amount of compensation depends on how long you are delayed. If you arrive at your destination more than an hour but less than two hours (four hours on international flights) after your original arrival time, the airline must give you either the equivalent of the one-way fare to your destination or $200, whichever is less. If you arrive at your destination more than two hours later (four hours on international flights), the compensation doubles to 200% of the one-way airfare or $400, whichever is less. You also get to keep your original ticket for either future use or a refund. You can also sue under state law for harm caused by the bumping.

To qualify for compensation, you must have a confirmed reservation and check in by the airline's deadline—which could be anywhere from ten to 90 minutes before the scheduled departure.

In a few cases, you are not entitled to compensation:

- the airline substitutes a smaller plane (no matter what the reason) than the originally scheduled plane
- on international flights bound for the U.S., and
- on flights between two non-U.S. cities.

Delayed Arrivals

In general, airlines to not have to pay compensation for delayed flights, particularly when the delay is caused by bad weather or other factors beyond the control of the airline. An airline may be liable to you, however, if the delay is caused by the airline—for example, if the plane sits on the ground waiting for a replacement part. The compensation amount is set by the airline itself. If you must stay overnight, many airlines will pay for meals and a hotel room. This isn't required by law, however. If the airline offers you no compensation or very little, be persistent—many airlines have relationships with hotels and can get you discounted rooms.

Delayed Baggage

If your baggage is delayed, chances are you'll get it within a few hours. Most airlines will make arrangements to deliver delayed luggage to you. If you receive your luggage promptly (within a few hours), don't expect compensation. For longer delays, when you have been seriously inconvenienced, you may be able to get a cash advance to purchase necessary items. (The amount given depends on whether you are away from home and how long it will take to return your bags to you.) If you can't get a cash advance, keep receipts for any necessary purchases for possible reimbursement later. If you have to buy needed replacement clothes, some airlines will reimburse you for half the cost and ask for the clothes. Don't ask what they do with used clothing—perhaps take a tax deduction by donating them to a nonprofit organization. Some airlines will only pay a portion of the cost, assuming you can use the clothes in the future.

Lost, Stolen or Damaged Baggage

Domestic Flights

If your baggage is lost or damaged, the maximum you can collect is $1,250 per passenger, assuming you can document that your belongings were worth this amount. Rarely will any airline actually pay that much. Some credit card companies (such as American Express) may cover baggage loss or damage if you used that credit card to pay for the airline tickets. Take out additional baggage insurance if you travel with lots of expensive items.

Airlines do not pay replacement value but, rather, depreciated value adjusted for wear and tear. Don't be surprised if the airline demand receipts to prove purchase price. Don't exaggerate the value of merchandise—your claim may be ignored or you may be given only a small refund. Airlines have a right to set their own policies and may completely deny a claim it feels is inflated or fraudulent. What the airline won't pay may be covered by your homeowners' or renters' insurance.

International Flights

If your baggage is lost or damaged, the maximum you can normally collect is $9.07 a pound, per bag—and virtually all airlines will assume that your bag weighed 70 pounds. That's not much when you figure how much bathing suits, silk blouses and silk ties (all of which weigh a mere few ounces) cost. The international rate of $9.07 a pound applies, even if your bag is lost in the U.S. during a transfer or stay in New York on your way to Europe. These liability limits are set by a treaty called the Warsaw Convention. Outrageous! But true.

A few years back, a New York court ruled in favor of two New Yorkers who sued airlines for $11,000 (rejecting the $9.07 per pound offered to them) after their baggage was lost on a trip to London. This case is unusual, however, and virtually all other courts have upheld the $9.07 per pound limitation. Don't get your hopes up about suing an airline for more. This is a very important issue for airlines and they will put up a big fight.

More Information/Where to Complain

The Federal Aviation Administration (FAA) can answer questions about airport security, airline safety, child safety seats and other FAA regulations. The toll-free consumer hotline is (800) FAA-SURE. Call between 5 a.m. and 1 p.m. pacific standard time, Monday through Friday. Or you can write to FAA, Office of Consumer Affairs, APA-200, 800 Independence Avenue SW, Washington, DC 20591.

To complain about an airline practice, contact the U.S. Department of Transportation, Office of Consumer Assistance, at 400-7th Street SW, Washington, DC 20590, (202) 366-2220. Call between 5:15 a.m. and 1:45 p.m. pacific standard time, Monday through Friday. It will contact the airline about your complaint, which may or may not result in your being compensated.

If your complaint cannot be resolved at the airport, write the airline a brief, businesslike letter (typed, if possible) with pertinent details. Send photocopies of documentation. Keep photocopies of your correspondence and the originals of your documentation. It helps to state what reasonable recourse you want. Long, nasty letters don't get results. The airline may take three to four weeks to respond. Consumer hotlines at newspapers or radio or TV stations can often be effective in nudging airlines into faster action. Also consider contacting an ombudsman from one of the travel magazines, such as *Conde Nast Traveler.*

If all else fails, you can take the airline to Small Claims Court. Sometimes, just writing a letter threatening to do so can produce desired results. But often you must file suit, at which point the airline will often re-evaluate your complaint and pay off if it's legitimate. ■

WILLS, TRUSTS AND FINAL ARRANGEMENTS

FUNERALS, BURIALS AND CREMATIONS

Most people avoid the subject of death—and are especially uncomfortable thinking about their own mortality. You, too, may be tempted to leave the details of your final arrangements to those who survive you.

But there are two good reasons not to do this: care and cost.

Letting your survivors know what kind of disposition and ceremonies you envision after your death saves them the agony of making such decisions at what is likely to be a vulnerable time for them. And many family members and friends have also found it to be a healthy relief to discuss preferences for final arrangements openly—especially if a person is elderly or in poor health and death is likely to occur soon.

Planning some of these details in advance can also help save money. Advance planning, with some wise comparison shopping, can help ensure that costs will be controlled or kept to a minimum.

Funeral Societies

Choosing the institution to handle your burial is probably the most important decision funeral-wise you can make, from an economic standpoint. For this reason, many people are choosing to join memorial or funeral societies, which help them find local mortuaries that will deal honestly with your survivors and charge prices that accurately reflect the value of their services.

Society members are free to choose whatever final arrangement they wish. Most societies, however, emphasize simple, dignified arrangements over the costly, elaborate services often promoted by the funeral industry.

While the services offered by each society differ, most societies distribute literature and information on options and legal controls on final arrangements.

You receive a prearrangement form upon joining, which allows you to plan for the goods and services you want—and to get them for a predetermined cost. The society also serves as a watchdog—making sure you get and pay for only the services you have specified.

The cost for joining and getting these organizations is low—usually from $20 to $40 for a lifetime membership, although some societies charge a small renewal fee periodically.

Look in the telephone book to find your local funeral or memorial society—or contact the Continental Association of Funeral and Memorial Societies, (800) 458-5563, for additional information.

More Information/Where to Complain

The National Research and Information Center (NRIC) is a national, independent, nonprofit organization dedicated to research concerning death, grief and funeral services. It provides a Funeral Service Consumer Assistance Program (FSCAP) to help you resolve complaints about your funeral service contract and related matters. In addition, it publishes a free pamphlet on common funeral-related questions. You can reach NRIC toll-free, Monday through Friday, 9 a.m. to 5 p.m. pacific standard time, at (800) 662-7666, or you can write NRIC, 2250 E. Devon Avenue, Suite 250, Des Plaines, IL 60018.

Plan Your Estate, by attorney Denis Clifford (Nolo Press), has a chapter on organ donations, funerals, burials, cremations and more. It is available in libraries and bookstores. Also, *WillMaker* version 5.0 (software published by Nolo Press), takes users step-by-step through the questions they need to answer to leave complete final arrangements for their survivors—including directions for body donations, body burial or cremation, and after-death ceremonies.

Cemeteries

If you have questions or complaints about the operation of or possible misrepresentation by cemeteries and crematories, or their employees, contact the California Cemetery Board, which licenses and regulates the industry. The Board also regulates trust fund care (money paid in advance for burial) and endowment care (a surcharge for perpetual care). The Board publishes a free guide to cemetery purchases and explains required disclosures. Contact its main office at 2535 Capitol Oaks Drive, Suite 300B, Sacramento, CA 95833, (916) 263-2660.

Mortuaries

The California Board of Funeral Directors and Embalmers regulates mortuaries, including their burial procedures and embalming practices. It also supervises pre-need trust funds (money paid in advance for funeral arrangements). Contact its main office 2535 Capitol Oaks Drive, Suite 300A, Sacramento, CA 95833, (916) 263-3180.

LIVING TRUST

A living trust, like a will, is a way to transfer property at your death. There are several kinds of living trusts; the simplest and most common is a probate-avoidance revocable living trust.

When you use this kind of living trust, no probate court proceeding is required after your death. Your heirs save money (lawyers' fees, court costs), and your property can be distributed much faster than if a court were overseeing the process.

Other, more complicated kinds of living trusts can save on estate taxes. California has no estate tax; the federal estate tax is assessed only on estates of at least $600,000. So you need to consider this kind of trust only if you expect to own more than $600,000 worth of property at your death.

Many lawyers charge upwards of $1,000 to prepare even a simple living trust. If you spend that much now, you may cancel out much of the savings that your heirs will eventually gain by avoiding probate after your death. You can, however, create a living trust yourself, without a lawyer.

More Information

Make Your Own Living Trust, by Denis Clifford (Nolo Press), includes forms and instructions for making a probate-avoidance or estate tax-savings living trust.

Plan Your Estate, by Denis Clifford (Nolo Press), discusses many estate planning issues, from simple probate-avoidance measures to sophisticated long-term trusts.

Nolo's Living Trust, by Mary Randolph (Nolo Press), software for Macintosh computers, lets users make their own probate-avoidance living trust.

PROBATE

Probate is a court proceeding to distribute the assets and pay the debts of a deceased person. Most property left by will (or by intestate succession in the absence of a will) must go through probate. Not only is the probate process time-consuming—it commonly takes a year or more—but fees must be paid to lawyers, accountants, appraisers and the court before the deceased's remaining assets may be distributed to the inheritors. If the amount of property left is less than $60,000, or property is left to a surviving spouse, streamlined procedures can be used to greatly speed the process.

Probate Avoidance Methods

Before your death, you can plan your affairs so that most or all of your property won't have to go through probate, but instead will be promptly distributed to the people and organizations you want to get it. The principal ways to avoid probate include:

- revocable living trusts
- joint tenancy
- informal bank account trusts (pay-on-death accounts), and
- life insurance.

More Information

Plan Your Estate, by attorney Denis Clifford, discusses many ways to avoid probate and reduce eventual estate taxes.

Make Your Own Living Trust, by attorney Denis Clifford, and *Nolo's Living Trust,* by Mary Randolph (software for Macintosh computers) contain do-it-yourself living trust forms.

How to Probate an Estate, by Julia Nissley, explains how to handle probate paperwork in California, and includes all the forms necessary if you are responsible for winding up the affairs of a deceased family member or friend.

These books and software are published by Nolo Press and are available in libraries and bookstores.

WILLS

Preparing a will is one way to ensure that your estate—a legal term for all the property you own at your death—is distributed to your beneficiaries in accordance with your wishes. If you should die intestate (without a will), your assets will normally be distributed to your spouse and children, or blood relatives if you aren't married and have no children, in accordance with state law. Because intestate succession rarely distributes your assets as you would have wanted, it is a poor substitute for a will.

A will enables you to:
- distribute your assets to the people and organizations you intend
- provide security for your survivors
- name a personal and financial guardian for your minor children and their property
- select an executor of your estate, and
- create trusts for your children so they won't inherit property until they reach an age you designate.

The disadvantage of wills is that they must go through probate, which is why alternative methods, such as living trusts, have become widely used.

Additional Resources

Preparing a basic will is the essential first step in planning any estate. Especially for larger estates, however, many more options are available.

Nolo Press publishes many resources that can help you with estate planning.
- *Nolo's Living Trust.* A software package that shows users how to create their own living trust documents.
- *Plan Your Estate.* Shows how to prepare an estate plan without the expensive services of a lawyer. It includes all the tear-out forms and step-by-step instructions needed to prepare living trusts and other estate planning devices. It contains considerable detail on federal estate taxes and simple strategies to avoid them.
- *5 Ways To Avoid Probate.* A 60-minute audio cassette tape covering the five principal probate avoidance techniques—joint tenancy, savings account trusts, insurance, living trusts and naming a beneficiary for IRAs, Keoghs and 401K plans.
- *Make Your Own Living Trust.* Provides a thorough explanation of living trusts—a popular probate avoidance device. Includes information on how a living trust works, how to transfer property to a trust and what happens when the person who sets one up dies.
- *Who Will Handle Your Finances If You Can't?* Contains tear-out, fill-in-the-blank forms and complete instructions for how to make a durable power of attorney for finances—the document that can give a person legal authority to handle financial matters for someone who is not able to do so.
- *Nolo's Law Form Kit: Power of Attorney.* Line-by-line instructions for preparing powers of attorney for finances.

- *WillMaker.* A software program that allows users to create a will and a living will, and leave instructions for body disposal and after-death ceremonies.
- *Nolo's Simple Will Book.* All instructions and forms needed to create a legally valid will, with examples of clauses to use to tailor your will to your needs.
- *Write Your Will.* A 50-minute audio cassette tape covering what provisions a will should contain, how to provide for children and grandchildren, how to assign an executor, how to have a will signed and witnessed.
- *Nolo's Law Form Kit: Wills.* Line-by-line instructions for preparing a simple will.
- *Beating the Nursing Home Trap: A Consumer's Guide to Choosing and Financing Long-Term Care.* A compendium of alternatives for those concerned about finding and financing long-term care. It discusses planning so that an elder's financial resources can supplement money available from public sources.
- *How to Probate an Estate* (California only). A simple explanation of how to read a will, handle probate paperwork, collect life insurance and other benefits, pay bills and taxes and distribute property left through trusts.
- *The Conservatorship Book* (California only). Guidance for determining when a conservatorship is necessary for a person incapacitated due to illness or age, and whether there are suitable alternatives.
- *A Legal Guide for Lesbian and Gay Couples.* A complete guide to understanding the specialized interpretations and laws that affect gay and lesbian couples, this book includes a chapter on estate planning concerns.
- *The Living Together Kit.* A legal and estate planning planning guide geared to the needs of unmarried heterosexual couples.
- *Nolo's Personal RecordKeeper.* A software program that provides structure for a complete inventory of all your important legal, financial, personal and family records. Having accurate and complete records gets you organized, makes tax preparation easier and helps loved ones manage your affairs if you become incapacitated or die.

In addition, the State Bar of California offers short, fill-in-the-blank will forms for California residents who are parents or married people with modest estates. There are two statutory form wills: a standard form and a will which sets up a trust for the care and support of children under 21. Both are available for $2 a copy. To obtain either form, send a check or money order (do not send cash) payable to the State Bar of California, and include a self-addressed, stamped, business-size envelope to Will Forms, Box 420411, San Francisco, CA 94142, (415) 561-8200. Enclose a note requesting either the standard will or the will with trust.

The State Bar also publishes two free pamphlets that answer common questions about wills and estate planning. To get a copy of *Do I Need a Will?* or *Do I Need Estate Planning?,* send a stamped, self-addressed envelope to State Bar Pamphlets, 555 Franklin Street, San Francisco, CA 94102.

DURABLE POWER OF ATTORNEY FOR FINANCES

When you sign a document called a power of attorney, you give another person legal authority to act on your behalf. That person is called your "attorney-in-fact."

A durable power of attorney for finances is a special kind of power of attorney. It authorizes someone to take charge of your finances and property. And, unlike regular powers of attorney, it stays in effect even if you become incapacitated.

In fact, many durable powers of attorney are written so that they go into effect *only* if you become incapacitated. For example, many couples create durable powers of attorney that name each other as attorney-in-fact. That way, if one spouse becomes incapacitated by illness, the other has authority to deposit the other's checks, pay bills and taxes, and exercise authority over the other's property. If there were no power of attorney, court authorization would be necessary.

It's not difficult to prepare a durable power of attorney for finances; the State of California has a fill-in-the-blanks form that's easy to fill out. You must sign the form in front of a notary public. It does not need to be filed with a court, but it should be filed (recorded) in the county recorder's office if it gives the attorney-in-fact authority over real estate.

Additional Resources

Who Will Handle Your Finances If You Can't?, by Denis Clifford and Mary Randolph (Nolo Press), includes tear-out forms and instructions for making a durable power of attorney for finances. ∎

Appendix

California Agencies

Attorney General
Public Inquiry Office ....(800) 952-5225
Registry of Charitable Trusts ....(916) 445-2021
Board of Accountancy ....(916) 574-2155
Board of Chiropractic Examiners ....(916) 227-2790
Board of Dental Examiners ....(916) 263-2335
Board of Funeral Directors and Embalmers ....(916) 263-3180
Board of Optometry ....(916) 323-8720
Board of Pharmacy ....(916) 445-5014
(213) 897-3125
Bureau of Automotive Repair ....(800) 952-5210
(916) 455-1254
(916) 323-7239
Bureau of Collection and Investigative Services ....(916) 445-7366
Bureau of Electronic and Appliance Repair ....(916) 445-4751
Bureau of Home Furnishings ....(916) 445-1254
Cemetery Board..(916) 263-2660
Commission on Judicial Performance ....(415) 904-3650
Contractor's State License Board....................................(800) 321-2752
Department of Aging ....(916) 322-5290
Health Insurance Counseling and Advocacy Program ....(916) 323-7315
Nursing Home Ombudsman ....(800) 231-4024
Department of Banking ....(800) 622-0620
Department of Consumer Affairs
Consumer Assistance Office ....(916) 445-1254
Consumer Information Line ....(800) 344-9940
Department of Corporations ....(213) 736-2741
(213) 736-3104
(916) 445-7205
(619) 525-4233
(415) 557-3787
(800) 347-6995
Department of Education ....(916) 657-2451
Adult Education Field Services ....(916) 322-2175
Department of Fair Employment and Housing ....(916) 445-9918
Department of Health Services
Licensing and Certification ....(916) 445-2070
Other information ....(916) 657-1425
Department of Housing and Community Development
Mobile Home Ombudsmen ....(800) 952-5275
Titles and Registration ....(800) 952-8356
Codes and Standards ....(916) 445-9471
Department of Industrial Relations
(Division of) Industrial Accidents ....(800) 736-7401

Department of Insurance .... (800) 927-4357 (HELP)
Department of Motor Vehicles .... (916) 657-7669
Department of Real Estate .... (916) 227-0931
(209) 445-5009
(213) 897-3399
(619) 525-4192
(415) 904-5925
(714) 558-4491
    Timeshare Division .... (916) 227-0864
Department of Savings and Loans .... (213) 897-8242
Department of Toxic Substances Control .... (916) 255-3545
(510) 540-2122
(818) 551-2800
(310) 590-4868
Department of Transportation (Caltrans) .... (916) 654-5413
Department of Veterans Affairs .... (800) 952-5626
(805) 395-2869
(510) 602-5070
(209) 445-5466
(805) 983-7477
(916) 224-4955
(916) 722-1841
(916) 262-2555
(909) 383-4282
(619) 627-3966
(310) 944-3585
Franchise Tax Board .... (800) 852-5711
Housing Financing Agency .... (213) 736-2355
(916) 322-3991
Medical Board .... (916) 920-6697
   Complaints .... (800) 633-2322
(916) 263-2424
    License verification .... (916) 263-2382
Medical Board Hearing Aid Dispensers
   Examining Committee .... (800) 633-2322
New Motor Vehicle Board .... (916) 445-1888
Office of Fleet Administration .... (916) 657-2318
Osteopathic Medical Board .... (916) 322-4306
Poison Control Centers
   Alameda, Contra Costa, Del Norte, Humboldt,
   Marin, Mendocino, Napa, San Francisco,
   San Mateo and Sonoma Counties .... (800) 523-2222
   Alpine, Amador, Butte, Calaveras, Colusa, El Dorado,
   Glenn, Lake, Lassen, Modoc, Nevada, Placer,
   Plumas, Sacramento, San Joaquin, Shasta, Sierra,
   Siskiyou, Solano, Stanislaus, Sutter, Tehama,
   Trinity, Tuolumne, Yolo and Yuba Counties .... (800) 342-9293
(916) 734-3692
   Monterey, San Benito, San Luis Obispo, Santa Clara
   and Santa Cruz Counties .... (209) 445-1222
   Fresno, Kern, Kings, Madera, Mariposa, Merced
   and Tulare Counties .... (800) 662-9886
(408) 299-5112

Federal Agencies

National Flood Insurance Program .... (800) 638-6620
National Highway Traffic Safety Administration
    Auto Safety Hotline .... (800) 424-9393
    Technical Reference Division .... (202) 366-2768
National Labor Relations Board .... (213) 894-5200
                                                     (310) 575-7351
                                                     (619) 557-6184
                                                     (415) 744-6810
                                                     (510) 273-7200

National Personnel Records Center
    Civilian personnel .... (314) 425-5761
    Army .... (314) 538-4261
    Navy, Marine, Coast Guard .... (314) 538-4141
    Air Force .... (314) 538-4243
Office of Thrift Supervision .... (415) 616-1500
Securities and Exchange Commission .... (213) 965-3998
                                                     (415) 744-3140
                                                     (202) 272-3100
Social Security Administration .... (800) 772-1213
State Department
    Citizens' Emergency Center .... (202) 647-5225
    Office of Consular Services .... (202) 647-3666
Student Loan Marketing Association (Sallie Mae) .... (800) 292-6868
Veterans Administration .... (800) 827-1000

Private Organizations
Academy of Textiles and Flooring .... (310) 698-1279
Advanced Carpet Specialists .... (510) 792-5758
Alberta Culver Corp. (Mrs. Dash) .... (800) 622-3274
American Arbitration Association .... (213) 383-6516
                                                     (415) 981-3901
                                                     (714) 474-5090
                                                     (619) 239-3051
                                                     (212) 484-4000
American Council of Life Insurance .... (800) 942-4242
American Movers Conference .... (703) 683-7410
American Resort Development Association .... (202) 371-6700
American Society of Composers .... (415) 574-6023
                                                     (714) 586-1632
Arbitration Forums .... (510) 825-0624
                                                     (714) 995-3614
Broadcast Music, Inc. .... (800) 326-4BMI
California Assigned Risk Plan .... (800) 622-0954
California Fabricare Association .... (408) 252-1746
California Moving and Storage Association .... (800) 672-1415
California State Association of Parliamentarians .... (415) 566-7826
Carpet and FabriCare Institute .... (800) 227-7389
Center for Auto Safety .... (202) 328-7700
Chemtrec Center .... (800) 262-8200
Consumer Action .... (415) 777-9648
Consumer Credit Counseling Service .... (800) 388-2227
Continental Association of Funeral and Memorial Societies .... (800) 458-5563
Direct Marketing Association, Mail Order Action Line .... (202) 347-1222

INDEX

...more books from Nolo Press

ESTATE PLANNING & PROBATE

Make Your Own Living Trust, *Clifford*	1st Ed	$19.95	LITR
Plan Your Estate With a Living Trust, *Clifford*	2nd Ed	$19.95	NEST
Nolo's Simple Will Book, *Clifford*	2nd Ed	$17.95	SWIL
Who Will Handle Your Finances If You Can't?, *Clifford & Randolph*	1st Ed	$19.95	FINA
The Conservatorship Book, *Goldoftas & Farren*	1st Ed	$24.95	CNSV
How to Probate an Estate, *Nissley*	7th Ed	$34.95	PAE
Nolo's Law Form Kit: Wills, *Clifford & Goldoftas*	1st Ed	$14.95	KWL
Write Your Will (audio cassette), *Warner & Greene*	1st Ed	$14.95	TWYW
5 Ways to Avoid Probate (audio cassette), *Warner & Greene*	1st Ed	$14.95	TPRO

GOING TO COURT

Represent Yourself in Court, *Bergman & Berman-Barrett*	1st Ed	$29.95	RYC
Everybody's Guide to Municipal Court, *Duncan*	1st Ed	$29.95	MUNI
Everybody's Guide to Small Claims Court, *Warner*	11th Ed	$16.95	CSCC
Fight Your Ticket, *Brown*	5th Ed	$18.95	FYT
Collect Your Court Judgment, *Scott, Elias & Goldoftas*	2nd Ed	$19.95	JUDG
How to Change Your Name, *Loeb & Brown*	5th Ed	$19.95	NAME
The Criminal Records Book, *Siegel*	3rd Ed	$19.95	CRIM
Winning in Small Claims Court, *Warner & Greene* (audio cassette)	1st Ed	$14.95	TWIN

LEGAL REFORM

Legal Breakdown: 40 Ways to Fix Our Legal System, *Nolo Press*	1st Ed	$8.95	LEG

BUSINESS & WORKPLACE

Software Development: A Legal Guide, *Fishman*	1st Ed	$44.95	SFT
The Legal Guide for Starting & Running a Small Business, *Steingold*	1st Ed	$22.95	RUNS
Sexual Harassment on the Job, *Petrocelli & Repa*	1st Ed	$14.95	HARS
Your Rights in the Workplace, *Repa*	2nd Ed	$15.95	YRW
How to Write a Business Plan, *McKeever*	4th Ed	$19.95	SBS
Marketing Without Advertising, *Phillips & Rasberry*	1st Ed	$14.00	MWAD
The Partnership Book, *Clifford & Warner*	4th Ed	$24.95	PART`
The California Nonprofit Corporation Handbook, *Mancuso*	6th Ed	$29.95	NON
The California Nonprofit Corporation Handbook, *Mancuso*	DOS	$39.95	NPI
	MAC	$39.95	NPM
How to Form Your Own California Corporation, *Mancuso*	7th Ed	$29.95	CCOR
The California Professional Corporation Handbook, *Mancuso*	5th Ed	$34.95	PROF
The Independent Paralegal's Handbook, *Warner*	2nd Ed	$24.95	PARA
Getting Started as an Independent Paralegal, *Warner* (audio cassette)	2nd Ed	$44.95	GSIP
How To Start Your Own Business:			
Small Business Law, *Warner & Greene* (audio cassette)	1st Ed	$14.95	TBUS

= Books With Disk

TO ORDER CALL 800-995-4775

THE NEIGHBORHOOD

Neighbor Law: Fences, Trees, Boundaries & Noise, *Jordan*	1st Ed	$14.95	NEI
Safe Home, Safe Neighborhoods: Stopping Crime Where You Live,			
Mann & Blakeman	1st Ed	$14.95	SAFE
Dog Law, *Randolph*	2nd Ed	$12.95	DOG

MONEY MATTERS

Stand Up to the IRS, *Daily*	2nd Ed	$21.95	SIRS
Money Troubles: Legal Strategies to Cope With Your Debts, *Leonard*	2nd Ed	$16.95	MT
How to File for Bankruptcy, *Elias, Renauer & Leonard*	4th Ed	$25.95	HFB
Simple Contracts for Personal Use, *Elias & Stewart*	2nd Ed	$16.95	CONT
Nolo's Law Form Kit: Power of Attorney, *Clifford, Randolph & Goldoftas*	1st Ed	$14.95	KPA
Nolo's Law Form Kit: Personal Bankruptcy,			
Elias, Renauer, Leonard & Goldoftas	1st Ed	$14.95	KBNK
Nolo's Law Form Kit: Rebuild Your Credit, *Leonard & Goldoftas*	1st Ed	$14.95	KCRD
Nolo's Law Form Kit: Loan Agreements, *Stewart & Goldoftas*	1st Ed	$14.95	KLOAN
Nolo's Law Form Kit: Buy & Sell Contracts, *Elias, Stewart & Goldoftas*	1st Ed	$9.95	KCONT

FAMILY MATTERS

How to Raise or Lower Child Support In California, *Duncan & Siegal*	2nd Ed	$17.95	CHLD
Divorce & Money, *Woodhouse & Felton-Collins with Blakeman*	2nd Ed	$21.95	DIMO
The Living Together Kit, *Ihara & Warner*	6th Ed	$17.95	LTK
The Guardianship Book, *Goldoftas & Brown*	1st Ed	$19.95	GB
A Legal Guide for Lesbian and Gay Couples, *Curry & Clifford*	7th Ed	$21.95	LG
How to Do Your Own Divorce, *Sherman*	19th Ed	$21.95	CDIV
Practical Divorce Solutions, *Sherman*	1st Ed	$14.95	PDS
California Marriage & Divorce Law, *Warner, Ihara & Elias*	11th Ed	$19.95	MARR
How to Adopt Your Stepchild in California, *Zagone & Randolph*	4th Ed	$22.95	ADOP
Nolo's Pocket Guide to Family Law, *Leonard & Elias*	3rd Ed	$14.95	FLD

JUST FOR FUN

29 Reasons Not to Go to Law School, *Warner & Ihara*	3rd Ed	$9.95	29R
Devil's Advocates, *Roth & Roth*	1st Ed	$12.95	DA
Poetic Justice, *Roth & Roth*	1st Ed	$8.95	PJ

PATENT, COPYRIGHT & TRADEMARK

Trademark: How To Name Your Business & Product,			
McGrath & Elias, with Shena	1st Ed	$29.95	TRD
Patent It Yourself, *Pressman*	3rd Ed	$36.95	PAT
The Inventor's Notebook, *Grissom & Pressman*	1st Ed	$19.95	INOT
The Copyright Handbook, *Fishman*	1st Ed	$24.95	COHA

LANDLORDS & TENANTS

The Landlord's Law Book, Vol. 1: Rights & Responsibilities,			
Brown & Warner	4th Ed	$32.95	LBRT
The Landlord's Law Book, Vol. 2: Evictions, *Brown*	4th Ed	$32.95	LBEV
Tenants' Rights, *Moskovitz & Warner*	11th Ed	$15.95	CTEN
Nolo's Law Form Kit: Leases & Rental Agreements, *Warner & Stewart*	1st Ed	$14.95	KLEAS

TO ORDER CALL 800-995-4775

HOMEOWNERS

How to Buy a House in California, *Warner, Serkes & Devine*	2nd Ed	$19.95	BHCA
For Sale By Owner, *Devine*	2nd Ed	$24.95	FSBO
Homestead Your House, *Warner, Sherman & Ihara*	8th Ed	$9.95	HOME
The Deeds Book, *Randolph*	2nd Ed	$15.95	DEED

OLDER AMERICANS

Beat the Nursing Home Trap: A Consumer's Guide to Choosing & Financing Long Term Care, *Matthews*	2nd Ed	$18.95	ELD
Social Security, Medicare & Pensions, *Matthews with Berman*	5th Ed	$15.95	SOA

RESEARCH/REFERENCE

Legal Research, *Elias & Levinkind*	3rd Ed	$19.95	LRES
Legal Research Made Easy: A Roadmap Through the Law Library Maze (2-1/2 hr videotape & manual), *Nolo & Legal Star*	1st Ed	$89.95	LRME

CONSUMER

How To Get A Green Card: Legal Ways To Stay In The U.S.A., *Nicolas Lewis*	1st Ed	$19.95	GRN
How to Win Your Personal Injury Claim, *Matthews*	1st Ed	$24.95	PICL
Nolo's Pocket Guide to California Law, *Guerin & Nolo Press Editors*	2nd Ed	$10.95	CLAW
Nolo's Pocket Guide to California Law on Disk, *Guerin & Nolo Press Editors*	Windows	$24.95	CLWIN
	MAC	$24.95	CLM
Nolo's Law Form Kit: Hiring Child Care & Household Help, *Repa & Goldoftas*	1st Ed	$14.95	KCHLD
Nolo's Pocket Guide to Consumer Rights, *Kaufman*	2nd Ed	$12.95	CAG

SOFTWARE

WillMaker 5.0, *Nolo Press*	Windows	$69.95	WI5
	DOS	$69.95	WI5
	MAC	$69.95	WM5
Nolo's Personal RecordKeeper 3.0, *Pladsen & Warner*	DOS	$49.95	FRI3
	MAC	$49.95	FRM3
Nolo's Living Trust 1.0, *Randolph*	MAC	$79.95	LTM1
Nolo's Partnership Maker 1.0, *Mancuso & Radtke*	DOS	$129.95	PAGI1
California Incorporator 1.0, *Mancuso*	DOS	$129.00	INCI
Patent It Yourself 1.0, *Pressman*	Windows	$229.00	PYW1

RECYCLE YOUR OUT-OF-DATE BOOKS AND GET 25% OFF YOUR NEXT PURCHASE
It's important to have the most current legal information. Because laws and legal procedures change often, we update our books regularly. To help keep you up-to-date we are extending this special offer. Cut out and mail the title portion of the cover of any old Nolo book with your next order and we'll give you a 25% discount off the retail price of ANY new Nolo book you purchase directly from us. For current prices and editions call us at 1 (800) 992-6656.

This offer is to individuals only. Prices subject to change.

TO ORDER CALL 800-995-4775

ORDER FORM

Code	Quantity	Title	Unit price	Total
		Subtotal		
		California residents add Sales Tax		
		Shipping & Handling ($4 for 1st item; $1 each additional)		
		2nd day UPS (additional $5; $8 in Alaska and Hawaii)		
		TOTAL		

Name

Address

(UPS to street address, Priority Mail to P.O. boxes)

FOR FASTER SERVICE, USE YOUR CREDIT CARD AND OUR TOLL-FREE NUMBERS

Monday-Friday, 7 a.m. to 6 p.m. Pacific Time

Order Line	1 (800) 992-6656 (in the 510 area code, call 549-1976)
General Information	1 (510) 549-1976
Fax your order	1 (800) 645-0895 (in the 510 area code, call 548-5902)

METHOD OF PAYMENT

☐ Check enclosed

☐ VISA ☐ Mastercard ☐ Discover Card ☐ American Express

Account #   Expiration Date

Authorizing Signature

Daytime Phone

Allow 2-3 weeks for delivery.

Prices subject to change.

SEND TO: Nolo Press, 950 Parker Street, Berkeley, CA 94710

TO ORDER CALL 800-995-4775